JULIE

SUCCESS FASTER ON FIRE HOT!

QUICKLY LAUNCH OR
RELAUNCH YOUR
REAL ESTATE CAREER

the
nelson
project

Copyright © 2020 by Julie Nelson and The Nelson Project Inc.

All rights reserved.

This publication, *Success Faster On Fire Hot!*, and subsequent publications or products sold are in no way affiliated with any particular real estate broker, brokerage, or franchise. All information within these pages is the creation of Julie Nelson and The Nelson Project Inc.

Book design: Kate Basart/Union Pageworks
Author photographs: Eleventh Box Media
Editing team: Portia Ryan, MS, ND and Dr. Virginia Monseau

ISBN: 978-1-7354886-0-8

thenelsonproject.org

Success Faster On Fire Hot! is for real estate professionals (current and those heading in that direction) and REALTORS®. Why the distinction? Because the National Association of REALTORS® (NAR) gives its members (of which the author is one) limited license to use the term REALTOR®. You see, REALTOR® is a federally registered collective membership mark which identifies a real estate professional who is a member of the National Association of REALTORS® and subscribes to its strict Code of Ethics. In preparation for publication, the author exhaustively studied the NAR Membership Marks Manual (42 pages) because she is a rule follower and takes compliance seriously. While the public uses the REALTOR® term casually (and often with three syllables, which is incorrect), it is actually, well, not supposed to be used that way in a registered trademark-ey sort of way. More specifically, "Compliance with the Context of Use limitation in the case of oral communication requires forethought and continued awareness that the term REALTOR® does not describe a vocation or profession." So the forethought and continued awareness here is ... you get the point.

Contents

Start Here ... 7

CHAPTER 1 The World as We Know It ... 11
    Shelter in Place ... 11

CHAPTER 2 Net Happiness, The True Bottom Line ... 19
    What to Expect ... 22
    The Short Game, Long Game Dance ... 27
    Working It Out in the Middle ... 30
    Borderline Obsessed ... 33
    Fast Beats Smart ... 34

CHAPTER 3 The Art (And the Mess) of the Pivot ... 35
    PIVOT 1: Year 3, Vision ... 38
    PIVOT 2: Year 8, Team ... 39
    PIVOT 3: Year 10, Acquisition and Help ... 41
    PIVOT 4: Year 12, Be Careful What You Ask For ... 42
    PIVOT 5: Year 17, Crash ... 43
    PIVOT 6: Year 18, Relaunch ... 45
    PIVOT 7: Year 18, Changing Brokerages ... 47
    PIVOT 8: TBD, You Never Know ... 49

CHAPTER 4 Some Things They Never Told You in Real Estate School ... 51
    Challenges to Getting Started (or Restarted) ... 52
    ONE: Ease of Licensure ... 53
    TWO: Unrealistic Expectations ... 54
    THREE: Cash Flow ... 55
    FOUR: Bossy ... 56
    FIVE: Your Energy, Your Power Score ... 56
    SIX: Never Fully Owning How to Do Sales ... 57

CHAPTER 5 Real Agent Stories — 59
- WE'LL START WITH ME: Thought About Real Estate for Years — 60
- STEPHANIE: Newly Divorced Mama Bear — 61
- WILLIAM: A Vision for His Life — 62
- MELANIE: VP Level Marketing Pro — 63
- SAM: Sixty-Something Non-Profit Executive — 64

CHAPTER 6 Success Stories... How Did These Rookie Sensations Kill It in Year One? — 65
- Rookie of the Year Profiles — 67

CHAPTER 7 Quickly — 73
- Clients First... And Fast — 75

CHAPTER 8 What Are You Telling Yourself? — 77
- Wildly Imperfect — 78
- I Heart Real Estate — 79
- Looking for Encouragement in All the Wrong Places — 81
- Full-time or Part-time, Showing Up Pro — 81
- Shifting into Full-time — 83

CHAPTER 9 It's a Race — 85
- IT'S A RACE FACTOR #1: Your Psyche — 86
- IT'S A RACE FACTOR #2: Sixty to Ninety Days — 87
- IT'S A RACE FACTOR #3: Your Bank Account — 88
- IT'S A RACE FACTOR #4: Confidence — 89
- IT'S A RACE FACTOR #5: Nothing — 89
- Your Shortest Job Description — 91
- Building Muscle Around What to Say — 92

CHAPTER 10 Who Is the Boss of Me? — 95
- You Are Your Own Boss — 96
- BOSS PERFORMANCE REVIEW: A Self-Assessment — 98
- You Are the CEO — 101
- Your Most Important Daily Meeting — 102

CHAPTER 11 Got Confidence?   111
   Confidence   111
   Power Score . . . Success from the Inside Out   112

CHAPTER 12 More Conversations = More Income   121
   Conversations   121
   What to Say . . . And How . . . And Why   123

CHAPTER 13 More on Practice   137
   Time on Task Over Time   138
   Speed vs. Perfection   139

CHAPTER 14 Bird Dogs and Your Next Few Clients   145
   Five People   145

CHAPTER 15 The Google   155
   Find Yourself   157

CHAPTER 16 Rinse and Repeat   165
   Sexy   165
   Not So Sexy   166
   Renew Your Joy   168
   Rinse and Repeat   170

CHAPTER 17 Where Are They Now?   175
   Fast-forward Five Years   175
   The Roadmap   178

CHAPTER 18 The $100,000 Recipe   181
   Ingredients   182
   Directions   188

CHAPTER 19 Getting Your License — 193

- Real-tor — 193
- It Takes HOW Much Time? — 194
- It Costs HOW Much? — 196
- Commission Structure, Do the Math — 199
- 60-90 Day Pay Cycle — 201
- Six-Month Reserve — 201
- Vital Resources — 202

CHAPTER 20 Broker Choice — 205

- Choosing a Broker, Newbies — 208
- Changing Brokers, Maybe — 210
- Brokers and Client Leads — 211
- More Things to Consider — 212
- How Are Brokerages Structured? — 219
- Ownership — 221

CHAPTER 21 On Fire Hot! — 231

- Sacred Pact — 232
- What's Next? — 234

- Reference: Action Items — 237
- Reference: Scripts — 243
- Online Resources — 253
- Disclaimers and Disclosures — 254
- Acknowledgments — 255
- About the Author — 256

Start Here

Success Faster On Fire Hot!

If you don't build your dreams, someone will hire you to help build theirs.

—Tony Gaskin

We built our dream home on three acres on the edge of Austin. We designed the modern farmhouse for years; we built it in 2013. We had a love-hate experience with our architect and his interactive spreadsheet that kept us humble and on budget. If we wanted to extend the laundry room three feet or widen the overall footprint of the home or add a fireplace or a dance hall, he clicked in a new number or two in his amazing technicolor spreadsheet and we could look immediately at the bottom line of what that particular modification did to our budget. The spreadsheet does not lie, and we would more often than not undo the most recent expensive what-if adjustment. We journeyed through this see-saw dream-reality process of tweaking our wants and needs in alignment with our very specific budget. I still think we need a dance hall.

We learned that you cannot build the perfect house, the first time. We learned that the only way to build the perfect house is to build it twice. That way, you get to improve upon everything that, in hindsight, would make it better or would at least move that one light switch that makes no sense at all or switch out that now obviously undersized ceiling fan that we just had to have. We love our modern farmhouse on the edge of Austin; it's not perfect, but it is the manifestation of a dream.

Think of something you have created or built in your life—a house, a relationship, your business, something you built with your hands, a recipe, a song you wrote, an athletic skill you refined—and all the reiterations of that thing from concept to fruition. Think through the phases of the initial vision and idea, then the first draft or drawing or verse or taste test, the discussions you had around it, the fifth draft or drawing, the first attempt or the prototype.

Imagine that thing was something as simple as building a tree swing for your kids. You build the first one, and it's pretty good, or maybe not quite good enough, so you redo it. When it looks good, you snap a photo with happy kids in full swing and post it on Facebook. And then your brother wants one, so you do another. And it's better the second time. And word gets out that you have mad tree swing skills, and your friends ask for one, with modifications because trees and kids are different, and now others are involved in the vision and the discussions. Books are this way.

Success Faster Quickly Launch or Relaunch Your Real Estate Career was published in spring 2018. Thousands of copies sold. Lives were modified, spirits lifted, squirrel chasing quieted, bank accounts righted.

The *Success Faster Workbook* was published on Amazon in fall 2018. This was incorporated into a new Success Faster class at the Austin Board of REALTORS®, spring 2019. Speaking engagements surfaced, the key topics evolved, and a new vision emerged.

I realized there was more opportunity to deliver a bigger version of *Success Faster*. More specifically, *Success Faster* 2018 does not reference the Workbook; the bossy performance review grew into a stand-alone interactive class, and COVID smacked us in the face first quarter 2020. I had a lot more to say.

I was already envisioning my second book, one based on crazy, funny, outrageous things that happen with entrepreneurs and I even have a URL so you can participate—crazystory.info. This storybook, or at least a blog series, will happen, but more *Success Faster* became the clear winner for what to do now, for what agents and other entrepreneurs need now.

I played around with titles before landing on *Success Faster On Fire Hot!* Success Faster Dammit. Success Faster Stronger. Real Estate is Rough: How to Thrive Anyway. Success and Faster was the right direction. But what's up with the On Fire Hot! thing?

If Gary John Bishop's *Unfu*k Yourself* was titled *Be N*ce to Yourself*, would that have the same effect? Would it have the same draw on the talk show circuit? If Jen Sincero's *You Are a Badass* was instead *You Are Excellent*, would you be more or less inclined to pick it up in the airport book store?

Exactly.

A brief disclaimer on some choice words—if you have zero tolerance for an occasional badass or bs or otherwise colorful language, I apologize in advance. I seem to be drawn to these edgy messages lately. I generally strive for appropriate. I am Midwest and Catholic and the youngest child, the trifecta of being careful and nice. I'm learning to be slightly less patient, more unapologetic, audacious when possible, and a bit more in your face when appropriate. Things seem to get done faster this way, and my goals materialized faster when I began to stand in my own power. It's like a psychologist who works with you over a long time to identify your underlying layers-deep issues versus the friend who calls you on your bullshit every time. Both approaches are effective for different reasons, but one is faster than the other. I find some of my favorite writers lean a bit inappropriate, and, well, they're my favorite authors, so, hello! I wanted to try on those shoes, find my louder more opinionated better-at-parties voice. What voice do you want to try on? I believe we all have a few voices, but which voice is running your life and your business and your bank account right now, and is that ok?

Oh, and let me throw this in real quick for the grammar police . . . the book is going to read like I speak, ellipses and all. And that means two things . . . one, it will not meet strict academic standards (my English professor editor loves me), and, two, it means I am keeping it real. Imagine we are sitting together on my back porch with a sweet tea having a conversation about your business and your amazing life. That is the voice, and the grammar, you will get in *Success Faster On Fire Hot!*

On Fire Hot! is you with your strongest most inspired unapologetic voice calling the shots. On Fire Hot! is you when your life and business are clicking, all cylinders firing. On Fire Hot! is that internal fire that gets you out of bed. On Fire Hot! is optimism without assistance, courage without chemicals. On Fire Hot! is pushing through the bullshit story you've been telling yourself and truly owning the success you knew you could be all along. On Fire Hot! is your bank account and profitability and net worth like never before. Can we agree that cash solves so many things? On Fire Hot! is that new car when that new car is not even a financial stretch. On Fire Hot! is joy solidly in place in your life and business, sometimes in that order. *Success Faster On Fire Hot!* is you truly becoming the on fire hottest version of yourself.

Success Faster On Fire Hot! builds on *Success Faster* 2018 with six new chapters including a healthy dose of calling you out on your bullshit, a slew of anecdotal stories, and an attempt at a COVID "new normal" roadmap. Not only are some of the original chapters re-written with extra spice, you will also get an interactive online bossy performance review (that may simply be the key to your on fire hotness), expanded online resources, more success stories, a few NINJA tricks, an elevated workbook do-this-next experience, and some "work" chapters. In other words, this is a whole new book to set your business On Fire Hot!

May I have your permission to hurt your brain a bit? The "work" chapters are somewhat operational in nature; they dive into the work and are, frankly, designed to hurt your brain a bit. I'll give you a little warning at the top of those chapters so you can get a glass of water or turn on your best work music—maybe Enya, a little Yo-Yo Ma, probably skip the Lizzo track—do whatever it is that helps you focus. This is IMPORTANT work!

Let's get started.

CHAPTER 1

The World as We Know It

The ultimate measure of a man
is not where he stands in moments of comfort and convenience
but where he stands in times of challenge and controversy.

—Martin Luther King Jr.

Shelter in Place

If someone had suggested I write about a highly infectious rapidly expansive global pandemic that overwhelmed hospitals worldwide, involved a screeching halt to the economy, shut down travel, closed every single school in the country for months, canceled March Madness and the Olympics, crippled supply chains, boarded non-essential businesses, plummeted oil prices, generated historical unemployment during a profoundly divisive election year all as a backstory to writing this book, I would have thought that was completely ridiculous. I would have said that high drama does not resonate with my writing style, is a bit much for *On Fire Hot!*, and that fiction is not my lane. No sci-fi for me, I'll stick to how to clear your head and build your life.

Well hell.

2020 will go down in history as the COVID-19 global pandemic and is the backdrop scene in writing this book. People are dying, health care workers are overwhelmed heroes. There is an ER doctor in Corpus Christi living in his kids' backyard treehouse to protect his family from the virus. COVID and shelter in place is altering our world, pumping the brakes on how we do business and live our daily lives. Friends and family are laid off or furloughed, jobless claims topped 40 million (this number keeps changing as I write), pretty much wiping out the number of jobs created over the last ten-year stretch. Every child in the US is home-schooled, parents are day-drinking while home officing, alcohol sales have spiked (nationally, tequila saw the biggest spike; I participated in this), and toilet paper is a commodity. No one had pandemic or stay-at-home-full-time-with-the-entire-family-for-months on their 2020 vision board.

Shelter-in-place, social distancing, and the new normal—at least the new normal until we have a vaccine—has forced a new way of being, the new abnormal. Families are reconnecting at home, mostly making that work, cooking more, building victory gardens, cleaning closets, reducing expenses, fostering dogs, simplifying life, simplifying entertainment, simplifying working out, just simplifying. It's almost refreshing, if it wasn't maddening.

Friends who live alone are struggling, even the introverts. Zoom fatigue is real. If a family was stressed before COVID, they may now have stress on top of stress. If a family was dysfunctional before COVID, they may now have layers of dysfunction. If a marriage was on the rocks before COVID, well maybe they're working it out in the midst of more time together.

And then there's business, work, jobs, income, the economy. Everyone is impacted. If you work for Zoom or a company that hosts online events or a company that makes masks or a service that delivers groceries, or you work for Amazon, then you have decent job stability. And you are most likely working your ass off. For real estate pros, it is a mixed bag.

Homes are selling. At least they are in Austin and Chicago, Cincinnati, Phoenix, Des Moines, Jacksonville, Nashville, New Zealand, and second-home markets like Aspen, and homes with pools. Of course, different markets will perform differently. The harder hit the local economy, let's say

Las Vegas, then the deeper the impact. And all of this is unprecedented and unpredictable. We miss precedented and predictable.

So how do you clear your head and build your life with this as the backstory? How do we tap into On Fire Hot! and push our businesses and lives forward?

Let's take a look at five ways professionals are adapting, five rules for the new normal.

NEW NORMAL RULE 1
Fluidity

In normal life, the ability to shift and adjust and reset and shake things off and start again and change course and then repeat—this adjustment acuity, this fluidity and flexibility, is perhaps the greatest gift, the greatest tool for overall happiness and life mastery. And now, in the midst of the greatest shake-up and smackdown of the century, your resilience and plasticity have become a necessity, your survival tool. It's like grit and flex had a baby and she was born in April 2020. We need that DNA in our toolkit.

Whether we like it or not, COVID has forced a reset on pretty much every single business out there. Even the essential businesses who stayed open had to reset, they had to adjust quickly. Real estate pros, entrepreneurs, the self-employed, everyone has had to adjust, reset, dig in and figure out how to make things work in the new normal, a new normal that is totally a moving target. And not normal. And very new.

So rule numero uno is to gut-check your fluidity. Get flexible, get creative, un-dig your heels, loosen your hard positions, recognize that everything and anything is up for close scrutiny. How you did business last year may be different from what works this year. Your goals may stay the same but the path to obtaining them just shifted.

Fluidity is not only your friend, she is now one of your greatest assets.

NEW NORMAL RULE 2
Being Human

Your greatest sales tool has always been simply showing up as an authentic, decent human. Always has, always will, and is now a necessity. So what does that mean in your business?

It means checking in on everyone you know. Calling all of them, no business chat allowed in these check-in conversations unless they bring it up. You're bringing humanity to other people's insanity. And stay in your lane, you're not a pandemic expert.

How are you doing? Do you have everything you need? How are your parents? How is homeschooling? Are you day drinking? (Kidding on that last one, unless it is your good friend then that's pretty funny, unless they are in recovery and then it's not.) As they say, in ten years we are going to be in trouble because we will be led by a bunch of homeschoolers who were taught by day drinkers.

Back to decent being human questions. Do you know anyone who has COVID? Do you have any family members who are health professionals?

If they ask about real estate, have your stats ready. People do want to know how's the market, how do I time this, and are we ok. Don't spin the market into something more than it is, and don't make it worse than it is; be the deliverer of the facts, keeping an even keel and seeing things as they are. Every day, look at the MLS weekly stats because that is the way it is.

I spoke with an agent in Omaha recently, in the early months of the COVID scene, and we were talking about what was working in his business and how he was using his time, since it wasn't the right time to talk business with most people. It wasn't right to make sales calls because people's lives were turned sideways, and parents were figuring out how to be homeschoolers, log in to their jobs at the same time, cut costs, and worry about their friends and family who were more sideways than they were. This agent, a very successful agent, admitted that he really did not like talking on the phone. But he had already talked with twenty people so far that day and none of those conversations had anything to do with real estate. He was just being a good human, checking in, making sure the family was ok, the kids were ok, the elderly parent had everything they needed.

We will look back at this time and realize that being a good human was one of our best tools all along.

NEW NORMAL RULE 3
Back to the Basics
I spoke with a friend of mine in Baton Rouge recently. I had interviewed her live as part of a company series featuring top-tier agents. I asked her how she had pushed her business from good to great and kept it there three years running. She said every Sunday evening she logged into her favorite Real Estate 101 class online. She spent one hour every week, on Funday Sunday evenings, re-visiting the fundamentals. She had realized that she had a tendency to overcomplicate the business, and when she overcomplicated, her business went down, and that when she just focused on the basics, her business grew, her bank account grew.

What would happen to your business and bank account if all you focused on for the next six months was the business fundamentals? If you did some version of Real Estate 101 every Sunday evening? And then you stuck with that program? What if all you focused on was lead generation, having conversations, what to say, adding to your database, communicating with your database, and having decent human conversations with those people?

Basics have always mattered, and they matter more in times of a market shift or a business relaunch or a pandemic smackdown. Put 101 solidly in your toolkit, own it.

NEW NORMAL RULE 4
Gut-check Your Leadership
How are you showing up as a leader for your clients and sphere right now? *On Fire Hot!* was published during the COVID scene. Perhaps you are reading post-post-COVID but the lesson remains the same. In times of crisis, and in times of not crisis, people need reassurance and facts, and they are looking for certainty and optimism. This is a call to up your leadership.

Tom Ferry, industry badass coach, says great leaders follow a schedule. He says there is not a single leader in a pressure cooker who does not follow a schedule, an agenda, a list of calls, objectives, and a tight routine. This is a call to up your leadership.

Great leaders over-communicate, they get out in front of the facts, they are knowledge brokers for what is going on in their market. You cannot be silent and let other people drive opinions not based on fact. You are, and always have been, in a keen position to deliver facts. How's the market? Where is this going? And what they really want to know is "will I be ok?" This is a call to up your leadership.

Huge corporations have crisis teams. These teams plan for ridiculously bad things to happen. The apple juice E. coli outbreak, a racial discrimination lawsuit, when KFC ran out of chicken in the UK, when teens started eating Tide Pods (yeah, that happened). And what is one of the main things we, as the consumer, witness with these crisis teams? We see them in front of the camera with information and leadership. They get in front of the news and lead the conversation and deliver data.

The new normal is your time to step up your leadership, lean in, lead the conversation.

NEW NORMAL RULE 5
Working Virtual

Companies have been expanding their virtual platforms for years, some more than others. But no one saw this coming. Hey, let's shut down the office for about eight months or so, and all work from home! We'll still pay the rent, the front desk staff, the phone system, and maintain the gardens out front, but let's take our entire operation and move it online tomorrow! And virtual it was. For everyone. Almost everyone, everywhere with little to no notice.

Zoom, Facetime, and other virtual venues exploded overnight. Wearing flip flops or house slippers, and perhaps dressed in business casual from the waist up, but in pajamas from the waist down became the work attire. Work commutes reduced to nearly zero, and air quality improved dramatically. And yes, that last statement is true! With shelter in place, I saved about $100 a month on gas. I never went to the gas station in April 2020, zero gas dollars on my April Visa statement. I had filled up in March, but still, zero for April. I figure I was getting about three weeks to the gallon.

So how is your setup for virtual? We can look at this from two angles, you personally and your company.

So, you personally. First and foremost, if you were all of a sudden home-schooling your kids, that's a pretty big gamechanger. I have seen some amazingly creative parents turned educator turning the dining room into a sophisticated learning lab. And I have seen parents really struggle and hope that their kids do not hurt each other today and celebrate when their kids cover half of what their school expected. Or maybe your college kid moved back in. How's that working for you? If your household is a bit quieter, sans little people or extra people, hopefully you managed to create a peaceful and productive workplace. At least for real estate professionals, many of us had things set up already, many of us have been working from home for years. I do have a couple of friends who had to upgrade their technology because their laptop camera was broken or did not exist—they probably needed an upgrade anyway, but if you wanted to take advantage of Zoom, and other virtual venues, on something other than your smartphone, then we had professionals (and parents) buying laptops when, at the same time, they were attempting to seriously lower expenses. The main point here, virtual at home means creating an environment that works.

How has your company adapted for virtual? Some companies and brokerages struggled with this, others adapted well, some were already virtual. My company was designed as a virtual model. We do not have a physical office, never have. We were built for virtual. We are seeing this play out in the industry. I witnessed the Austin Board of REALTORS take their entire curriculum online quickly, and they did it well. I witnessed brokerages offering Zoom classes, streaming video, and online broker hours. It will be interesting to see how this plays out, see who reopens when, see who figures out that virtual actually works really well in so many ways.

While the COVID dynamics are unique, unprecedented, and a moving target, the lessons are evergreen. These new normal lessons of fluidity, being human, getting back to the basics, gut-checking your leadership, and stepping up virtually, all of this matters for you and your business and your success, your success faster.

There are many ways to measure your success in any business. In *Success Faster On Fire Hot!*, we will dance between measuring your success financially and measuring your success with the most basic of human needs, your overall happiness.

CHAPTER 2

Net Happiness, The True Bottom Line

Tell me, what is it you plan to do with your one wild and precious life?

—Mary Oliver

Yale University's most popular course ever, Psychology and the Good Life, had over 1,200 students enrolled when it first rolled out. You would think that being at Yale alone would solidify the happiness factor, as in these smart kids hit the higher education lottery, right? Turns out, happiness can be elusive for the lottery winners too. Psychology and the Good Life is an elective course, but it looks like there's a waiting list. I think it should be required freshman year and then a refresher senior year. Good news for us, there is a free version of this course online, The Science of Well-Being. The free online version, a series of lectures, includes rewiring techniques, and if you pay for the $49 version, a certificate. It seems that my theory of drive-your-happiness-as-much-as-you-drive-your-overall-success passes the Yale test.

So one of the cornerstones of *Success Faster On Fire Hot!* is an assumption and belief that, at the end of the day, end of your hard-working, hit-the-grind day, that the true measure of your and my success is simply being happy. For me, the goal is to be outrageously and infectiously happy. If you are considering real estate as a career, are about to get your real estate license, or are currently a practicing real estate professional, but you are not insanely happy with where you are with your business or your bank, this is your book.

This is your book because I believe *Success Faster: On Fire Hot!* can change your perception of really what it takes to succeed in this amazing business. And who doesn't want to be On Fire Hot!? For the experienced agent, On Fire Hot! may be a simple course correction or a slight shift in priority. For the new agent, On Fire Hot! can be a seriously valuable roadmap.

In business, we talk about net income as the top line and net profit as the bottom line. I believe the true bottom line is net happiness. Are you truly happy with your business and your life?

The thing with real estate career net happiness is that, for many, it is an elusive slippery slope. Success and momentum and client leads and cash flow here this month, missing in action the next, happy then frustrated, confident then not, cash flow then cash tight. I have some theories around this.

The first theory is that an increase in sales tends to fix everything. Don't you just love a good theory, especially an over-simplified one? But can we agree that theories can be a little challenging to put into practice unless you live in a bubble? We will dig into all sorts of things around you owning your bubble and owning your environment in order to put all this into practice, but back to the sales-fixes-everything theory.

I know, it's not an advanced business concept, but it is business school 101 and I have seen it in action for years. I have seen this pattern play out many times with agents and, uh, maybe with myself. I see frustrated agents desperately seeking coaching, cash, and encouragement. They have an ongoing whack-a-mole approach to fixing issues in their business, and then a couple of weeks later they have three new clients and now they're happy and postponing coaching. We ride the client wave for a while, not necessarily addressing the underlying issues in our unpredictable pipeline, then scarcity and uncertainty creep back in, and we question whether we are destined for greatness or really have what it takes to succeed or at least to be happy and somewhat stress-free in this business. Our internal dialogue delivers uncertainty—a drip, drip, drip of self-sabotage. Conversations with family members allow doubt to creep in, and then we hold back our frustrations from our significant others as we attempt to protect ourselves from outside concern and harbor all the concern and uncertainty internally, at a time when we are in the greatest need of support, input, direction, accountability, and encouragement. This is a messy and exhausting pattern that most agents, myself included, know all too well.

I am not immune to these issues. I can write and talk and coach about these at times painful issues because I know them on a cellular level. My experience with the woes and frustrations and the mind games I have had to personally overcome, and then overcome again, and then overcome again dammit, make up a large pizza pie portion of my career learning curve and my qualifications to deliver On Fire Hot!

That cycle of frustration—from skip-in-your-step, back to unsure, to momentum, then back two steps—is exhausting and all too common. For the newly licensed agents, doing whatever they can and pushing through to quickly gain three or ten clients and then the next three or ten makes all the difference in the world. Garnering an increase in sales quickly may be the secret sauce. Clients now, build later. Hence the title, *Success Faster*, "faster" being the operative word. I have other theories around this success formula, and we will kick that can around throughout the book.

So how does this net happiness thing work? Business fundamentals teach us to focus on sales first (clients faster), the top line, and then, at the end of the day, or at least once a month, when the bookkeeper (if you do not have one, then you are one) delivers your financial statements to your inbox, focus on net income, the bottom line. (My English Professor editor is going to frown upon that last sentence. My run-on sentences push the boundaries of her academia standards.) One thing I will hammer away at in *Success Faster On Fire Hot!* is the true bottom line of your net happiness, your joy and internal dialogue at the end of the day. Sales may solve everything (that's business 101), but happiness is the ultimate measure of your success (that's life 101).

It turns out that net happiness has a compounding effect. When you improve the trajectory and overall enjoyment of your business and your life, you end up changing your world. It's that simple. And when you change your world, you set things in motion that inevitably change another life. This change-your-world-change-someone-else's-life domino and compounding effect is, to say the least, powerful. It's one of the greatest gifts of being human. I believe we are all on this planet to participate in this happiness compound process. My sacred mission is to help you do that.

What to Expect

You will run into a couple underlying premises here in *Success Faster On Fire Hot!* One premise is that no one taught you the happiness factor in real estate school. Heck, real estate school barely taught you how to drive sales let alone how to get started.

The other premise is that our real estate industry, and probably other industries, so heavily promotes the top 1 percent superstars that the bulk of agents in the middle end up tuning out the majority of industry advice and guidance because someone else's $20,000 per month marketing budget and personal video crew does not quite resonate with what you need now. You are not going to get stories of multi-millionaires in *Success Faster On Fire Hot!* I do want to mention that some of the top superstar producer agents read *Success Faster*; they still review the basics and revisit the happiness thing. And they give the book to their team and their little sister or neighbor or favorite client who is about to get her real estate license.

Here is what you will get with *Success Faster On Fire Hot!* You will get authentic, relatable, practical, and actionable real advice and guidance for the launching or relaunching real estate professional. You will get less of how to make the cover of *Realtor Magazine* and more of how to have a solid business and a life.

Success Faster On Fire Hot! is for everyone who wants to succeed in the world of real estate. That especially includes those considering real estate as a career, the newly licensed, those who have yet to reach their goals, and those in need of a reset or a simple calibration or a gentle push to get things done. We will call these categories prelaunch, launch, and relaunch.

Prelaunch is the maybe or soon-to-be licensed pro, the launch is the newly minted pro, and the relaunch is the agent, however seasoned, who needs to or is choosing to hit the reset button in his or her business. A reset can be a beautiful thing and *Success Faster On Fire Hot!* will act as the reset tour guide.

Some brokers have robust training and coaching programs to help the launching and relaunching agent. Other brokers, not so much. There are programs online and in person, programs that are free, and those that are costly. There are programs that have been around for years and new options surfacing all the time. You could spend twenty-four straight hours on YouTube on the topic of jump-starting your real estate business. You could spend thousands of hard-earned dollars on programs from top coaches. The body of real estate knowledge, advice, and direction is not one size fits all, and it certainly is not one budget fits all. Find the tools, programs, resources, and brokerage that work best for you, your life, your budget, your business, and your vision of the life and finances you are building. *Success Faster On Fire Hot!* will help guide you in this process.

Success Faster will provide newcomers with a leg up on getting started faster, with insight into the mindset, skills, and panache it takes to get into a groove (and stay there), in this fast-paced high-attrition business.

Success Faster will provide relaunchers with a fresh platform to reset and move forward, to recommit to the joy you experience when things are working nicely in your favor. You know that little skip in your step when things are working in your favor? We are going to tap into that as we build your bank account. Happiness and bank, most of us are happy to hang with that conversation. We will cover success stories, challenges, what to do, setting up your success plan, the habits that matter the most, what to say, how to garner clients quickly, and more.

Success Faster On Fire Hot! can help. Let's take a closer look.

Prelaunch

You are considering real estate as a career or are in the midst of moving in that direction. You may have hit a huge employment bump in the COVID road, and now is the time to move toward a new career. I am working with two new agents right now who fall into this COVID career realignment category. The fact that you have *Success Faster On Fire Hot!* in your hands during your pre-launch phase is an indication of great things to come. You are a planner, you are forward-thinking, you are starting a new chapter in your life.

A new chapter in your life... take that in for a minute. Whether in your twenties, your forties, or your sixties, a new license, a new direction, a new career is definitely a new chapter and that, in and of itself, is profound. Congratulations. Regardless of which decade of your life you now occupy, congratulations on moving your life forward. Your new chapter (and your psyche and your family and your bank account) deserves a solid foundation, a solid launching pad. *Success Faster On Fire Hot!* will provide a framework for a successful start.

Start telling your story now! I cannot emphasize this enough. Share your vision, passion, and motivation for why you are taking your life in this direction. Tell your story now so by the time you have your license and are ready to go, your world is already supporting you and aligning itself with your new path. Start your momentum now.

If you have ever run a race with a starting line, whether a high school track meet or a ready-set-go backyard race as a kid, you know there is a starting line and everyone stands ready at that line, poised to bolt with their toe on the line, ready for the official start of the race. And then there is that kid that saw the race materializing and started running behind you before you and your pals were lined up and ready, and when you said "Go!", that kid, your older brother or that friend who was always pushing the edge of cheating, blasts past everyone because he already started and lands at the finish line all victorious and braggadocious claiming the win. Well, guess what? That running before the start is NOT cheating in business and your life. Your life, your party... you get to call the shots. The running before you start will be one of the smartest things you ever do for your business. *Success Faster* will help you line up that fast start, that win.

Launch

You are a freshly minted agent in your first year or two, or you have been dabbling in real estate and now you're all in. Congratulations, you have started a new chapter in your life. You may be the young kid starting out in the business, or the retiree starting a new career, or the "employee" finally making the leap into self-employment. (You do know that most real estate professionals are self-employed, right?) New life chapters, they're a big deal in limited supply in your life, and you owe yourself a pat on the back for having the wherewithal to get here.

The learning curve can be steep; cash flow and your lead pipeline are everything. The first one to three months is the honeymoon phase of starting something new. The reality that your real estate license school did not teach you how to thrive in this business settles in relatively quickly. Mentors are critical. In most cases, you are now your own boss. Where do you capture your next client, your next ten clients? *Success Faster On Fire Hot!* will serve as a launching pad to help you succeed and thrive in this amazing business.

I have taught the *Success Faster* material, in various forms, for many years now. When we first rolled it out, there were typically two versions of the class—the version for new launching agents, and the version for not-new agents. I initially had two versions because I thought their needs were different. Their needs are different in a few ways.

The new agent has a steeper learning curve, needs to learn what to say, and needs to build a base of tools, all as quickly as possible. The not-new agent should have most of that down; they may need to revisit it, but they at least have the tools in their toolkit.

What they have in common is the need to line up sales and cash flow as quickly as possible in a sustainable way. If this was all we focused on, for everyone all the time, we honestly would all be On Fire Hot! and our bank accounts would reflect that!

So I started combining the classes and the material. So whether you are launch or relaunch, spend time with all of the *Success Faster* material to move your business, your mindset, your bank account, and your life forward.

Relaunch

Success Faster On Fire Hot! is ideal for the relaunchers, for those of you who for some reason are starting over or pushing through to the next level or tweaking or simply resetting your beautiful mind. It could be the maternity-leave parent re-entering the business, the agent who diverted onto a leadership path and is now back in production, or the agent who six-figure status in real estate, often lost traction and their seat on the six-figure bus the longer they were in the business. He thinks they were spending too much time on short-game (more leads, always more leads) versus long-game (more value, more service, more impressive value-laden market knowledge).

In the short game, you are always chasing your next sale; in the long game, consumers will seek you out, friends will send their friends. Every seasoned agent knows that the repeat client and the referral lead are the best opportunity, the most cost-effective, and a sign of a value-driven business.

SHORT GAME	LONG GAME
chasing the sale	customers seek me out
hot & cold	steady build
luck & hustle	systems & discipline
quantity focus	quality focus
sales focus	delivery focus
the sprint	the marathon

We are going to straddle this short-game long-game dance throughout *Success Faster*. Your ability to finesse this loose dichotomy in building your business is part art and part science.

A successful agent is the one who focuses on true value and delivery and, thus, builds a sustainable pipeline of clients, repeat clients, raving fans, and referrals. Think of the large corporation who has both a large and competent sales force (the short game, the pipeline builders) and amazing product development, engineering, service and delivery teams (the long game). If that corporate sales team cranks out the sales but the product or delivery teams fail to deliver, then it's broken. You get the picture.

In *Success Faster*, we are going to walk the fine line between short game and long game, between gaining your next lead and client and sale quickly (this is important) and building competency and quality (this is critical and ethical). These two concepts are not oppositional. Rather, they must work in tandem. The short game, in any sales profession, is foundational.

There is an old business adage of sales fixes everything. And it's true, but never at the expense of quality and sustainability. Short-game success without long-game quality and foundation is simply lousy business.

Success Faster On Fire Hot! is designed for any agent who is working to create (or recreate) a solid real estate business with a healthy client pipeline, predictable cash flow, and a life.

You've already started . . . you're reading this book. You're ready to take action. You're ready to make money. You're ready to build your life through the success of your real estate business. *Success Faster On Fire Hot!* is practical, actionable, and may be just the thing you need to make real estate really work for you, to gain or regain your seat on the success bus.

Success Faster will hit you with business insights, tips, action plans, what to say, how to build, and includes a dose or two or five of tough love.

The *Success Faster* Workbook

> *Inaction breeds doubt and fear. Action breeds confidence and courage. If you want to conquer fear, do not sit home and think about it. Go out and get busy.*
> —Dale Carnegie

Action, my friends, is everything.

Have you ever read a great business or self-development book and never really did anything with it? You took in the information, sort of, dropped some of the information into a cell or two in your brain, and left it there. We do this all the time, don't we?

Our brains are inundated with information and data 24/7. Whether that information is sensory intake walking down the street or information intake reading a book, your short-term memory can hold maybe five to ten things, max, at a time. Then your brain does some processing and moves some of the relevant things to long-term memory but even that will fade in time if not accessed or exercised. If left to itself, your unconscious brain is going to decide what to do with the information it takes in. You have some control over this.

Action, my friends, is everything.

One of the primary reasons for more *Success Faster* is that when the original was published in 2018, the companion workbook did not yet exist.

The *Success Faster Workbook* (available on Amazon or easy access and some free downloads through thenelsonproject.org) is designed to help you take the information and shift it into action and build business muscle and results. More action, more opportunity. More action, more muscle. More action, more bank. So the best opportunity with *Success Faster On Fire Hot!* is not your first read, it is what you do with that information, the work and application, that will put gas in the tank, clients on your doorstep, and cash in the bank.

Action, my friends, is everything.

Working It Out in the Middle

You may be wondering how *Success Faster On Fire Hot!* is different from the hundreds of books, blogs, videos, and other online resources on the topic. You may be wondering how *Success Faster* differs from what your brokerage delivers in the training, coaching, mentoring arena. You may be wondering how *Success Faster* varies from some of the world-class programs available in this great big real estate world. First, let me tell you what *Success Faster* is not.

Success Faster is not a book of superstar centerfolds, what they did to get started, how big their marketing budgets are, what their plan is to expand into other cities, and how awesome they are today. With all due respect, those superstars are some amazing business people who have worked their tails off to get where they are today, many of them had humble beginnings, and some of them almost failed out of the business before they succeeded. While I will sprinkle in some impressive success anecdotes, the *Success Faster* read will not be dominated by the top 1 percent super producers. Here's the deal: The top 1% has changed considerably over the years. The top 1% ten years ago is almost chump change today. Today's top 1%, they are running empires. Empire building is another book written by somebody else. If you are into empire building, find me online and let's chat because I have a few thoughts on that topic, too.

I have found there to be a tremendous need in the industry for advice and guidance for the agents who are working it out in the middle. If this speaks to you, you are in the right place.

Depending on your market, the middle could be $3 million in sales, or the middle could be $20 million in sales. Middle is simply the group of agents who are not beginners and are not the top-rated in their market. The middle of the real estate pro rankings has some serious way-above-average talent.

I have read hundreds of articles where the author bio says "I was top 1% in the country"... seriously, how many top 1% is out there, and is that the model and motivation and right approach for the 80% of the agents in the middle? My professional story is a story of a solid competitive agent in the middle, working her way to success and sustainability, knowing I could do more and knowing I could have better bank, better balance, and a better life. I knew I was a good agent and I wanted more; not all, just more. I did not desire to be top 1%; I just wanted to achieve and push my financial and life balance goals and found myself constantly in search of the right business tools and opportunities and the message and messenger that spoke to my place in the world, that spoke to my intentions and goals.

What the real estate industry needs more of is a voice and the right support system and opportunities that speak to the bulk of agents fighting for stability and awesomeness in the middle. In 2016, Brad Inman (I'm a fan-girl) of Inman News acknowledged the Everyday Realtor as the Person of the Year:

> "... shout-out to the entrepreneur, the young kid starting in the business, the individual Realtor who doesn't have a paycheck every two weeks, no benefits, 100 percent commission, the true entrepreneur. These extraordinary people earn a living without receiving a salary or even minimum wage. They are entirely commission-based—they wake up every morning without a paid job. They must dig deep and reach high to find the fortitude to keep it going. Theirs is not easy work. No one is paying for their health insurance, sick days, paid time off or maternity leave. No one buys them a computer, a cell phone, or a company car."

I ran a top 10 percent real estate practice in Austin, Texas. I still do. Besides an occasional dreamy thought of what if I was in the top 1 percent club, that really was never my aspiration. I wanted a healthy bank account, a decent vacation fund, I wanted to make a difference in people's lives, and I wanted a life with some breathing room. As the years go on, I want an even healthier bank, an even better vacation fund, I want to make a big difference on the planet and want even more breathing room. And a retirement strategy. And a ski cabin and to help my family. And less time looking at my cell phone. Does this speak to you? From personal observation, I believe there are a lot of agents out there in this pack.

As my career progressed to include leadership, coaching, and training, I became more and more enamored with and committed to the new and middle agents. I found significant meaning and tremendous reward working with the new, emerging, launching, relaunching, pivoting agents in the middle of the pack.

Whether new and emerging, beginning or middle, getting the right things done is critical to moving forward. To support your forward progress, one of the key things you will find in *Success Faster On Fire Hot!* is action and reference to the *Success Faster Workbook*. Most chapters give you tasks, ACTION ITEMS designed to help you move toward client leads now and tasks designed to build or improve your foundation. The key here is that as soon as you have more leads and a more consistent pipeline, most of your other problems will solve themselves. That is a life lesson, right? Fix the foundation and everything else seems to fix itself.

You can take the best class ever, but all the progress, the muscle building, the clients happen with what you do with it after the class. This applies to *Success Faster* or any business book. It's not the book itself, it's what you do with it afterward that puts money in your bank account and swagger in your step. Hence, ACTION and the workbook. I will drive this point home throughout the book.

The other key that *Success Faster* addresses is the reality of how you are showing up in the world. I have seen well-meaning, hard-working entrepreneurs completely sabotage their business because their energy is low, or they are trying to be someone they are not, or they are simply being lousy bosses in their own businesses. *Success Faster On Fire Hot!* spends time on authenticity, time on being a better boss, and time on a tool I call your power score. How you are showing up in the world is huge for you moving forward with your quest.

Borderline Obsessed

I am borderline obsessed with this success topic. I am obsessed with this real estate success and sustainability thing. I am obsessed with financial freedom, obsessed with the idea of reduced stress and increased happiness, obsessed with what might happen for you when you tap into the most awesome, audacious, and inspired version of yourself.

I have spent countless hours on the topic of new and emerging agent success, researching every possible resource and angle and mindset and best practice out there. I have explored every imaginable rabbit hole regarding the launching or relaunching professional. I have hired some of the best coaches. I have trained and coached hundreds of new agents in the largest real estate office in the world. I have delivered and sat through training after training on the topic. I have spent countless hours consulting with agents who have traction, and countless hours consulting with agents who have little to no traction. In this years-long process, I have found there to be a few critical differences among agents who succeed and those who do not. We will explore these differences throughout *Success Faster On Fire Hot!*

Success Faster On Fire Hot! is an invitation for you to take inventory on your principles and beliefs and disposition and standards and ask, does this serve me now? What pieces of me are serving me best? What ingredient do I need to move forward? What family ethos serves me and which belief manifestation do I need to dump? We are going to clean the palate so that your best possible self is driving your success bus.

My ultimate mission is to help you succeed. This really means that my ultimate mission is to help you make a difference on this planet. When you chose to get your real estate license, in one way or another you were making a decision to change your life. In writing and delivering *Success Faster On Fire Hot!*, I get to help you change your life. When this book is the difference-maker for one agent, one family, one future, then I have succeeded.

Your success is my obsession.

Fast Beats Smart

Let me explain the title, *Success Faster*, in a bit more detail. The theory behind this book (and my experience) is that acquiring clients faster may be THE biggest success differentiator.

In the beginning, faster overrules smart.

In the beginning, faster overrules talent.

In the beginning, faster overrules perfection.

The fast B-minus hustler will make bank and gain confidence and momentum faster than the A-plus perfectionist.

Smart and talent will catch up, but the agents who gain clients and momentum faster will have all sorts of things working in their favor, and this will be a burr in the waistband of the smarty-pants and the chronically organized. Let me paraphrase, hustle wins. Clients faster.

> ⊗ **WARNING LABEL!**
> Real estate involves people's lives, money, and legal contracts. While fast and hustle are part of the business success formula, broker and mentor support go hand-in-hand until you have a dozen transactions under your belt. Be smart!

So what does that hustle look like? How do you gain clients quickly? *Success Faster On Fire Hot!* provides actionable steps you can take today to gain clients faster. Clients faster leads to gaining traction faster, which leads to all sorts of sexy things in your business ecosystem, which leads to more clients, which leads to you taking a decent vacation, and so on. It is a beautiful cycle of making things happen in your business and your world.

Success Faster is designed as a roadmap, a to-do guide for gaining momentum. If you engage in the action, if you really, truly do the work outlined throughout the book and the workbook, I will bank on your success.

First, let me tell you more of my story and the various pivots, some more poetic than others, that got me to where I am today.

CHAPTER 3

The Art (And the Mess) of the Pivot

> *Are you one of those people who say you have fifteen years' experience, when actually you mean you have one experience fifteen times? Repeating yourself year after year after year. Do you keep doing the same thing? Do you keep showing up as the same person this year as you did four years ago? You keep repeating yourself. Your job is to be better and better every year. Your job is to figure that out.*
>
> —Caroline McHugh, TedTalk, Be as good at being you as possible.

My imaginary career start headline looks like this: "Seduced by success, Julie Nelson breaks records, achieves top honors, sets new standards, funds non-profit animal rescue in two years, runs a marathon, takes long vacations, makes it look easy, writes a book."

My truth-o-meter career start headline: "Seduced by success, perfectionist extrovert-leaning rosy glasses agent had no idea what she was getting herself into, restarts business multiple times, funds chicken farm in fifteen years, stops running, makes it look easy, writes a book." More on the chicken farm later.

I have been in real estate since 1999. Based on industry standards, I had a good first year. Seduced by success, I had $3,798,315 in sales volume my first full year in the business. I have trained Rookies of the Year who did three or four times more volume than that, but at the time, it was a solid respectable first year. It was more money than I had been making in my previous career, I was having a blast, and this working from home on my own schedule thing was the greatest invention ever. I was professionally grinning from ear to ear. Fist bump, high five!

And then I sold $3.3 million in my second year and $3 million my third year. I was sliding backward. I realized I had no plan, was lacking focus, was being a lousy boss to myself, and that my business was running me. The honeymoon was over. I had no control over my pipeline, had zero training on the concept of pipeline or database, had few if any tools, my website was meh, my cash flow was completely unpredictable, I had little control over my flexible (air quotes) schedule, and my business was running me and my life. I was a mess and needed solutions.

So I started over. Some sort of business intuition or personal fortitude kicked in, and I simply started over. That was my first significant pivot in my real estate career.

I can track seven significant pivots in my real estate career and have absolutely lost count of all the minor pivots. The major pivots are these personal and professional inflection points where everything changed, when the conditions and mood and vision clarity became undeniable. Some of these pivots were fluid, a bit of an art; some were more on the messy side. In looking back, I believe I pivoted a lot. Whenever I hear pivot, I think it should be a drinking game. Or a dance. That would be fun. As it turns out, business pivoting is a bit of a skill, a survival technique of sort. Two steps forward, one step back. Not always linear, sometimes sideways, sometimes messy, sometimes by design, sometimes because life shows up or sometimes because the market or economy shifted. It's a bit of a business cha-cha-cha.

My story is not one of uber top 1 percent production. It is not one of mega team super stardom. Top 10 percent always felt like a good target for me. My story is one of pushing through to make more money than I had ever made before, of pushing through to secure my future. I wanted security, I wanted cash flow, I wanted meaning in my professional endeavors. My story is one of being bound and determined to get balance and into the top 10%

and stay there. And then falling off and then getting back on and each time a bit smarter. My story is a story that cycles from balance to out of balance, back to balance, and so forth, round and round. See, sort of a dance.

The number of times I pivoted, reset, and a few times completely relaunched my business, is a significant part of this story. Sometimes the best thing to do is simply start over. Or pivot.

Your diet is not working? Start over. Get a new accountability partner and start over. Your working out is not working out? Try something different. Your relationship is not working? Tweak it. Or start over. Your sales are under target? Then pivot. Your sales are way under target? Then fire yourself and start over with your new self. You're not happy? Then evaluate and start over. This process is the letting go of things that no longer serve you and starting over.

Oh my God, the simplicity of this is beautiful! Stop over-complicating your life or your business and just start over! If it's not working out yet, at a high level, if you're not happy and financially stable, then you're not done! It doesn't matter if you're twenty-seven or fifty-seven. Dig in and start over. It doesn't matter if you're chronically single or twice divorced. Step into your happiness. It doesn't matter if you're lost or found. Step into your quest. Step into your unshakable spirit. Step into getting it right. Step into knowing you're worth it. Step into knowing that pivoting is one of the greatest gifts life has to offer. Keep going. Step into your success.

> *So I just showed up to invite you to give the world notice that you're coming*
> *Give the world notice that you've been here*
> *Give the world notice that you've played polite long enough*
> *Now is time to play full out*
> *Give the world notice that unapologetic just showed up*
> *Give the world notice that non-negotiable just showed up*
> *Give the world notice that if they can't handle your light*
> *That you're tired, you're not going to dim your light*
> *If they can't handle your light, put on some shades*
> *I'm just sayin.*
> *Are you willing?*
> —LISA NICHOLS, *I WAS BROKE AND BROKEN*, YOUTUBE

I find that most successful business owners, most successful real estate professionals pivoted a lot or wish they had pivoted sooner. This is common. Some of the top agents in the country, the superstars, the mega teams, I've seen hundreds of them on stage all espousing a similar story of the early years being quite messy. I have heard the best of the best say they almost left the business, they almost left before they pivoted, they failed before they succeeded.

The business pivot topic is not new. There is a *Forbes* article from July 2015 on the business pivot that says: "According to one estimate, as many as 15–20 percent of startups pivot from their initial business plan. In some ways, pivoting a company can be like pressing the restart button on your laptop, and it can breathe new life into a failing venture." That 2015 *Forbes* article references a 2012 *New York Times* article on the topic of how startups often fail their way forward. It's the fail-forward concept of "... sometimes the first try doesn't go as planned."

I am a big fan of the restart button, a big fan of the hit-the-reset-button approach to getting what you want. Not happy? Change something. And when you change something, or something is changed for you, the speed of your life changes.

Let's take a closer look at my pivot record.

PIVOT 1
Year 3, Vision

I loved my first brokerage. It was a small boutique run by two dear friends, and they were generous in mentoring my start in the business. Former educators, the mentor thing came naturally to them. And I was a good student, I was a talented junior agent. With $3.8 million in sales volume in my first full year (all personally generated), I awarded myself the Rookie of the Year award. The problem with that self-assigned award is that, besides being self-assigned, I was the only rookie. I had no competition. So it was a bit of a fake award, but I assigned it to myself and it was what I needed at the time.

As with many agents, it took me a year or two to begin to form the vision of what I really wanted with this new career. Did I want my own brokerage? Who did I want to be as an agent? How could I make the biggest impact?

What sort of specializations interested me? What was I good at? What sort of customer experience did I want to provide for my clients? How could I bring more value? How would I attract the ideal client? How in the heck do you take time off in this business? Realistically, how much money could I make? What was I building and how was I going to get there?

I came to the realization that I wanted a bigger platform to build on my vision. I was with a small brokerage and they were, and still are, successful, professional, trustworthy, generous, good people. But I was itchy and my business was flat. I did not know how to get to the next level, and I'm not sure I asked. I felt the need to be exposed to different ways to do this thing called real estate. I was curious about and wanted to be surrounded by top producers, movers, and shakers, a variety of agents. I felt insulated and wanted a bigger platform to create the customer experience I was starting to piece together. Because of how I learn, I came to the realization that I needed to be around more agents, top producers so that maybe their success would rub off. You hang around the barbershop long enough and sooner or later you're going to get a haircut. So in the sophomore year of my real estate career, I moved my business to the biggest game in town.

This was not an easy decision for me. I hate disappointing anyone. I am a nice, loyal, youngest child, Midwest girl, and I lost sleep over disappointing my business partners, my friends who believed in me, who had mentored me for two years. Loyalty matters, but I realized that my commitment to my family and our financial goals took precedence over loyalty to my colleagues and broker, and I needed to have the courage to make a meaningful move toward my goals. I knew I needed to make a dynamic move to another business model. So I made the business decision. I pivoted.

PIVOT 2
Year 8, Team

> *If you do not have an assistant, you are one.*
> —SAID EVERYONE WHO HAS AN ASSISTANT

A lot happened between year three and year eight. With a new focus and a huge training push, I pulled my business out of the slide hitting $5 million, then $7 million, then $9 million over the next few years. How did that happen? It was all about the brokerage move and a mindset shift and my life and business speeding up. I tapped into training and mentoring times ten. I grew into myself, grew into my future self. I was hungry. The brokerage move upped my technology, tricked out my website, and put me in a position to observe (and copy) some of the best agents. And it worked.

And I was killing myself. I was working all the time. The perceived issue was time, the real issue was leverage. I needed help. What I was doing, how I was operating was not sustainable. So the second major pivot in my real estate career was building a team. It started with an assistant (always start with an assistant; actually, start with a closing coordinator, then an assistant) and then a buyer's agent. I was learning how to leverage and how to incorporate that into my business.

A little clarification here on hiring, on your first hire. Typically, the best and safest and lowest financial risk leverage is hiring a contract-to-close specialist on a contract-only basis. This person is not an employee, not technically a hire, but is definitely leverage. This key person is your right-hand angel who does the heavy lifting and detail checklist monitoring to get your buyers and sellers safely from under-contract to here-are-your-keys. And, assuming they are licensed, you get to tell your clients that they get two licensed professionals for the price of one and you look more like a business to your clients.

Perfectionists and control freaks, pay attention here. I am not saying that perfectionists are control freaks, but most control freaks are perfectionists. You know who you are. Chances are you are proud of your perfectionist leaning tendencies and that wiring has served you well. And that wiring can hold you back in growing your business. Your ability to let go of some of the minutia, will free you up to tend to higher dollar activity. Otherwise, you'll just be working more and more hours, the quality of your life will be compromised, and your ability to grow your business even further will have critical time restrictions. Sometimes we have to loosen our grip to move forward.

So I hired a contract-to-close specialist (I think it was $350 per contract, and that is still pretty much the cost today), then I hired a paid assistant (my first employee . . . now I do not like to have employees, only contract help), then I added a buyers' agent onto my team. I stepped from solo agent to small team.

The shift from solo to not solo is actually a really big shift. Not only is it a shift in leverage and sales trajectory (it should always have a sales trajectory; if not, fix it fast), but it is the psychological shift of you moving from solo entrepreneur to CEO, from solo to boss, from lead myself to lead a team, from I do everything to I am running a business, from I am responsible for myself to I am now responsible for other people that will ultimately, if you do it right, have the biggest impact on your business.

PIVOT 3
Year 10, Acquisition and Help

In 2009, I had the opportunity to acquire another agent's business. The agent was a top agent in my office and she had a unique opportunity to move her family back to California. To make that happen, she needed an Austin business partner to adopt her client relationships, and I was the right match. Think of it a bit like a second marriage and growing your family. In the acquisition, I gained a seriously talented buyers' agent. I started my team over.

The team lineup changed four or five times over the years. To be brutally honest, I was really good at real estate and sort of okay running a team. Note, my personal shift from solo entrepreneur to boss lady to CEO was one I had to really work at and required mentors and coaches to help me see the way, or stumble along the path. I see this a lot in the general agent population . . . good at real estate, not great running a business. Being a good boss, running the team was not my strongest suit. But the team members were good, smart, hard-working people, and we all liked each other, so it worked.

In hindsight, the models that exist today for building and running a team, for being a good real estate boss, are amazing compared to what I was working off of at the time. But again, a pattern re-emerged, and I was working all the time. (Here's a hint: Look for your patterns.)

I was out of balance and seeking direction for my team. So I hired a coach, an interim CEO of sorts. I hired a coach because I did not want to keep repeating my patterns. I hired a coach because I feared, if left to myself, I would keep doing what I had been doing. I hired a coach because I needed help to create change and stay the course. I hired a coach to run less of a squirrel farm and stay focused on the goals. I hired a coach because being the CEO required growth. I am made up of a seriously distractible attention span; I was beginning to learn how to run a team and grow a business and I am pleased to say I had help navigating that ship. Year after year, your job is to be better at who you are and that doesn't mean you have to do that alone.

PIVOT 4
Year 12, Be Careful What You Ask For

> There are certain times in life that lend themselves to change, that make change quicker, deeper. I call them intervals of possibility. You know there are times in your life when you come to bifurcation on the path, and you sense that the potential for change is heightened.
> —CAROLINE MCHUGH, TEDTALK

I believe there are magical times in life when the stars align and opportunities and blessings show up in your path. Sometimes these happen to you because you stepped in that direction, and sometimes these happen to you, catastrophically, without warning or choice. Without fail, these blessings show up when you are ready and, in my experience, when you finally have the clarity and wherewithal to ask the Universe or yourself for direction or insight.

In October of 2010, I was seriously restless and had a meaningful conversation with my business coach. Typically, my conversations with my coach were specifically business related—accountability, goal progress, obstacle maneuvering, situational dissecting, and mindset tweaks. Occasionally, the coaching conversation was deeply personal. For me, this is the right coaching balance, left brain and right brain, business and get my head on straight or talk off some cliff or deal with my baggage. As it turns out, this particular coaching conversation was personal and pivotal, and I tell this story all the time.

I told her I had two very distinct goals for the next year. Goal one, get my life back in balance (a repetitive theme). I felt like I was in the midst of or at risk of a self-imposed implosion. I seemed to have misplaced my happiness, and stress was kicking my butt. And goal two, increase my business and bank account. In that order. Happiness, health, and balance first, business and bank second. I was staring at a burnout cliff and had every intention of fixing it. Jon Gordon, best-selling author, says we don't get burned out because of what we do, we get burned out because we forget why we do it. Pivots are often about just that, realigning ourselves with why we do what we do. I had profound clarity around these two goals.

And a profound thing happened. See the connection there? Clarity and solutions are inseparable.

Seriously, the very next day, within twenty-four hours after this deeply personal and pivotal coaching conversation, I get a call from my Team Leader (similar to a managing broker). A leadership position had opened up, and I was a possible candidate. I had the opportunity to take on the Director of Career Development position in the largest real estate office in the world (at the time, the largest for agent count and volume of real estate sales). (A little precursor here, I had been voluntarily running the Education Committee in this office for years, working closely with the Director to drive that program.) I asked the universe for balance, and this was the very loud answer, the show-up-in-my-voicemail-within-24-hours answer.

All the lights went on. This was a super big pivot.

This was a coveted full-time staff coaching position within the Keller Williams Realty franchise system. This type of opportunity rarely surfaces, and I ran with it. I knew it was what I was supposed to do and that it would change the trajectory of my business and my life. I quickly partnered my business with another top agent in the office and started working on that transition.

PIVOT 5
Year 17, Crash

My go-to analogy for stress repetitively showing up in my world is that I am a sprinter. I am a sprinter, not a marathoner. Literally and figuratively. I was a bit of a track star in high school. I could crush the 100-yard hurdles, and would completely bonk on the third turn in the 400. It has always confused me that the quarter-mile is considered a sprint. Fifty yards is a sprint; the quarter-mile always kicked my ass. And there was that one fall I was on the cross-country team . . . not my thing. I prefer the short distances to the long. I am wired with fast-twitch muscle fiber and a high metabolism and have often wondered if this translates to how my brain is wired. When I take on something, I go full-on, pedal to the metal and I keep going. And I have a tendency to say "yes" a lot; I take things on. This bodes well for the short distance, and is a failure ticket for the marathon.

I was running the largest new agent training program in the country. For five years, I helped nearly 150 brand new agents each year get their start in real estate. This was super meaningful work, I helped agents change their lives. And I oversaw the overall training effort in this big office. I was sprinting. And saying yes a lot. Sprint, yes, sprint, yes, sprint, yes. And I hit a wall. A lot like that wall on the third turn of the 400, I crashed. Interestingly enough, there were other leaders in that office who were health crashing too; it was definitely a go-go-go environment.

I landed at the cardiologist. I am a healthy, sporty, trim, 50-something and my heart was racing, my chest was tight.

I was at a coaching workshop just outside of Austin with about 300 coaches and trainers and industry leaders from around the country. I remember the exact seat I was sitting in, middle left aisle about ten rows back, blue backpack, black suit jacket, shiny silver Italian loafers (I have a shoe thing). And something was off. Something was physically off. I was pretty sure it was not right for a healthy, sporty, well-hydrated gal to have a racing heart and tightness in her chest. I tried meditating in my seat. I tried breathing exercises. I ate a healthy snack, drank some water. And it persisted.

So I walked out of the big room shaking. I was practically in tears. I knew a lot of the folks running the conference, so I asked for help. In the back hallway, I told someone that I was having trouble breathing. They immediately summoned one of the top coaches at the conference, my former health coach. When she set eyes on me, she literally had to look twice because when she got the message that someone at the conference was having chest tightness and breathing issues, frankly, I think she expected to encounter an older or heavier or not particularly healthy conference attendee, and I did not fit the profile. I remember the questioning look on her face. I think the first word out of her mouth was simply, "Julie?" as she looked quizzically around to see if there was someone else standing nearby having breathing issues.

Fast forward, it was not a heart attack. I get to the hospital, pass all the tests with flying colors, get assigned to a cardiologist for more tests. Everything checks out fine. Turns out that sprinting and sprinting and sprinting is not sustainable. Go figure. I was exhausted, and stress was showing up in my body. I landed at the cardiologist again five months later with the same thing. Same symptoms, same test results, same diagnosis. It was a wakeup call. A huge wake up call. I felt a little train-wrecky, something had to shift. It was time to let someone else figure out how to take the program to the next level, the next more manageable level, and time for me to do something else. It was time to pivot.

So the next big pivot in this story is how I decided to go back to being a solo entrepreneur, formalize The Nelson Project training and coaching company, and start writing a book that could help more than 150 agents per year.

PIVOT 6
Year 18, Relaunch

My training and coaching company had been a part of my work for years. Helping real estate business people grow their successful careers has been a long-time passion that fuels my inner fire. The time was right to pull it all together and relaunch. In 2016, I generated the first published version of this very book, designed a couple online courses, became a contributing writer for Inman News, blogged, podcasted, spoke nationally, got my life and health back. And made very little money in the process. It was a bit of a sabbatical year. And I loved it.

As a bit of a side note, I want to make a comment on the sabbatical concept. I think we need more of this in our culture. I've done it twice and it helped me channel a slightly less uptight version of myself. Academia prescribes it. Australia calls it a gap year. Europe practically shuts down in August. We are such a hard-working, driven society, and I have seen so many people with the work/life balance thing not balanced at all. And when that work/life balance thing is not balanced at all, it's a slippery slope for happiness, health, and family. It's a challenge in real estate. Work, work, work. Disrespect the family, the kids, your health. Sprint, sprint, sprint. Skip meals. Sprint. And life flies by. And then you land at the cardiologist.

If you can afford it, consider a sabbatical. It doesn't have to be a year, perhaps it is a month in Europe or a long RV trip with the kids. When you are about to relaunch, it is super valuable, if not critical, to get your head right, your health right, your priorities straight, catch your breath, and reclaim your life. Relaunch with a solid foundation.

Back to my story.

I realized that I needed and wanted to redesign and boost my financial path. My spouse had recently retired, at 53 from a 29-year teaching career, and we were taking a close look at our 10-year plan. It was very clear to me what I needed to do. I would continue some training, writing, and speaking, but what is it that I know how to do best? Real estate. With renewed vigor, health, and clarity, I relaunched my *real* real estate business in 2017.

When I first wrote the original e-version of *Success Faster*, I was relaunching my business, my real estate practice. If anyone could do it, if anyone could efficiently and successfully relaunch their real estate practice, the director from the one of the largest agent training programs in the country could. Or should. I felt some pressure, but in a good way.

True to form, I gave the real estate relaunch a theme, even a logo (compliments of WordSwag), because a nice visual helps me stay focused. And is part of my squirrel tendencies. I'll be working on an idea or plan and somehow find myself in WordSwag or Canva working out some graphic or social media post to support it. Happens all the time on my squirrel farm.

The theme for the relaunch was "zero to ten in ten months." My plan was to go from $0 sales income (starting over) to $10M in sales in 10 months. It was an aggressive goal, but was doable for an experienced agent fresh off of sabbatical with a vision, the right leverage, a logo, a catchy theme, and a backpack full of best practices. Why 10M in 10 months? Well I was sure I could do $6M, I could most likely do $8M, and $10M sounded like a nice stretch goal and was catchy with the approximately 10 months left in the year.

PIVOT 7
Year 18, Changing Brokerages

I did not see this coming.

In the midst of my 2017 relaunch (Pivot 6), I hired a coach. An amazing coach! I had the 0-to-10-in-10 plan in place and moving along. I needed some accountability to stay on pace, fuel to get to the next level financially, and help in formulating my five-year plan. And I was still working out some noise from the Pivot 5 crash. Hint, identify your noise, recognize it, own it, and deal with it. My coach is highly skilled with noise reduction, highly skilled with working some of the underlying issues in order to push through to a better version and the next level. She's a lifesaver, my secret weapon.

The relaunch was working, but I was still trying to figure out the other pieces . . . my coaching practice, teaching opportunities, writing the book, how to do a slightly easier version of real estate, creating an accelerated retirement plan, and continuing to make a difference in the world. How can I make more money in less time? Or how can I help agents make more money in less time? I wanted help pulling all that together and occasional conversations with my personal and professional besties, while valuable and insightful and sometimes involving happy hour, those conversations were not resulting in the formulation of a clear plan. Hiring a coach is leverage to get somewhere faster. I knew I needed more than the slow drip, drip, drip financial progress that was completely reliable on my next real estate sale. I desired a seat on a faster train to freedom with multiple sources of income. Millionaires, on average, have seven streams of income, and I sort of had two or three, and those were somewhat inconsistent.

We laid out all of the pieces I was attempting to weave together, some of those pieces more successfully than others, and we jumped in as a team to dissect and reassemble the tapestry into something I could wrap my arms and heart and bank account around. And an interesting thing happened.

I came to the realization that I was bumping into walls and ceilings at my current brokerage. I felt that the company vibe and rules had shifted over the years, as had mine, and I was questioning whether it was still the best fit for me and my business and my five- to ten-year plan. Things change in all organizations, so I did not have a lot of judgment going on—well, some—but for the most part, I was experienced enough to know how businesses and organizations and people change over time.

I felt at a bit of a crossroads. Do I stay with my sixteen-year brokerage for the rest of my sales career, another five to ten years, or is there another model that has the potential to move my business, my goals, my bank account and investments ahead faster? Do I recommit and stay in this place, where I really care for these people and have built up friendships and a national reputation, or is there another industry vehicle I should consider? I am a fan of independently studying the industry and knowing what else is out there; this is normal business. Ford should understand Ferrari. Dell should understand Apple. The traditional brokerage should understand new emerging models.

I found myself looking at other brokerage models, but I really had this loyalty thing going on. It was my intention to stay, but I was starting to realize that I probably had some blinders on in terms of how I was perceiving or interpreting my five-to-ten-year plan and my options moving forward.

It is human nature that we filter things based on what we know and based on our experiences. If you grew up in a large and happy and Baptist family, then you filter your world and how you perceive things based on everything that is built into large and happy and Baptist. If you grew up in a dysfunctional and financially lacking environment, then you filter (sometimes for your entire life) based on the set of beliefs that tend to accompany dysfunction and lack. So what is your set of beliefs that you carry with you today, personally and professionally, and do they still serve you?

I had this sense that I just wasn't all that happy. And very few people knew this. I was either going to need to adapt, or I would need to create a new solution. I felt like I had been adapting and then adapting some more, adjusting to continue to fit in, and realized I was morphing away from myself and starting to play small. Anyone who knows me, knows I am not hard-wired to play small.

As I moved through this soul-searching business and personal re-evaluation exercise, I realized that the process was a tremendous amount of work. The work-through-your-baggage process is heavy lifting for introspective-leaning fiercely loyal types like me. For other folks who are all business, perhaps this type of exercise is natural, and you easily move onto another opportunity... for me, it took some time.

Methodically, my coach helped me work through my noise and my vision. One of the main benefits of doing that hard, introspective work is that I fully vetted my needs, my thoughts, my financial outlook, and my five-to-ten-year plan. My resolve was solid and I moved my eighteen-year license to a newer emerging technology-driven agent-owned cloud-based brokerage. New chapter!

PIVOT 8
TBD, You Never Know

Who knows if there will be a Pivot 8? Late in the process of writing *Success Faster*, and after much introspection (believe me, write a book and you'll be in introspection overload, years' worth of introspection wrapped into the hundreds of hours and months and months of brain space!), it had me wondering what my next pivot might be. Why wouldn't there be another pivot out there? What other opportunities will surface? My mindset could shift. What lovely sabbatical may present itself? I could win the lottery. I dream of an RV trip. A month of skiing has been on the bucket list for some time. So I add Pivot #8 as a place-keeper for my next move or opportunity. And how lovely to know that it is there, that place-keeper for something awesome, something new, something unknown.

So back to the truth-o-meter career start headline, I am writing this book for you.

I am writing this book for the beginning and middle agent who has a dream.

I am writing this book for the relaunching agent who has a vision.

I am writing this book for the independent broker who is tired or financially strapped or struggling to keep the right agents on the bus and keep them productive and happy and engaged.

I am writing for that independent broker who is tired of chasing people to help them be successful.

I am writing this book for the pivoting professional.

I am writing this book for the real estate pro who has not yet found her groove.

I am writing this book for the real estate pro who has found her groove but is always striving for the next level.

I am writing this book for those who seek financial freedom.

I am writing this book for those seeking solutions and tools and direction and a roadmap.

I am writing this book for those who seek a voice and an ally.

I am writing this for the agent who is a bit over the over-abundance of mega mega mega superstar agent advice out there that applies to almost no one.

And writing for the mega mega superstar who is re-embracing the basics and resetting and realigning with net happiness.

If you are that person who has the vision of creating some amazingness in your life through real estate career success, then you are in the right place.

Regardless of the size, shape, or color of your sales goals, 3, 5, 10, 20 million... it's your goal, own it, and don't let anyone tell you that you are not thinking big enough!

I write this book for anyone who has pivoted and judged themselves for it or anyone who thinks they may need to pivot and is judging that as some sort of failure, set-back, or falling short.

Pivot can be brilliant, refreshing, and life-changing.

Let's take a closer look at how *Success Faster On Fire Hot!* will help you get on track to building something amazing in your life.

CHAPTER 4

Some Things They Never Told You in Real Estate School

If you have a dream, you can spend a lifetime studying, planning, and getting ready for it. What you should be doing is getting started.

—Drew Houston, founder DropBox

When you made the decision to start in real estate, whether part-time or full-time (more on that later), you were making the decision to change your life. You realize that, right? You may have started full-on or on a whim or as a side gig or a fill-in after a layoff. Regardless of the reason or circumstance, that decision, that move shifted the trajectory of your life.

Any new career choice is a choice for your future. Any new career choice, new career beginning, is you making an exponential move toward your future. When you started in real estate, the day you decided to get your license, the day you signed up for your first real estate class, the day you actually got your license, the day you signed on with your broker, the day you told your best friend what you wanted to do, you were making the decision to move your life forward.

If you were or are going in full-time, then you made the decision to leave the safety, the financial safety and ceiling of the traditional workforce, and enter this amazing business. You made the decision to enter this business that, frankly, is a bit easy to get into, and much harder to stay.

In *Success Faster On Fire Hot!*, we will plow into techniques and best practices that are designed to help you succeed in real estate, designed to help you gain clients and momentum quickly, designed to help you stay and thrive, designed to help you create something amazing in your life, designed to help you have the courage to pivot. *Success Faster On Fire Hot!* is practical and actionable and is designed to help you get a leg up in an amazing business that, frankly, has a high fallout rate. That fallout rate does not need to include you. We are here to help.

But there are some things they never told you in real estate school. Let's take a look.

Challenges to Getting Started (or Restarted)

Let's get the bad news out of the way fast. Statistics for first-year success are abysmal.

It is a common industry belief that the likelihood of a newly licensed agent still being in the business one or two years later is around 10 percent. Simple math tells us that one out of every ten newly licensed agents will actually remain in the business.

I do not fully buy into that statistic. I have spent hours trying to find the source of that widely-held number, the one-out-of-ten success thing. I even emailed back and forth with NAR (the National Association of REALTORS®) researchers. NAR knows that the industry throws these statistics around like Hell's Kitchen throws fire, but they said it did not come from them. I am a bit skeptical of the 90% attrition position. I am skeptical because there are so many licensees around the country that do other things besides full-on traditional real estate sales. There are property managers, administrators, and researchers. But let's say even if that attrition number is closer to a 75 or 80 percent dropout rate, that maybe only one in four of the newly licensed actually stick around, it's still a daunting number.

It is my personal mission to crush fallout, improve retention, positively impact the professional landscape, and significantly increase the odds of your success in this business. It is my mission for you to be part of the winners' circle who make this into a viable, sustainable, and rewarding business. The true endgame and vision is that your thriving real estate career will put money in your bank, will reduce or eliminate your debt, will get your kids through college, will fund your vacations and your dreams, and will change your life. Your thriving career and your thriving life, they go hand in hand. Ask for and outline everything you've ever wanted, and then some. We are going all-in with your dreams. They say you can't have too much of a good thing (wish I would have been part of that study), but we are not buying into that with *On Fire Hot!* And then the greatest bonus, the icing on the good-thing cake is that when you change and build your amazing life, you will change and build someone else's. I feel an obligation to participate in that success circle of life.

What are some of the reasons for the sobering industry fallout? I think it comes down to these six things: ease of licensure, unrealistic expectations, cash flow, being a good boss (or not), your energy, and never fully owning how to do sales. I'll expand here a bit, and throughout the book in significantly more detail, on how you can overcome these potential hazards.

ONE
Ease of Licensure
In most states, it is very easy to get a real estate license. Almost too easy. Fill out an application, pay some money, take four or five or six classes online (none of which are called How to Succeed in Real Estate), pay a little more money, pass a state exam, a national exam, and a background check, maybe some fingerprints, pay a little more money to join a board and MLS, find a broker, and ta-da! You're in business! Now what?

This happens in many industries. I asked my favorite doctor, my go-to doc who runs her own small practice, Did they teach you how to run a business in med school? No. I have asked my therapist friends the same question, Did they teach you how to run a business in your masters or PhD program? No. I asked my massage therapist. No. I asked my nephew, Ian, who is a professional chef in Chicago. One class. You get the picture.

In your real estate classes, did they teach you how to run a real estate business? In real estate school did they teach you how to generate leads and build a healthy pipeline? In real estate school did they teach you what to say when someone says "Why should I hire you?" or "I am interviewing three agents." or "How's the market?" No, they did not. Or that class was optional. Your real estate school taught you contracts (although they missed nuance and negotiation), they taught finance, legal and ethics, and how to pass a state and national exam.

TWO
Unrealistic Expectations
Your real estate license classes taught you how to pass an exam. You learned real estate ethics, real estate law, real estate contracts, and real estate finance. You may have learned some marketing. All very important things. But your pre-license real estate school missed some very important and foundational things.

Your classes did not teach you how to attract and retain clients, how to build a pipeline of qualified clients, or how to run a business. Additionally, your pre-license classes most likely did not cover any sort of financial model instruction including expense and profit targets. For some of you, your past experience—sales, college, your corporate jobs, family experience—may have prepared you for sales and successful real estate; but, for many of you, not so much. Arguably, I would like to see Business 101 and Sales 101 added to the pre-license course requirements. Newly minted agents show up eager to jump into their new business and realize, very quickly, that it costs money to run a real estate business, that no one taught them about a sales pipeline, and attracting clients is harder and slower than they thought.

And what about your broker? Does your broker teach you how to run a good business? The old real estate brokerage model, which still exists today, does not produce business owners; it simply produces salespeople who are dependent upon their broker. I have a friend that I work with who spent her first five years in the business working part-time with a small mom and pop brokerage that had 4–6 agents at any given time. She said no one ever taught her about a database or a lead pipeline and she never had her own website. Know what you are getting from your broker and know that you need a lot more training in your first few years.

Today's real estate model is different . . . you must learn to be a good business person. Did anyone tell you, before you got your license, that you were in a lead generation business first and a real estate business second? You are actually in the business of having conversations with people about real estate . . . but school did not teach you what to say! Did they teach you about CRM's and a pipeline and an efficient follow-up system? If so, you're one of the lucky ones. If not, you learned that super fast, right?

THREE

Cash Flow

These unrealistic expectations can lead to the third reason, cash flow. Everything in real estate, every payday, is sixty to ninety days out, at best. That means that the work you are doing today, will result in your paycheck in 2-3 months. Or 6-12 months for new construction. Or 1-3 years for commercial transactions. My record is 8 years, from gaining the lead from a friend and then 8 years later when she finally decided to sell her rental property.

Conversely, the work you do not do today, will not result in a paycheck in 2-3 months. The work you do (or do not do) in the fourth quarter will show up (or not) in your bank account in the first quarter, your first quarter work will show up in your bank account in the second quarter and so on. If it is new construction, that paycheck can be nine months out. If it is a commercial contract, six to twelve months is not uncommon. If a brand-new agent starts on January 1, will she have a paycheck in March or April? It depends on what she is doing in January.

If an agent is slow to start or is cautious or lacking confidence or is a bit of a perfectionist, that agent may not have a client lead in January. Or the agent may have two or three leads but none of them convert, yet, to an active client. I am regularly working with buyers and sellers that I have been in conversation with, off and on, for six to twelve months. You get the picture. Cash flow, or the lack thereof, is very real for most new agents. Agents who start in the business with very little cash reserve basically have a cash flow problem on day one. Cash is king, and sales solve everything.

FOUR
Bossy

And the fourth reason, in my opinion, for the abysmal first-year success rate for real estate pros is the failure to be a good boss. This is a huge topic that gets its own chapter later in the book.

We have all pretty much worked for someone else in previous careers or jobs, so we know what it looks like to be a good employee. And hopefully you have had a good boss or two over the years. We treated our former boss or bosses with respect, we were reliable employees who knew how to show up on time (hopefully you were that person), and we were consistently responsible about getting the most important things done. We did these things not only out of a sense of doing the right thing, but we did these things for job security. Right?

But this strange thing happens with too many agents. Suddenly you are your own boss, but instead of the discipline of getting the most important things done every day (and hint, that thing is not your new marketing plan, new logo, or making a cool new flyer), you're off running a complete squirrel farm, chasing shiny objects all day long with little to no progress on creating client opportunities.

So many agents are not holding themselves accountable to a strict schedule and a reliable daily lead generation effort. I will dive deeper on this topic, but for now let's agree on a couple of things. First, the good news about your new career choice is that you are your own boss. The bad news? The bad news is that you are your own boss. Don't be a lousy one.

FIVE
Your Energy, Your Power Score

The fifth challenge may be your energy, your confidence, how you are showing up in the world. I call this your power score or intensity score, and we will do a deep dive on that later in the book. Here is the basic premise . . . you are in the people attraction business. You are in the business of having conversations with people about real estate (you will hear this statement *ad nauseum* in *Success Faster On Fire Hot!*).

This takes a certain amount of energy, of people-attraction juju. Does being around and engaging with people bring you energy or completely zap you? How well do you adapt when someone's behavior style is different from yours? Do you like to be in the mix, or do you prefer solitude, quiet, and an impressive spreadsheet?

When I was in the training director seat, I had new agents in my office all the time. I could usually read someone's energy, their power score, within minutes. The power score walked in the room before their seat hit the chair. How were they carrying themselves? What was their energy? How was their eye contact?

This is not an introvert-extrovert thing. I have trained introverts whose power score was high; I have trained extroverts who seemed to misplace their confidence in the newness of the situation and steepness of the learning curve. In early chapters, we will dive into taking inventory of how you're showing up in the world. As with any big task, goal, new chapter, starting a new business, training for a marathon, preparing for grad school, or planning a family, taking inventory on where you're at in comparison to probably where you need to be can make all the difference in the world. Do you need to evolve to accomplish that big task, to become who you want to be? Or is it more an enhancement of who you already are? How are you showing up in the world?

SIX
Never Fully Owning How to Do Sales

When I first got into real estate, I told myself that I was never going to be that salesy sort of agent. I was very clear that I did not want to have anything to do with the fast-moving, slick-talker, car-salesy persona. I never saw myself in the sales business; the house would sell itself.

I saw my role as a trusted advisor, solutions provider, industry expert, and friend. And that is how I approached my business in the first few years. Until my business started falling off, strong one month, weak the next, non-existent the next two, then back to two or three clients, and rinse and repeat. I was working all the time and my cash was not reliable or wiped out because I had my head in the sand regarding income taxes. (Most agents I know got hit once, early on in their career, with a failure to plan for taxes; please avoid this rookie mistake.)

Nowhere in real estate school did they teach or even mention a sales pipeline. My business minor in college covered Accounting 101 (hated it, but now I get it), Marketing 101, some sort of professional writing course (actually a super valuable class), and Intro to Law (a really tough course; you know, weed out 19-year-olds who think they want to go to law school).

I think every two or four-year degree should include a graduation requirement of Entrepreneurship 101 for all students. The art students, the musicians, the teachers, the engineers, the athletic trainers, the athletes, the mechanics, the chefs ... all of them. Seems that so many people eventually end up opening their own business, end up as an entrepreneur because of skill or passion, but have no clue how to run a business and drive sales. Just because you're good at your craft, your skill, doesn't mean you're decent at building sales.

When I first started in real estate in 1999, I was not even familiar with the concept of a sales pipeline. How did I have a business minor and not even really understand this basic business lifeline concept? Of course, I did have an awareness of whether I had my next few clients lined up or not, but I was not aggressively driving that bus. Rather, that tricked-out bus was just sitting on the side of the road assuming people would get on.

An important part of my business journey is when I finally began to recognize how the most important thing I could do for my business and for my bank and for my psyche was to get in the driver's seat of that sales bus.

Are you ready to own and drive that bus, take ownership of your energy, shift into the best bossy version of yourself, address your cash flow, and drive sales?

The good news is that you can do this. You can do this, and it is a super cool business with limitless opportunity. The good news about your success? It's what it will do for your life, your family, your independence. Your success in your real estate career will change the trajectory of your life.

Let's take a look at some changed lives, see if you relate to any of these stories.

CHAPTER 5

Real Agent Stories

Your past does not have to dictate your future;
write your own story.

We all have our stories. Some of them are true. We have the real factual stories, the abbreviated stories, the exaggerated stories, and the stories we tell ourselves. You have your story of how you got to where you are today. Someone else may have a different version of your journey. You'll have a story at the end of this year, and another one two or three years from now. You have, or are about to have, your getting started or getting restarted or hitting the refresh button story, or your On Fire Hot! story. Most getting started stories are a bit messy. Most success stories started with a few failures. You have your story on paper, what really happened, and you have the story in your head, what you are telling yourself happened. Be careful with the stories you are telling yourself; some of them are true, some of them are baggage showing up in the form of the story you keep telling yourself. Your story matters, but the story that matters the most is the one you are currently writing.

Success Faster On Fire Hot! is about writing your next story. Let's take a look at some getting started stories.

WE'LL START WITH ME
Thought About Real Estate for Years

> Often when you think you're at the end of something, you're at the beginning of something else. —FRED ROGERS

Before I got into real estate, I had a career in high-tech. It was a career that chose me, I did not choose it. I was the liberal arts grad in a sea of engineers and was lacking a vision of where I wanted to go, of how I wanted to live my life. It was a good company with good people. I was paid well (or so I thought) and had amazing travel opportunities. In a growing company where I was a bit of a utility player, I seemed to have a new title every six to twelve months. They even had me as the accounting manager for a while, which was just wrong; what were they thinking? I was a leaf in the career stream flowing downstream with few navigational tools, taking on whatever came my way with little vision of what I wanted or what was around the next bend. I was lacking a steering device and a compass. I was beginning to think that my career path, my professional life would never fill my soul, that professional bliss was not in my cards. I was starting to settle. And I was restless.

And then I got laid off. After eight years. The layoff day was a good day for me. I actually had a smile on my face, sort of had a smile on my face, as I was aware that it was supposed to be a somewhat somber conversation, but I already knew that it was my freedom ticket. My layoff day removed so much stress, just gone. I could breathe again, and that day is the day when I turned the corner toward real estate. I turned the corner to the rest of my life. I turned the corner toward doing something that I actually loved.

I had thought about real estate off and on for years but had been talked out of it a couple of times. And besides, I had a good job, so why replace good income, opportunity, and benefits with a 100% commission entrepreneurial endeavor that was harder than it looked? And get this, at age 16 I took a career assessment test that rated me low on entrepreneurial... and that actually stuck with me. I believed it to be true. That assessment result was part of the story I had been telling myself. Please, do the world a favor and intervene with your teenagers who are taking career assessments. They're young! Who knows what will motivate them at age 30! What age 16 messages do you need to dump? What programming in your psyche is no longer serving you or never served you in the first place?

I had been wondering for a long time what really, truly my path was supposed to be. I felt like I was a career wanderer stumbling upon various opportunities. I almost gave up believing that I would find work happiness or believing that I would make a difference or be famous or wealthy. It's like I was driven, yet I was lost. I was motivated, yet without a vision. I was degreed, yet without a target. I was confident, yet struggling. I had faith, only to misplace it. This cycle seemed to go on and on.

Until age thirty-eight and the layoff.

When I finally decided to get started with real estate, it's as if all the lights went on. Everything finally clicked, everything was in place to make this happen. Thanks to the layoff. I had to have a setback to make a meaningful step forward.

I was about to have a career that spoke to me at a deep level, that made sense. I was no longer that leaf in the corporate stream. I had a vision, I had a target, I had faith, I had joy. I was in charge of my professional life. I had never felt this way before. I never before had the courage to be self-employed (age sixteen baggage), and now here it was right in front of me. It completely made sense and dramatically changed the trajectory of my life.

STEPHANIE
Newly Divorced Mama Bear
Single mom with two teenage daughters in a high-end neighborhood, Stephanie needed solutions fast. With a medical sales background, she knew how to talk to people. Stephanie needed a financial solution for her family, and she needed to show her daughters that women can be professionally successful. She intended to set a tone with her daughters that the divorce was not a setback; it was a launching pad. She needed to show her daughters what empowerment looked like, needed to show courage in the face of change, that starting over could be a very good thing. I think she also had a little dose

of "I'll show you" to the ex who, for years, undermined her aspirations and enthusiasm. Stephanie was about to take charge of her oxygen circle and her life and write her own story and build a new story for her daughters.

Stephanie crushed it her first year. She was all mama bear, fierce and fearless and powerful and clear.

You see, Stephanie was not the top of her real estate class; she had to work harder to learn the business. She took most of my training classes twice. But she ran circles around some of the brainiacs because of her clarity and gumption. Mama Bear is a powerful force when starting over. Angela Lee Duckworth calls this grit in her TED Talks, "Grit: the power of passion and perseverance." Stephanie had grit, and her real estate career changed her life and laid a new foundation for her daughters.

WILLIAM
A Vision for His Life

A single father with two small boys. When William first walked into my office, our first coaching session, I had a hard time reading him. Either his energy was a bit low, or perhaps he was a quiet observer. He was pleasant, soft-spoken, good eye contact, a bit unclear on his direction, a man of few words, a bit loose on his ability to name a goal. He wasn't sure where he wanted to take his real estate career or what it would take for him to go full-time.

There was something compelling about William, something that made me think his well ran deep. I soon learned that not only would William talk to anyone (he is currently working with someone he met at the gas station), his roots in east Austin, his family ties, were extensive. His parents, his brothers and sisters (eight kids!) knew everyone in the rapidly changing and gentrifying east Austin. William had connections that some agents only dream of. Every possible community leader, every auto shop, hair salon, restaurant, little league coach, someone in William's family knew someone and they all looked out for each other. They had learned, from poverty in the early years to family crisis later on, that they needed each other, and that family and community were everything.

Identify what you're good at, identify your assets, identify your wheelhouse, and double-down. For William, his wheelhouse was his network in one very specific geographic area. In his first year, William did $3 million in volume as a part-time agent. He did something like $6.5 million and two flips his second year. His goal for year three was $10 million, three flips, and getting those two young sons into the best schools possible. William was writing an amazing story for his sons.

MELANIE
VP Level Marketing Pro

Marketing pro. Former VP of Marketing for national e-commerce leaders, Melanie had an impressive 25-year high-end marketing career in Dallas. Full disclosure here, Melanie is my business partner and sister-in-law. A couple things were happening in Melanie's world that were causing her to reassess. She was consistently working eighty hours a week, and her father was aging in Austin, her father was declining.

For years, Melanie had thought about relocating back to Austin, but VP-level marketing positions were few in Austin and plentiful in DFW. When the personal pull finally outweighed her high-end resume, Melanie bit the bullet and moved back to Austin.

Melanie had been a real estate junkie for years. She studied homes and design and the market and pricing in her spare time. She stopped by every open house. She knew as much as some experienced agents. She knew architecture, design, pricing before she even considered getting her real estate license. I had been telling her, for years, that real estate may be the solution to her next professional chapter, that a real estate career could free her from the corporate marketing world and create her Austin solution.

Melanie's real estate decision was a gradual one. She kept having short-term marketing opportunities through her various professional connections. She would start moving toward real estate, then have an opportunity to do a six-month marketing gig for big bucks. Then move a little more toward real estate, and one more corporate project would show up in her inbox. Not a bad problem to have, right? But Melanie wanted something more and different; she was ready for her next story and eventually went full-on with real estate.

SAM
Sixty-Something Non-Profit Executive

Sam had a successful career as a non-profit executive. His LinkedIn profile reads like a laundry list of getting things done—from business operations management, strategic leadership, and market development, to process enhancements and client relations. Married, two teenage sons, silver-haired, a bit nerdy, a serious punster, everyone likes Sam and you want him on your team. Sam's non-profit career hit a bump in the road, a bump called funding, and Sam found himself needing solutions. At the time, the funding environment for big non-profits created an oversupply of qualified director-level candidates. The resume-to-opportunity ratio was seriously lopsided in favor of the non-profit, lacking for the candidates, especially the higher salary candidates. So Sam turned to real estate in Austin, one of the most robust economies in the country.

With Sam's confidence, fearlessness, and people skills, he gained traction in real estate pretty quickly. Give him a task, he would do it. Show him the best practices, he would jump in. Put him in the toughest training program you offer (the one that is competitive to get in), and he excelled. He had enough of a training and HR background that he trusted the training programs and best practices recommendations. He assumed those programs had teeth and proven records, so he simply did everything that he was taught, without hesitation. He was the best student ... no ego, ready to emulate the top agents, willing to run with the industry standards.

Right away when he started, he was exposed to some of the top agents in Austin and saw that many of them and their teams were following the model of hitting the phones first thing every day. He embraced the foundational principle of more conversations equals more business. Sam quickly developed mad authentic phone skills and was cranking out calls for two to three hours every morning and showing property to buyers most afternoons.

These stories and your story are representative of many starts in the business. Some of the stories are unique, and some are common life changes and choices. Your story represents the foundation of your start, the lens on your vision, the beginning of your path. We will get back to these vignettes later in the book for an update on how they are doing a few years into their careers. Let's continue this theme and look at some first-year agents who hit it out of the park.

CHAPTER 6

Success Stories ... How Did These Rookie Sensations Kill It in Year One?

Sure, you need enormous amounts of technical expertise to be the best in the world. But to accomplish mindfulness, you just need something you already have: the willingness to quiet down, clear the crap and trust yourself.

—Danny Gregory, artist, author

I attend a lot of real estate conferences, and my favorite sessions, the speakers and panels I seek out the most, are those that feature the rookies of the year, the amazing out-of-the-box successes, the momentum grabbers, the freshman freaks. Refreshingly, most of these freshmen MVP's were humble, not salesy. In most cases, they were authentic in that their success was derived primarily from something close to home, something very close to their true selves.

When you're a kid, you're fantastic at being yourself. And then gradually we have a tendency to get away from that and become something that we think we're supposed to be but then, hopefully, you somehow find your way back to your authentic self. It's why I think we get more and more fabulous as we get older. What if you applied this to your real estate practice and simply capitalized on who you truly are? Many successful agents have done just that.

Let's take a closer look at some of these rookie success stories. A couple of these successful agents hit it way out of the park, a couple simply owned a solid start worthy of attention. Most of the names escape me, yet I have always remembered their stories.

As you read through these, pay attention to the narrowness of their focus. With maybe one exception, each of these award-winning freshmen did one thing particularly well. They took one aspect of the business, or one aspect of something true and close to them, or a major aspect of their personality and went all in; it's all they did, nothing else. While there are many real estate career starts out there who embraced a much broader approach—the I'll-talk-to-anyone, the leave-no-corner-untouched, the try-everything-or-anything, the try-this-or-this-or-that-until-something-sticks approach, and that works—there are thousands of stories out there that support the go-narrow approach to success.

Do not be afraid to narrowly define your sales target, to have a singular focus. You work with investors purchasing fourplexes in south Minneapolis. You work with high net worth families in Mexico City purchasing rental property in San Antonio. You work condos in the Logan Square area of Chicago, anything else you refer out to your business partners. Eighty percent of your marketing and your efforts is focused solely on the two schools your kids attend, and this results in 80 percent of your client opportunities. A quick note on this last one, when you focus on a school, you end up with a nice tight geographic focus, which makes it easier to be an expert, easier to know every single house in the area, easier to service your clients, easier on your gas tank, easier to jump on an immediate need versus one that requires a 45-minute drive across town, easier to be an expert quickly.

There's that quickly word again. When your focus is narrow, you will be an expert much faster than a wide-scope approach. When your focus is narrow, you'll be confident faster and, often, confident on day one because you are already working with something you know well or something that comes naturally or something you have already had your hands on in one way or another over the years.

Rookie of the Year Profiles

THE MINISTER GUY IN MISSISSIPPI
One Call Per Day

This first story has a story within the story, a bit of a side story.

When I first wrote this out in probably 2016 with the first draft of the first version of *Success Faster*, I had pulled this story from my business journals. I always remembered this guy's story and told it often in classes, but I never remembered his name, and I had failed to write it down in my journal. When I am writing those journals, they are simply notebooks full of notes from conferences, speakers, and classes. They are very quickly written notes meant simply to remember pertinent points that I would be able to take back home to my agents. If you're like me, you do not always catch the person's name unless they leave it on the screen for a while. Otherwise, it passes by as you quickly scribble down some of the pertinent points. I did not realize, at the time, that those notebooks would one day morph into book material.

Fast forward a couple of years after publishing *Success Faster* in 2018, and I get an email from Mark Metcalf, a broker in Jackson, Mississippi, and he says, "Hey, a friend of mine showed me your book, and I think I am your rookie preacher guy. Call me." I called him, it was a super fun conversation, and, yes, I found my rookie preacher guy. And, it turns out, we are with the same brokerage, so the extension of this story is running into him at a conference a year later. It's a small wonderful world.

This thirty-something's real passion, his mission, was coaching and training pastors. He helped ministers and churches bring more people in the doors. He started in real estate because he needed a flexible financial solution that would fund his mission. Real estate was not the end, it was the means. And here was his key: he knew everyone.

Some agents are phone volume freaks; this guy, seriously, he made one real estate lead gen phone call per day. One. And each daily real estate lead gen phone call typically resulted in an appointment. There are agents that it takes twenty phone calls to garner one appointment; Mark's ratio was close to one-to-one. His script was something like "In order to continue making an impact on churches and ministers in our area, I have to have three real estate appointments every week with someone who may need my services. Who do you know who is thinking of buying or selling and will you make the introduction, ask them to meet with me?" It worked. Rookie of the Year finalist.

THE DOOR-KNOCKER IN CANADA
New Shoes Every Three Months

This thirty-something guy used to sell air conditioners door-to-door in Toronto or Vancouver, somewhere cold. AC's in Canada, take that in for a minute. It's like selling expensive winter coats in Phoenix; not everyone needs one. His previous sales career was solely door-knocking. He was used to going door-to-door for eight hours a day. He said he wore through a new pair of shoes every ninety days. He was the top AC sales guy in his company. Knocking on doors was all he knew how to do, and he was really good at it. When he realized how he could take his current activity and seriously increase his paycheck, seriously increase the ROI on a pair of shoes, he jumped industries. When he learned that the lead generation benchmark for a top producer in real estate was three to four hours per day—in other words, door-knocking for half of the time he was accustomed to, half the shoes, half the doors with a much higher paycheck—he was all in. Mr. Canadian door-knocker was a National Rookie of the Year finalist.

THE INVESTOR IN VEGAS
Soft Spoken

This fifty-something guy was mild and soft-spoken and had been personally investing in real estate for years. On the side from his full-time casino job, he had rentals and flips, and his friends and colleagues were regularly asking him for help—help to find the deals, partnering on flips, negotiating with a FSBO, finding financing and investors. He was the go-to helpful guy before he even had his license. He was creating a healthy portfolio and was beginning to help his family and friends do the same. The writing was on the wall. He had a zero marketing budget, was low-tech, definitely not salesy. He was the smart, nice guy who people trusted. All of his clients were people he already knew or that they knew. Rookie of the Year finalist.

THE TEACHER IN SOUTH DAKOTA
Home Every Day at 3

This forty-year old mother of three was tired of teaching and wanted to meet her kids at the school bus. I've always said there is a teacher or two or three out there right now in every state who, five years from now, will be a top producing agent in his/her town.

Teachers make great real estate professionals. They're hard-working, know everyone, and negotiate their way through every day. Yes, the skills a teacher learns in managing twelve-year-olds and parents and administrators come in handy in real estate. Most teachers I know, and I'm married to one, have personal fortitude beyond their years.

So this gal in South Dakota, her price point, the average price of a home in her area, was much lower than Mr. Door-Knocker Canada and Mr. Investor Vegas. She sold twice as many homes as those guys. Her key was really two things... her hustle, and she knew everyone.

And she caught the veterans off-guard. While the veteran agents in Sioux Falls or Rapids (or what is the capital of South Dakota? I forget what town she was in...) were cruising on their reputations, she was steadily gaining market share. She started running circles around them, and they were not even aware of that until her sign was showing up more than theirs. She hired an assistant early on because she was innately aware that she needed to spend most of her time face-to-face with buyers and sellers. And it was a non-negotiable that she would be home with her kids at 3 pm... her clients understood this. She would not allow herself to get buried in the deets and she was committed to having a schedule that kept her priority on her family. Rookie of the Year finalist.

THE HIGH-END IN LA
Spending Money to Make Money

Every year it seems there is a Rookie of the Year finalist who is super high-end. A talented rookie who goes after the multi-million dollar market right out of the box. None of the "Oh I have to earn my stripes in the middle before I venture into luxury" mindset. Often, these luxury rookie superstars are already in that genre of wealth, a sort of real estate silver spoon.

I already know what you're thinking. You think these multi-million dollar price point lucky dogs have it easy, that they only need a deal every other month to rank as a top producer, that there is more luck and family tree involved than talent and hard work. You think that by some unnatural chain of events, they got to list Oprah's estate, end of story. Not this 30-year old success story.

Mr. High-end in LA knew he wanted this market and knew he had to have top-notch, high-end, expensive marketing and support to make it happen. Mr. High-End in LA spent a lot of money to make a lot of money. Rookie of the Year finalist.

THE INTERNATIONAL IN NYC
Power Package

This forty-something female phenomenon in Manhattan was European, drop-dead gorgeous, and had some sort of advanced degree in international business. She dressed to kill. She was a power package in high heels and went after one very specific market, international buyers. She was multilingual (so American of me to point that out, like that is actually a resume highlight, when most Europeans are multilingual) and did 100 percent of her marketing attracting international buyers online. Yes, a high price point and a very narrow focus. Rookie of the Year finalist.

THE FSBO GUY
Twenty-One in Three Months

This guy had twenty-one for-sale-by-owner listings within three months of being licensed. FSBO, it's all he did. Narrow focus. I do not remember anything more about him. I simply remember that FSBO is all he did, and he had twenty-one of them signed up for his services within three months. I seem to recall that he did not want to work any other part of the market besides listing FSBO's; he referred everything else out. Rookie of the Year finalist.

ONE CAR
One Neighborhood

There is one other gal I remember where all she serviced was her immediate walkable neighborhood because she did not have a car. She and her husband had one car, and he needed it to get to work. Cash was tight, at first, so all she did was what was walkable. I love that business plan! And she rocked it because she went all in, one neighborhood.

I have shelves full of notes from real estate conferences. Stacks of notebooks, blog articles, plus a 145-page perpetual online journal of notes and industry insights. In fact, that 145-page running journal was this book in its infancy. Think you have a book in you? Start journaling or blogging on the topic every day and see where you are in six months. Fortunately, that journal is searchable, and I was able to resurrect the Rookie of the Year gems, advice, and words of note from some very successful first-year agents and insights from endless hours spent on blogs and webinars and observing agents get their start.

As you can see from the stories above, these success stories come from all walks of life, with varying journeys, specialties, and interests. The success stories represent all ages from a few knock-your-socks-off millennials who killed it online, to the hustling 30-something Canadian door-knocker, to the humble soft-spoken fifty-something investor in Vegas, to the international specialist in Manhattan, to the former teacher, and the hometown preacher boy who knows everyone in his west Mississippi town. Here are a few rookie success gems, quotes, and insights from my journals and notebooks:

- It started with mindset.
- I ask this all the time: "Who have you talked to in the last 30 days that has mentioned real estate?"
- Expect more referrals from your top twenty-five people and treat them accordingly.
- My biggest mistakes: time management and fear of signing the buyer agreement.
- No one told me my first listing could not be a $2 million mansion.
- I knew that I was simply going to attempt to out-hustle everyone, and I prepared my family for an intense year.
- My broker told me I had to sign a new client every week. So that's what I did. For eight straight weeks I signed a client every week. And then on the ninth or tenth week I did not. So I sheepishly went to my broker to ask for help, and he said that no one signs a new client every week... I just told you that to motivate you.

- I was home every day at 3:00 to meet my kids off the bus because that was my job, too. This was non-negotiable with my clients, and they understood.

Look for more rookie gems scattered throughout the book. When you find a gem that works specifically for you, a message that causes you to pause, advice that seriously captures your attention, a quote or comment that simply is a message custom-designed for where you are right now or tailor-made for where you are going, then pause for a minute. Write it down. That one message, that one idea, that one moment of clarity could be the one thing that shifts your mindset and your business to the next level.

For example, there is an agent I coach in Texas who has pulled herself out of a major and scary financial slump (scary because she is a single mom, one source of income in that household). She had gone to sleep on her business because of some family issues, and two years later pushed through to top honors in her company by focusing daily on two Julie-isms (her word). She said she could hear my voice in her head and kept repeating this:

- Where are my next three leads?
- Two hours per day.

I am now working with her to solidify these two cornerstones and move her toward owning her role as National Sales Manager (of her solo business) and then we will work on COO, then CFO, then CEO, in that order over the next couple years.

Throughout *On Fire Hot!*, keep a keen eye out for your a-ha's and your break-through moments. I recommend that you take notes, keep a log, grab a highlighter, keep a journal. Your journal will begin to serve as your roadmap, an easily referenced collection of business insights, your business insights. One of my goals is that your insights, your a-ha's and takeaways will be the catalyst for your next wave of momentum and, ultimately, a key tool for you creating awesomeness and success faster in your business and your life. If I can have just the tiniest impact on the evolution of your awesomeness, then I am doing my job; I will have lived large. If *On Fire Hot!* has a big impact on what happens next for you, then I want to hear about it.

CHAPTER 7

Quickly

"Grit is passion and perseverance for very long-term goals. Grit is having stamina. Grit is sticking with your future, day in, day out, not just for the week, not just for the month, but for years, and working really hard to make that future a reality. Grit is living life like it's a marathon, not a sprint.

What I do know is that talent doesn't make you gritty. Our data show very clearly that there are many talented individuals who simply do not follow through on their commitments. In fact, in our data, grit is usually unrelated or even inversely related to measures of talent."

—Angela Lee Duckworth, "Grit: the power of passion and perseverance,"
April 2013 TED Talks

So how do you succeed in this business? You succeed by following simple models and getting into action quickly. The bigger picture of this business includes client experience, service, relationships, systems, marketing, market knowledge, and how you are contributing to your community. These bigger picture items are key and represent the long game of surviving and thriving in this business.

In *Success Faster On Fire Hot!*, we are working closely with the short game of gaining clients quickly. The faster you gain clients, your short game, the faster you will get on your feet (or back on your feet) and can then work on your long game. Short game first, clients quickly.

The faster you gain clients and momentum, then the sooner you will have the green light to work on your long game. Play red light/green light with this. Almost everything is red light until you have some clients lined up. All those other projects you have lined up, like improving your social media game, reworking your marketing plan, maximizing your CRM, researching newsletter services, redesigning your website . . . absolutely none of that matters until you have clients in hand and a few more lined up behind them. Yes, a bit of an oversimplification, but trust me on this concept, as I think it may be one of the most important business rules ever. Clients quickly.

Pause for just a moment and write this down in your notes, or highlight it . . .

Clients Quickly

Heck, write it out one hundred times. Find your whiteboard and write it down.

Say it out loud.

Walk around the house saying it out loud for an hour.

Put it on a sticky note on the bathroom mirror.

Do all of this until your entire being, until every cell in your body believes the concept. Do what you can to grasp this at a cellular level. Repetition and practice and doing and sticky note reminders strengthen the synapses, where neurons connect and memories begin to take hold. When you can take the concept of clients quickly and move it forward to a belief and a practice, from concept to belief, from belief to practice, all sorts of things will come together and work in your favor. Any time sales are down or cash is tight or you find yourself adding too many things to your docket, always come back to this business 101 rule.

This is a foundational principle of *Success Faster*, a foundational principle of business success. It's all about building your client pipeline quickly. If you are in retail, it's all about getting people through the door. If your business is online, it's all about getting click-throughs. In your real estate career, it's all about building a pipeline of client leads. Quickly.

Let's use my 0-to-10-in-10-months 2017 relaunch as an example. I knew to successfully relaunch, and having a lot of people observe that relaunch (the pressure was on to succeed), I needed to feed my pipeline quickly. I could not waste time. I knew my systems and tools and software and marketing would all happen quicker with a client in hand; clients first, systems second or, in this case, dusting off my systems second. The systems-then-clients approach would be too slow, I would lose valuable time.

If you have a big corporate background, an impressive marketing background, are super detail and systems-oriented, an engineer type, a spreadsheet junkie, double-dipped in the perfectionist department, then beware. You know who you are. I see you. Your natural tendency (or one that was built into you in the corporate world) will be to organize the hell out of your new business. Remember the mama bear Stephanie story earlier? You are smarter and more experienced than Stephanie, but she is going to run circles around you because she is gritty and has urgency and is building her pipeline while you work on your marketing plan.

Clients First...And Fast

In my relaunch, I needed to simply hustle and find my first ten leads and clients quickly. And then my next ten. This simply involved having meaningful conversations with the key people in my life, with my professional friends and clients, with my connected and influential friends, with my agent network around the country. And not letting any of my spreadsheet tendencies or marketing ideas get in the way or rob me of my time. I used a not-sophisticated-at-all technique to drive my relaunch bus. I had a sticky note on my laptop that read:

Julie, what is your fastest route today
   to a lead, client, contract, or paycheck?
Do that thing first.

Go ahead, you can borrow this fabulous idea. Grab your sticky note now and then send me a photo of it. (I bet no one sends me a photo of their sticky note, but I really am secretly hoping you do.) This sticky note anchored my day and my morning activity. Five months in, I had $6M in the pipeline. It was a solid start.

You can succeed in this high-attrition business by gaining clients quickly. You can succeed by having more conversations than the average agent. Conversations, that is the other key ingredient that we will tackle in a few chapters or so.

If you are just getting started in the business, then it's your first ten clients. Quickly. If you are in year two, year three, year ten, re-starting, re-booting, relaunching, then it's your next ten. Quickly.

You are always working on finding your next ten leads. And then following up. And then you are working on finding your next ten leads. And then following up. And so on and so on. This is the key activity you will do every day. It is not sexy, it's work, it's your job. This cycle never ends and is the key activity of all successful agents. It's a very simple roadmap. Stop overcomplicating this business.

More clients, quickly, will resolve most problems in your business and your bank account. Half of the chapters in *Success Faster On Fire Hot!* tackle the specifics of clients quickly. The book outlines specific actions you can take now to make this happen in a more expeditious manner than what you are currently experiencing.

I see quite a few agents gain little traction in their first year and then super take off in year two, sometimes year three. This delayed momentum, while common, has one significant caveat . . . cash flow. Some agents can afford a sluggish first year, others not at all. And this is where your urgency needs to come into play.

Because of cash flow and definitely because of mindset, the momentum club is a really good place to be. Get in that club and stay there.

CHAPTER 8

What Are You Telling Yourself?

You are not really the CEO of your brain, you're more like the press secretary.

—Paraphrased from *Seven Stories Every Salesperson Must Tell*, Mike Adams

Let's explore this press secretary concept for just a minute. The press secretaries of the world dispense information, select information they want to dispense with a marketing spin here and there to make sure they drive their message and, at best, impact and drive the beliefs of those who will listen. The press secretary has very little control over the content, maybe some control over the spin. Hang in there with me on this analogy. We all have an internal press secretary that is constantly delivering messages, often with a spin, to our internal audience of one. And we tend to believe what we tell ourselves. I saw a meme recently that said we should listen to ourselves less and talk to ourselves more. So what are you telling yourself?

Your mindset will make or break you. Every day. Some days your mindset is your greatest ally, some days the villain. Some days your mindset moves you forward, some days it sabotages your progress. Make sure your mindset points you, and keeps pointing you in the right direction every day. Train your brain muscles to have this mindset:

- I came here to succeed.
- I will do what it takes to create my success on purpose.
- I will take a meaningful step toward my goal every day.

Your mindset is your foundation, so of course we are going to spend some time here. A bit of my personal philosophy, my compass, my foundation looks like this:

Life is fair, fair and beautiful. I believe this, and the more I say this, the more I attract people who think the same way, and then fair and beautiful manifests itself more and more right before my eyes.

Everything is easy and belongs. I choose to believe this, and the more I say it, the more it manifests itself before my eyes.

I am creating massive financial opportunity and the life of my dreams. I believe this and so it is.

I do something concrete every day that moves me toward my goal.

I got this! (usually accompanied by a fist pump).

What are you telling yourself? What is your philosophy that grounds you as you pursue your dreams? You can borrow mine if you like, especially the last one.

Let's cover a few foundational concepts as we build your success plan.

Wildly Imperfect

If you are new-ish to the business, your job is to work only on clients and traction; your broker or mentor works with you on contracts and process. For the new-ish agents, there is a slightly counter-intuitive dynamic about getting started . . . you need to be gaining traction before you really know what you're doing. There is a life lesson in this somewhere, but in real estate, if you wait to get started with your first client, if you wait until everything is perfect and you feel super prepared and your knowledge base is super ramped up, you'll be too late. It's like waiting for only the perfect date, and then you have no dates while someone else, who's not as hot as you, has all sorts of dates. Guess who is going to find the perfect date first? Progress is better than perfect, wildly imperfect works.

When you get stuck in prep mode, we call this the getting-ready-to-get-ready syndrome. I can write about this because I have way too much experience with this, the getting-ready-to-get-ready thing. If you lean perfectionist or have a tendency to over-analyze, you'll relate. I find folks who have strong corporate backgrounds easily fall into this mode because they worked in an environment that was built on planning and perfect execution. In this real estate launch thing, it will serve you well to loosen up on the perfection planning cycle. You can get to perfect or ready later, you can circle back around.

You must get started fast. Your broker or mentor will/should help you with your first few clients; they better help you with your first few clients. Your job is to go get them quickly. More on this support topic later.

If you are a seasoned or somewhat seasoned agent, then you already have the contracts and process down, and we are simply focusing on traction and an improved pipeline. Real estate school taught you the legalities—contracts, ethics, finance, etc. It taught you how to DEAL with business. School does not teach you how to FIND business. This program is all about consistently FINDING business. Wildly imperfect works.

I Heart Real Estate

> *You can only become truly accomplished at something you love. Don't make money your goal. Instead, pursue the things you love doing, and then do them so well that people can't take their eyes off you.*
> —MAYA ANGELOU

I heart real estate, homes, people, success, my bank account, being an entrepreneur. Pick one. This mindset parameter is a test of identifying what motivates you to be here and assessing if that motivation is sustainable. What is the candy that is wooing you to real estate? You only need one solid motivation, one that a few bumps in the road, a challenging client or two, a learning curve, or an intense year of building a new business, will not shake. Let's take a minute and identify your core motivation.

This is not a pass-fail test. Find the one or two that speak to you, that represent you at a deep level. Which of these apply to you:

- I love to talk houses with anyone who will listen.
- I attract people.
- I like to talk to people.
- I am generally a confident person.
- I stop in to open houses just to see how people live or decorate.
- I spend hours on real estate websites.
- I re-design houses when I'm in them. "Oh, you could move this wall, open up this room, add a window and a French door!"
- I like to win.
- I am financially motivated.
- I am known as a hard worker.
- I want to own my own business.
- I am motivated to support my family at a new level.

What is your motivation for this business? While not a pass-fail test, the concept here is your commitment, your resolve. Are you really committed to making this career choice work? Over the years of working with agents getting their start, I have seen agents succeed at high levels while others get frustrated and fall out. As with any big endeavor, getting in touch with your core motivation can be the cornerstone of your success and your ability to stick with it.

And there may be people in your world who attempt to talk you out of your new career path. I ran into this. This is not necessarily a bad thing. If the people in your life can easily talk you out of something, then it's an indication that either you are not yet clear and have not fully and convincingly presented your case and vision, or you do not yet fully embrace it yourself. Or it may be possible that the key people in your life lean negative or risk-averse; deep down they have regrets for the things they never did. It is a false agenda to expect people in your life who have never taken a risk, to line up with encouragement behind your big goals. Perhaps well-meaning, but the risk factor of a 100% commission career may not rest well with someone in your life. Getting in touch with your resolve is foundational to any new chapter and will help you power through the naysayers. Build your vision board and show it to big thinkers; if you show it to small thinkers, your vision board will shrink.

Looking for Encouragement in All the Wrong Places

I spent years looking for encouragement, cheerleaders, a nod of approval, a sign that now was the right time to jump into a real estate career. Perhaps your process was shorter than mine. Mine took years. Before I even looked at my first real estate license class, three different people talked me out of real estate as a career . . . a family friend, the agent who sold me my house, and it seems the biggest culprit was me.

The family friend was a thirty-plus-year veteran of the industry. Her message was consistent, "It's harder than you think." And, in a parental sort of way, I think she wanted me to have some impressive corporate career.

My first agent, whom I contacted to explore real estate as a career, talked me out of it. His position was more of the it's-harder-than-you-think position with a dose of stay with a regular paycheck and benefits.

And so I kept talking myself out of it. My cornerstone motivation, while developing, was not yet firmly in place. And so I kept talking myself out of it. I stayed in the corporate world well past my enjoyment of the corporate scene.

And then, finally, years later, it was my friends who owned the small brokerage who enthusiastically said, "You would be great!" that finally hit home at the right time. I had found my cheerleaders. Line up your cheerleaders.

Because I had been laid off with a severance package and had a couple of contract gigs, a European travel stint, and the pleasure of living inexpensively, I was in a position to start my real estate career full-time. Let's take a closer look at part-time versus full-time.

Full-time or Part-time, Showing Up Pro

For various personal and life reasons, some agents start out part-time and some are part-time by design. There is the stay-at-home parent who is shifting back into the professional world and the investor agent who works a few personal flip properties, and there is the agent who is somewhat dipping their toe in the real estate pond to see if they like it. Sometimes those agents stay right where they are because it's exactly where they want to be, it fits their life and their goals, and some of them build a bigger business later. But what really is part-time?

The full-time/part-time thing is somewhat relative. I know full-time agents who, by design and desire, work with maybe four to six clients per year. And I know and coach agents who can work six clients per week.

I want to reiterate a couple important points here for the agents who are either part-time or just getting started or for agents who, by design and desire, choose to do maybe four to six transactions per year. First, there are many very successful agents out there who started part-time. Second, what is part-time? For hours worked in the "job" world, we accept that forty hours a week is full-time. For real estate professionals, there are no industry definitions of full-time; you get to determine that for you and your goals and your family.

Don't let the industry tell you what success is or is not. Only YOU get to define YOUR success in YOUR terms. Your broker may determine a minimum standard for that brokerage, so if there is a mismatch there, then I guess you either need to shift your goal and activity to satisfy your broker or find another brokerage that is a better match for your goals and needs.

While there may not be an industry-wide definition of full-time, there is an industry definition of professional, and that is the NAR REALTOR® Code of Ethics. In its purest form, the Code says we have to know what we are doing in order to represent our clients at the highest level, to be their fiduciary. And this is the mindset piece, since this is a mindset chapter.

It is logical that the agent who helps twenty clients this year will build up a greater working knowledge faster than the agent who helps four clients, but both agents need to know their market and the contract and the process the same. So everyone, regardless of the number of clients or the size of our goal, needs the same professional body of knowledge, and that is what "showing up pro" is about.

The volume of information real estate pros are held accountable for is staggering. As we have an obligation to our fellow professionals to uphold our industry, we have a substantially larger obligation to the public and the public trust to be consummate professionals. I know full-time agents who are clueless, and I know part-time agents who have an amazing knowledge base. The client always deserves a knowledgeable professional.

For most people, a real estate transaction represents the largest financial transaction of their lives. I have often thought it should be much more difficult to get a real estate license. The enormity of what we do with a buyer or seller, the amount of money involved, the legality of that contract and that deed and that title, the estate, the investment, the financial plan, the life event—be it a marriage, a divorce, a new child, empty-nesting, an estate, a move-up, a size-down—is hugely significant.

I want all agents to have this mindset: We each need a phenomenal knowledge base regardless of how many clients we are serving each year. If you are working six clients per year, you need the same knowledge base as the agent doing six clients per week. Failure to study and pay attention can seriously screw up a deal and put your client and broker at risk. So we all, regardless of client volume or goals, need to put in the same amount of time staying current and informed and educated.

Shifting into Full-time

If you are starting out part-time with the intention of growing into full-time, *Success Faster On Fire Hot!* can be your roadmap to make that happen.

When agents start part-time, I always like to help them identify a jumping-off point, the point at which they will go full-time. The jumping-off point tends to be one of two things; either pick a date on the calendar, or identify a certain amount of money in the bank. Or both. Such as I will have $20,000 in the bank by January 1, or my target is to resign from my other job May 31st.

So what would it take for you to go full-time? Is it January 1? Is it the end of the school year? Is it the beginning of the school year, when the kids are finally back in school? Is it $10,000 in the bank? $30,000? Setting a target and writing it down helps tremendously. Write it down, set that benchmark in your brain, and start organizing your world around it. Even your psyche will organize around it. Remember, your brain believes what you feed it.

Do yourself a huge favor and build in some accountability. Tell your friends and tell your family about your target, at least the friends and family members who will cheer you on—bypass the naysayers, you know who they are. Send me a message online with your target (see links in the last chapter). And then send me another message when you hit your goal.

I want to make a comment on that last concept, the idea of actually sending me a message with your target. I put this out there with the first book. Very few people took me up on it. But the ones who did, they were all strong and confident. And yes, I emailed them back, every time.

And what if insurance is an issue? This can be a tough one, a real reality check. If you or a family member has a serious medical issue, you need to fully understand your medical insurance options before venturing into self-employment. Some brokerages have insurance programs available. You may need to assess this before you make a move. This alone keeps many people in employee mode. Understand this important detail and how it impacts you and your family before you jump from part-time to full-time.

If you are just starting out, keep in mind that every single successful agent out there had a first year in the business, a year with a steep learning curve and maybe a solid support and broker team. Whenever I teach a class in person, I like to ask the room, "Raise your hand if you had a first year in the business." This keeps us humble.

CHAPTER 9

It's a Race

I have been impressed with the urgency of doing.
Knowing is not enough; we must apply.
Being willing is not enough; we must do.

—Leonardo Da Vinci

What if the agent success quotient, the key to who stays in the business and who doesn't, was speed? What if the speed at which you gained your first ten clients had more to do with your longevity in the business, your likelihood to have a year two and three, than talent and intelligence? Not the strongest will survive; rather, the swiftest will have the most sustainable real estate career?

What if speed was the number-one indicator of a first-year agent's success? What if the key was simply who found clients quickly? And then more clients quickly? This is my argument ... that the key to your success is gaining clients and a pipeline quickly. I have seen this play out many times. It is a bit of a race.

Like any race, you can train for it. Let's look at five specific race factors, and how you can best position yourself in that aspect of the race.

IT'S A RACE FACTOR #1
Your Psyche

It's a race because of your psyche. Remember, I have trained hundreds (probably over 1,000, I lost count) of first-year agents with thousands of observations and conversations. And here is an important insight: Gaining a few clients quickly will do more for your psyche than the best self-help book out there.

How long did it take you to get your license? How long had you been thinking about it before you took your license classes? How long did it take you to really decide to take this step toward a new profession? And how much money have you spent in that process? For most of you, it's been a while. At least months, and in some cases, years.

Your behind-the-scenes brain has been working toward this for a long time. Your brain is ready. Your brain needs a client quickly. Psychologists will call this your reticular activating system, your RAS. Your RAS is a loose collection of neurons connected somehow to your brain stem. The general sleep regulator, your RAS is also directly related to how your brain processes information. Your RAS is in play when your brain is actively searching for the right information or experience to fill the gaps. It's the same thing as researching that blue Mini Cooper S convertible with the white stripe that you so desire, and all of a sudden you're seeing them everywhere around town. Your RAS was looking for them; your RAS was processing that information. By the way, although you'll look cool, that Mini Cooper is a bit small to haul clients around on property tours (although it seems—liability, COVID—folks are embracing the two-car tour with buyers these days). I know this firsthand. I brought a tape measure with me to the Mini Cooper dealer so I could measure the back and make sure it fit my yard signs. I did not, however, measure that Mini for my 150-pound Great Dane, Groovy; I have a photo of that in my blog online.

In your new or renewed real estate endeavor, your brain needs clients quickly; it needs to fill in the blanks. Without clients and client leads, your brain will have a tendency to fill in the gaps with noise; the committee inside your head, the inner chatter that is not your ally, will start messing with you. Your RAS will always work to fill in the gap; it will fill it in with anything somehow relevant.

If you are saying to yourself repeatedly "ten clients, ten clients, ten clients," your brain becomes your advocate in making that happen. Same thing goes if your inner dialogue is, "I'm not sure I like this." or "This is hard." or "I'm tired." Then your brain will support that mantra. You think your mantras are only those things that fulfill your dreams and motivate your world, but really your mantras are anything you are regularly telling yourself. So take some inventory on how you talk to yourself. Does it serve you and your goals, or is it of the self-sabotaging sort? "Ten clients, ten clients, ten clients." "I got this." "I'm living the dream." Get that committee inside your head working in your favor.

If you are thirty days in without a solid client lead or two or ten ... let's just say it gets noisy in your head; the committee gets messy. I could make a list of a hundred agents who would give a nod of understanding to this noise concept. If you have been in the business for a bit, you may be nodding your head right now. Avoid the noise and that annoying committee by getting your first ten clients as quickly as possible.

It's a race.

IT'S A RACE FACTOR #2
Sixty to Ninety Days

It's a race because everything in this business, every paycheck, is sixty to ninety days out. And that is a fast client. For most people, having a paycheck every two weeks makes sense, and the only way this happens in real estate is to build a healthy pipeline of leads and clients.

The majority of leads that show up will benefit you or materialize as a real client much further down the road, months down the road. It is definitely delayed gratification. Your cousin's friend who is probably moving to town next summer. The neighbor whose elderly mother is declining. The investor who intends to purchase two properties sometime this year. Your friends with two kids and one on the way who are still in their starter home and have a long list of repairs before they're ready to put the house on the market. The family about to put two kids through the local university. The new construction that won't produce a commission check for ten months. The rental property where the lease expires next spring. Your PhD-candidate friends who will most likely move somewhere next year. This is the reality of a pipeline. When you find a lead that is ready today, such as a for-sale-by-owner or a motivated and financially qualified and unrepresented open house guest or your friend who calls and says "OMG, I found the house I want to buy.!" That is as good as it gets.

Motivated, Qualified
The ideal focus in your real estate business is the client lead who is ready in 30–60 days. That is a motivated short-term lead. Your pipeline will include short-term and long-term leads. It will also include motivated and not motivated leads, qualified and not qualified leads, people who respect our time, and those who do not. Your pipeline will include leads that result in a client and leads that were never really a lead in the first place.

So how does the pipeline concept line up with your financial cushion and the need for your next paycheck? Most of us have been used to a paycheck every two weeks. If your real estate paychecks are sixty to ninety days out, then how does that work for you? What are your monthly expenses? Are you tapping into your savings and, if so, for how long? It's definitely a race.

If you're one of the lucky ones where your financial cushion is not really an issue, you still need clients quickly because of the other race factors. If you're one of these "lucky" ones, beware as you'll have a higher risk of getting caught up in the getting-ready-to-get-ready syndrome.

It's still a race.

IT'S A RACE FACTOR #3
Your Bank Account
It's a race because of your bank account. You can get varying opinions on this topic. Everyone talks about the financial cushion needed to get started. You have living expenses saved up, right?

Four-month financial cushion. Six-month cushion. Nine-month cushion. I lean toward the six-month cushion for getting started in real estate and here's why. Two months' reserve can be gone in a nanosecond. Let's just agree that time flies and that you can get sucked into the learning and ramp-up portion of this business (which we are going to avoid . . . see getting-ready-to-get-ready section). Whatever your cushion, just subtract two months to make room for error. So if you have a six-month cushion, treat it like it's a four-month cushion because two months can slip away easily, and it's sixty to ninety days out for any given client to turn into a paycheck. I think you get the picture. Assume that time will fly faster than you think.

It's definitely a race.

IT'S A RACE FACTOR #4
Confidence
It's a race because you'll gain skills and confidence faster by doing. You will gain infinitely more confidence faster by doing than you will in the classroom. Experience is the best teacher. I have heard of brokers who tell their new recruits, go get your first client then come see me. I prefer the brokers who train the recruits on how to find and engage and convert that first client, but the point is that the most critical learning and confidence-building starts with a client in hand.

Don't wait until things are perfect and you're beginning to feel confident. John Maxwell speaks to this is in his book *Failing Forward: Turning Mistakes Into Stepping Stones for Success*. He deftly challenges us to fail often, faster, and better. Get out of prep mode and into ACTION. You WILL get better. Get out of your head and into action.

It's a race.

IT'S A RACE FACTOR #5
Nothing
It's a race because nothing leads to nothing. You may be fabulous with people, a great listener, an exceptional advocate, a PTA badass, a twenty-year marketing professional, super smart, super detailed, organized, a market expert, a leader in your field, maybe you've been a mortgage professional or designer or builder for ten years. You're awesome, you have game, you have skills. This is good.

But without a client, or three, or five, or ten, and a pipeline of potential clients, you have nothing. Nothing. It's like having an impressive degree, but no job; an amazing voice, yet no song to sing.

Can we agree that you intend to have a paycheck, earn commission, and be profitable? Right. It's a business. This is really simple . . . CLIENTS QUICKLY. It's a race. Treat it like a race. Get there faster than everyone else.

Now that we are clear on race day and urgency, let's explore some steps you can take to move in that direction immediately.

> ✔ **ACTION ITEM**
> **An Introduction to Action Items**

In the introduction, I said *Success Faster On Fire Hot!* is practical and actionable. So far, we laid a foundation for your success, your launch or relaunch, and now it is time to go deeper, time to add the magic of what we actually do to gain clients quickly. We are now going to physically and verbally get busy with the right things. The goal here, whether new or relaunching, is to gain traction quickly, and the ACTION ITEMS are designed to help you create that traction. The more you engage in the ACTION ITEMS throughout the book, the more traction you will have by the time you get to the last chapter.

Here is how critical this ACTION thing is . . . it has everything to do with the cause and effect delay in the life cycle of real estate sales. All your habits today, the things you are doing, the conversations you are having, the schedule you are keeping, the shiny objects you are avoiding, will show up as opportunity, and hopefully cash, sixty to ninety days from now. So your ability to course-correct when you realize that next month is thin on or void of paychecks, is critical, and it has a delay.

In retail sales or a restaurant business, you may be able to course-correct a lot faster by putting a big and bold new banner outside or running a margarita special in August or a teacher special in September to get people through the door. That service industry course-correction may be more like a speedboat revving its engines to make a solid push toward increased cash flow. The real estate sales cycle correction is more like turning a sailboat around. When you realize you need to get from point A to point B, it's a bit of a big somewhat slow three-point turn to get there, and that is why we start now or actually why we never stop.

In your efforts to gain traction, what you do today matters. Actually, what you did sixty to ninety days back matters most, what you do today matters next. So I want to encourage you to shift from reading and introspection to reading and doing.

Let's get started.

> Every Day: "The main thing is to keep the main thing the main thing."
> —STEPHEN COVEY, THE 7 HABITS OF HIGHLY EFFECTIVE PEOPLE

Your Shortest Job Description

You are in the business of having conversations with people about real estate.

EVERY...SINGLE...DAY you must do something that has the likelihood of finding a client or client lead (or three, or five, or ten). Write that down. What is important is the extent to which you are doing something every single day that has a strong likelihood of you gaining a client. Clients faster.

Remember this: traction and clients quickly.

Embrace the 8:00 A.M. everyday mantra of traction and clients quickly. Put a sticky note on your forehead, laptop, bathroom mirror, cell phone screen that reminds you what your job is today. I have a bit of a daily mantra, practically tattooed on my wrist, that says, "What is my fastest route to a solid lead, client, contract, or paycheck today?" It's how I start my day so I get the most important things done first.

In this chapter, we roll out the gold with an ACTION ITEM, and then that ACTION ITEM thing is what you'll see play out in almost every chapter moving forward. So get your running shoes on because this is where you will gain traction. A little guidance with the ACTION ITEMS . . . I recommend that you do not proceed to the next chapter until you have completed the ACTION ITEM in the current chapter. Let's just say it's a bit of a board game, and you do not get to proceed to the next level without completing that ACTION ITEM. No cheating. Trust me on this. Just do it. Unless you're going to read through the book then circle back around for ACTION ITEMS, then that works, but only if you promise yourself and make it happen. The money is in the ACTION.

Building Muscle Around What to Say

Most chapters will include some scripts, what to say samples. It's like working out; you have to build some muscle here. Let's scuba dive into the what-to-say topic for a minute.

When I first started in real estate, I rejected the concept of scripts. Even the word, script, was a bit of a four-letter-word thing for me. I was very clear that I never wanted to be that salesy sounding type of agent. Being authentic was super important to me, and I was going to succeed in this business on my terms. I was not going to memorize the book of sales-pitchy things to say, I was just going to talk to people; I was going to be myself.

You may have some sort of corporate sales background. Or maybe you have experience in retail or a call center or a medical setting. And on day one of your new job, your boss or sales director placed a manual on your desk with the directive to memorize, quiz on Friday. You memorized what to say because in that environment, on that team, everyone said the same thing the same way. The team or the industry had figured out the most effective way to communicate, and you were expected to be up to speed quickly. Failure to do so could cost you your job.

Here's what I did with the script manual when I first started in real estate . . . I ignored it. Or so I thought.

Someone had given me a set of real estate CD's, and I started listening to these in my car. When I listen to non-fiction books in my car, I tend to listen in a somewhat passive manner, and the same CD or track or chapter or podcast will play two or three or four times in a row, sometimes over days or weeks, before I realize that I am on a merry-go-round with the material. This is not a bad thing; the repetition suits my learning style. I had been listening to this material over and over and over again. And a funny thing happened.

I was with clients, and they threw some objection on the table. I do not remember what the specific objection was. It would have been something like, "Why should we hire you?" or "We think we'll wait." or "We are interviewing other agents." or "Will you reduce your commission?" Again, I do not remember the actual question, but what I do remember is that some near perfect and poetic words came out of my mouth at the right time, and I handled the objection like a pro. I remember almost being startled like someone else was in my body delivering the scripted prose. It was a huge bump in my confidence, and I knew, at that moment, that I had been practicing scripts. The words that came out of my mouth, without hesitation, in that moment of need, were directly from the CD's that had been on replay, replay, replay mode in my car. I had been building muscle around what to say. I had been lifting weights almost every day on what to say.

At that point, I became more intentional with practicing what to say, and I started spending more time with that script manual.

So let's get started with what to say.

We have scripts scattered throughout the book and a full reference section near the end of the book. Let's cover one of the basics of all basics of what to say.

> ✓ **ACTION ITEM**
> **Call Your Mother**

Call your mother. Seriously, call your mother (or your sister or BFF), and here's what you are going to say:

"Mom (sister, BFF), I just started at [broker name] today! OMG, I am so excited! Wish I had done this earlier. I need your help. This is day one of the training program, and the very first assignment they gave me was to call you! This business is seriously referral-based, and I have big goals. Will you help me? It's now my job to know the real estate needs of my friends and family and their friends and families, so there is a basic question, actually, two questions, that I need to ask you. 1. Are you anticipating any real estate needs this year? 2. Who do you know who may need my services this year? It's pretty much my job to ask these questions, and who better to start with than you? I really super appreciate your support."

If you read this to her or sort of read it while you're talking to her, it will be really weird and ineffective. You need to have a genuine personal high-energy conversation with her where you are sharing your goals and your inspiration and explaining your business a bit, and you are asking for her help. In other words, your genuine natural approach to the call-your-mother script. And then call your sister and your BFF and your next BFF and do the same thing.

We'll talk more about scripts throughout the book, but I need you to trust me on this call-your-mother (or the other people who love you) task. I have brand-new agents who get their first piece of business all the time because they called their mother and asked. If the actual wording of this script, or any script, does not really work for you, just tweak it . . . make it work, modify it to make it authentic for you. But DO NOT SKIP.

This call-your-mother script is the foundational lead generation question (or some form thereof) that you will be addressing all the time. Write it out a few times. Stand up, walk around and read it out loud a few times. Find your version of it. Own it, internalize it.

Keep calling your mother or your designated BFF. Get these folks in your court. As soon as there is a glimpse of them supporting you at a high level, then send some flowers or a personal thank you note or make them dinner or do something special. Get them in your court and keep them there. This is not a one-time phone call; this is an ongoing conversation. Call your mother.

CHAPTER 10

Who Is the Boss of Me?

The most successful entrepreneurs I know are optimistic. It's part of the job description.

—Caterina Fake, founder Flickr

> ⊗ WARNING LABEL!
> This is one of those "work" chapters I mentioned early on. It means we are going to dive into the work! Remember, and fair warning, this chapter is designed to hurt your brain a bit. So you may want to get a glass of water or turn on your best work music, quiet the kids . . . do whatever it is that helps you focus. This is IMPORTANT work that is designed to move you forward with your on fire hotness! Do I have your permission to help you actually move forward toward something better? I thought so.

You Are Your Own Boss

You are a licensed professional. You're an entrepreneur, an independent contractor. The good news about this? The good news is that you are your own boss. But what is the bad news? The bad news is that you are your own boss. Don't be a lousy one.

You've worked for someone else before. Most of us have. You showed up on time, you got the most important things done every day, you planned out your vacations carefully, you figured out how to run your life and get important things done—buying groceries, taking kitty to the vet, driving kids to school early, meeting the repair guy, preparing for family visiting over the holidays. You figured out what to do when your child was sick. You made the most out of your weekends. You figured it out. You may have been tired, but you figured it out. For years, you figured it out. You were amazing with that forty to fifty-hour or more obligation every week. You had to . . . it meant job stability; it paid the bills.

And then you become a self-employed independent contractor, and you start behaving differently with all this freedom and flexibility. You're running a business, YOUR BUSINESS, the most important business you have ever had your hands on. So are you running it as well as you used to run someone else's?

Why would you treat your own real estate business, that you own, any differently than you had treated someone else's business when you were an employee? Why would you treat someone else's business with more respect and reliability than you treat your own? This chapter is about holding a mirror in front of our faces identifying where our opportunities lie.

Once I really grasped this concept, I started holding the mirror and regularly asking myself these questions:

- Am I being a good boss?
- Was I a good boss today?
- If I was a lousy boss today, what got in my way?
- Am I doing the things I need to do today to build my pipeline?
- What is my fastest route to a new client or paycheck today?
- Am I maintaining a full-time schedule?
- Do I look busy, or did I actually gain traction this week?

- How many hours did I actually work this week?
- Did I do what I said I was going to do?
- Did I add to my pipeline today?
- If I were to give myself a performance review for today or the past week or month, how would I rate?
- And the kicker... Based on what I did today or this week, would I hire me?

> **NINJA TRICK**
> Ask yourself this "Would I hire me?" kicker question at the end of every day, followed by, "What is one thing I could have done differently?" or "How can I course correct tomorrow?"

NOTE: When I say NINJA, it is usually an indication that, when fully embodied and implemented, the NINJA thing could actually result in generating business, building your pipeline, creating fans.

I'll outline the expanded version of the Boss Performance Review here in a minute, but you may want to know that I have a hands-on version in the *Success Faster Workbook* (Amazon), as well as a downloadable version on thenelsonproject.org. This is a great tool as a solo exercise, and an even better tool when done with a small group of like-minded professionals all trying to move their businesses forward. While not a particularly feel-good activity, it is a get-my-business-back-on-track activity, so consider the bossy performance review as your friendly course-correction tool and a great big hug, or kick in the pants, from Julie.

There are five sections to the review and the kicker as follows:

- Sales Goals and Systems
- Busy
- Schedule/Balance
- Focus
- Financial
- The Kicker: Would I hire me?

Boss Performance Review: A Self-Assessment

Am I being a good boss in my own business?

RATE YOURSELF ON THE FOLLOWING STATEMENTS	1 (LOW) ——— 10 (HIGH)
SALES GOALS AND SYSTEMS	
I have sales goals, and I track them.	1-2-3-4-5-6-7-8-9-10
I have tools in place to track my pipeline.	1-2-3-4-5-6-7-8-9-10
I reference my pipeline daily.	1-2-3-4-5-6-7-8-9-10
I add to my pipeline every week.	1-2-3-4-5-6-7-8-9-10
I have conversations about real estate every day.	1-2-3-4-5-6-7-8-9-10
I am consistent with lead follow-up.	1-2-3-4-5-6-7-8-9-10
Right now, my pipeline is healthy.	1-2-3-4-5-6-7-8-9-10
BUSY	
I get back on track quickly and easily.	1-2-3-4-5-6-7-8-9-10
I get the most important things done every day.	1-2-3-4-5-6-7-8-9-10
I am busy with the right things.	1-2-3-4-5-6-7-8-9-10
I have income-producing activity every day.	1-2-3-4-5-6-7-8-9-10
I have minimized distractions.	1-2-3-4-5-6-7-8-9-10
SCHEDULE/BALANCE	
I maintain a full-time schedule.	1-2-3-4-5-6-7-8-9-10
I time-block my schedule.	1-2-3-4-5-6-7-8-9-10
I honor my time-blocked schedule.	1-2-3-4-5-6-7-8-9-10
My work/life balance is in check.	1-2-3-4-5-6-7-8-9-10

FOCUS

I do what I say I am going to do.	1-2-3-4-5-6-7-8-9-10
I rarely get distracted by social media.	1-2-3-4-5-6-7-8-9-10
If I say I am making ten calls, I make ten calls.	1-2-3-4-5-6-7-8-9-10
I have leverage (help) in my business.	1-2-3-4-5-6-7-8-9-10
I am in business with the right people.	1-2-3-4-5-6-7-8-9-10
I consistently educate myself.	1-2-3-4-5-6-7-8-9-10

FINANCIAL

I have a monthly P&L.	1-2-3-4-5-6-7-8-9-10
I regularly review my financial statements.	1-2-3-4-5-6-7-8-9-10
My expenses are in check.	1-2-3-4-5-6-7-8-9-10
I am making all the money I want.	1-2-3-4-5-6-7-8-9-10
My bank account is healthy.	1-2-3-4-5-6-7-8-9-10
I have at least one form of passive income.	1-2-3-4-5-6-7-8-9-10
I have investments and add to them.	1-2-3-4-5-6-7-8-9-10
I have a five-year plan.	1-2-3-4-5-6-7-8-9-10
I have a solid retirement strategy.	1-2-3-4-5-6-7-8-9-10

WOULD I

Based on today (week, month), would I hire me?	1-2-3-4-5-6-7-8-9-10

The Would-I-hire-me question is powerful. I like to ask myself this question at the end of every day with something like, "Based on today, would I hire me?" Sometimes the answer to that question is "Hell no!" And more times than not it is "Yes, rock star, good job!" You could ask this version every Friday, "Based on this week, would I hire me?" Or you could do the Monday morning version with "What will I need to accomplish today/this week in order to ace the Would-I-hire-me question?"

Your personal ratings can change often and can be impacted by what is going on in your life at the time. So be kind to yourself. What we are doing is looking for key opportunities for you to improve the results of your business and then making plans to focus on one or two of the opportunities. I like to take a bite-size approach to this process. I'll take one or two items that I want to focus on, and that will be my 30-day project. As I do this, I lean toward the things that will help me financially the quickest. You got this!

Remember, this is YOU reviewing YOU on how good a boss you are being in your own business. This performance review is designed to help you assess and quickly adjust to get focused on income-producing activity. Your assessment can vary from day to day, week to week. Your performance can be situational.

What is most helpful here is not the pursuit of perfection, but rather improvement and quick course corrections... to get back on track quickly with activities that actually add to your pipeline and bank account.

A reality-check (or kick in the pants) exercise like this would not be complete without a solid follow-up assessment and an action plan. *The Success Faster Workbook* provides additional questions to help you dig deeper with your assessment and outline a simple course of action, an improvement plan.

Awareness is curative. Use this assessment on a regular basis to help course-correct your business and your results. This review is handy for individuals, teams, assistants, and mastermind partners. The review can be done weekly, monthly, quarterly, or you can ask yourself the last question at the end of every day... based on today, would I hire me? Look for the things that are working in your favor, and look for the opportunities to improve as a boss and improve your financial state.

You Are the CEO

You are the CEO of you. And the COO and the CFO and the National Sales Manager. As the boss, ask yourself, What can I do today to gain a lead? Do that bossy foundational thing first every day.

For a minute, let's pretend that I am your boss. Me, Julie Nelson, I am your direct supervisor. Not that I want that job; I really don't want to ever be anyone's direct supervisor. It's not my thing and tends to involve drama. We'll just pretend for a hot minute in order to make a point.

As your supervisor, what if I told you on your first day that, in order to keep your job, you have to sign one client per week, and that is what everyone else at the Julie team does when they start? And because you did not know any better, you took my authoritative word. Or maybe I said you need two appointments and ten substantive real estate conversations every week. And that you had to turn in a report every Monday morning. And if the report was short, then you would be on a performance-improvement program because I only wanted producers on the bus. So what if the golden rule for keeping your job was to sign one client per week? Would you do it?

If you were on a real estate team, there would be performance metrics such as in the office and on the phones by 8:00 A.M., fifty phone calls by noon, and setting a minimum of three appointments every day. This is somewhat how the big, big teams work. (More on teams later.)

Alright, now I am done being your supervisor—just those few minutes stressed me out. This is simply an exercise in setting a performance standard or two for you and setting daily or weekly performance targets and then making sure you hit them. This is what a good boss does.

The main message here? Be a good boss.

So give the Boss Performance Review a shot and remember, you can use this as a weekly or monthly tool to reset or realign your business.

> **🥷 NINJA TRICK**
> Successful people review themselves and course-correct all the time. You can download the Boss review on thenelsonproject.org

Your Most Important Daily Meeting

> *I have been truly blessed with the ability to compartmentalize the many competing agendas in my mind. Because of this, I can shut it off and enjoy the moment.*
> —ARLENE DICKINSON, ENTREPRENEUR, MARKETER, TV PERSONALITY

Now that we have the basis set for this boss or bossy concept and the role it plays in you hitting your goals and calming your squirrel farm, we are going to talk about the most important meeting you have every day with your executive team—the CEO and COO and CFO and National Sales Manager (that's you, all four of them)—and how compartmentalization is actually your friend.

What the Psychologists Say

A ways back in my life, I dated a psychologist. Overall, it was a good thing, but you better like to talk and get all introspective, often, and get called out on your body language, and recognize theirs, because this is how they hang in the world. They are trained and wired to hold mirrors in front of people and to create safe spaces around that process, and most of them, in my experience, incorporate this skillset into their everyday stuff. It is part of what attracted me to the doctor in the first place. I learned a lot and helped edit a dissertation somewhere in those three or four years. When you are personally close with these trained professionals, whether family, friends, or friends with benefits, you start seeing things differently.

For the longest time, I thought compartmentalization was bad. Or maybe useful in the short term, like blocking out something that was too much to handle at the time, and then much later it morphs into baggage no longer serving its original protective covering. In the psych world (I did not say psych ward; I have never been to one of those), compartmentalization is really this thing that you work through or fix or, at the very least, identify. Awareness is curative, I have learned, and I now love that phrase.

I am not a psychologist, but I have seen one or two, maybe three, and I have dated one (just one) so I have developed my personal set of amateur psych opinions along the way.

In the therapy world, so much of the effort is in helping people make peace with their past or their troubles or simply an awareness of what is, especially when those things are getting in the way of life or happiness or jobs or sobriety or effective parenting or getting out of bed. But I have come to recognize the other side of the compartmentalization coin, the part that helps us traverse complicated issues and be more productive at work.

The Meeting

This daily stand-up meeting is simple and short. The agenda: What will I do in the next two hours that will specifically and concretely move me toward my goal? And then you do that thing, and only that thing, single-tasking for the next two hours. You can multitask your way throughout the day and your life, but you single-task the first two hours of each work day.

Here are a few modifications of your daily stand-up meeting agenda; pick one that resonates with you:

What is my fastest route to a lead, client, contract, or paycheck? Do that thing first.

What is my fastest route to six (I just grabbed that number, you'll find yours) decent real estate conversations? Do that, and only that, in the next two hours.

What is my fastest route to a $10,000 paycheck today? Do that, and only that, in the next two hours.

What two things will I do today that foster genuine real estate questions and possible active business? Do that, and only that, first.

What is one concrete step I can take today that moves me toward my goal?

That's it. This is how you will start every work day. You start with this meeting and then proceed accordingly for the next two hours. Every other meeting comes after that task is complete. That's it. I should just end the book here. That is, sort of, all you need to do.

> **🥷 NINJA TRICK**
> Two-Hour Pipeline-Building Meeting Every Day

That's Another Meeting

And then there is all the other stuff, right? Getting back with vendors, answering email, working that repair amendment, paying bills, tending to your new contract, responding to texts, negotiating a deal, your Facebook or Instagram posts, mowing the lawn, going for a run, picking up dog food, marinating the chicken for tonight's dinner; every one of these things is another meeting at another time.

I am far from mastering this, but I find it tremendously useful to temporarily compartmentalize all of this stuff, and the placeholder for that is simply, "that's another meeting."

This is handy in both business and personal and especially handy when someone brings up a new topic when the first topic is not yet complete. Start paying attention to how often you may do that, introducing other topics before the first one is addressed, because it can be an annoying little habit bordering on rude.

You are talking about technology and someone brings up marketing. That's another meeting. You attend a neighborhood meeting on the new road design, and that one neighbor only wants to discuss the proposed bylaws. That's another meeting. You are discussing homework with your teenager, and he wants to talk about the car. That is a clever diversion, and the car is another meeting; this meeting is about your homework. You start a discussion with your sister about Mom and Dad's health, and you start solving all the world's problems or talking politics. Definitely another meeting.

And this is where compartmentalization is your friend. The most successful agents compartmentalize the hell out of their days.

We need to compartmentalize when dealing with buyers, sellers, and vendors. It's the one-thing-at-a-time concept. There are all these moving pieces, so many moving pieces in real estate and then this is us thinking that we can sort of deal with all of it simultaneously. Your squirrels, your squirrel farm. The best agents quarantine the squirrels for a few hours every day.

Today's Meeting and Your Lead Generation

So many agents have this start and then stop pattern with their lead generation, and so much of it is because of the space between their ears and all the stories they are telling themselves. I understand you have reasons for why you did not do lead gen last week... and, guess what? That's another meeting!

The meeting today is, What are two things I will do today that are genuine real estate conversations to potentially bring clients to my business? This is the repetitive meeting. Give yourself the ability and permission to tend to what needs to be attended to. It is temporary compartmentalizing, finishing the task at hand.

Your marketing... that is another meeting.

Your spreadsheet... that is another meeting.

The email campaigns you want to build into your CRM... that is another meeting.

And the repetitive meeting that happens every single day is, What are the two things I can do right away to generate some decent real estate conversations?

You're running a business, and your first meeting every day is this meeting. Stop overcomplicating! You're running too many meetings, or your other meetings are getting in the way of your most important daily meeting.

> ✔ **ACTION ITEM**
> **The Fastest Route to Your Next Client**

Most of you are independent contractors, and by now you recognize that you are in the business of talking to people about real estate. If you have no conversations, then you have no clients. So let's start at the top.

The vast majority of agents have a referral-based business; the majority of their clients come from folks they already know or that those folks know. Statistically, eight out of your first ten clients will come from someone you already know or someone they know. Those folks are most likely in your phone right now.

Let's explore some of the fastest routes to gaining a client.

FASTEST ROUTE ACTION ITEM 1
Your Phone is Power

The fastest route to gaining a client today is your phone, with your contact list already in your cell phone, the people you already know.

Keep this super simple, do not overthink. Here are some options of what to say:

"I have an announcement; do you have a minute?"

"I have a quick business question; do you have a minute?"

"I have two questions, one personal, one business; do you have a minute?"

"Did you see my Facebook post? Big announcement!"

"Are you anticipating any real estate needs this year, or who do you know who may be in need of my services this year?"

"I want to add my name to the list of people you call when you have a real estate question."

"I have big goals. I need your support."

To engage the people I know, I typically text first to set up the call. I shoot a text something along the lines of, "Hey, it's Julie. Want to run something business by you real quick. Can you chat?"

For the best people in your phone, particularly the folks you have on speed dial—if they are on your speed dial, your favorites list, they deserve to hear your full story, your why; they deserve to hear your passion. Tell your story. Engage them in your story and your motivation, and your goals, and your excitement.

Your job is to talk to people about real estate. What if your framework for every working day was to simply talk to ten people? See if they have any real estate needs or know someone who does or knows someone you should be talking to? How hard is that? Keep it simple and on task. You could walk the block, go to the park, the mall, your church, the kids' school, hold an open house. But the fastest route is your phone. You can crank out ten conversations in a minimal amount of time over the phone. In person may be more effective, but it's slower.

FASTEST ROUTE ACTION ITEM 2
Why For Sale By Owner is a No-Brainer

The next fastest route is the For Sale by Owner (FSBOs) and expired listings. Why? Because these folks are ready to sell today. These folks have already raised their hand and said I am selling my home and am well into the process. Most of them are motivated. And many of them are already frustrated because buyers have called and set appointments and then no-showed. And the buyers have a house to sell first. They are frustrated because so many agents are calling them pretending that they may have a buyer, but they really want the listing. Industry research says that approximately 70 percent of FSBO's end up hiring an agent, and NAR says only 30 percent of FSBO's say they would FSBO again.

FSBO is definitely an opportunity. Check the professional standards in your area and with your brokerage before reaching out to FSBO's or expireds.

Right away, start stopping by and calling on FSBO's in your area. Here is what you say:

"I am Susan with ABC Realty (you always have to disclose your credentials). I live in the area and saw your sign. I wanted to ask you a couple of questions; do you have a minute? Can you tell me a little about the house? What is the price? If I had a qualified buyer, are you prepared to pay a buyer agent commission? Are you considering hiring an agent? I'd like to come see the house real quick... can I swing by this afternoon?"

One of my first clients came from a FSBO across the street from me. I was nervous. I did not know these people, but I knew the street. I called them. They wanted to give it a go by themselves for a couple of weeks. I stayed in touch. They got tired of the process and buyer no-shows. It became my first listing.

Be a resource to FSBOs, build the relationships, and make these conversations a regular part of your business.

With any of these niches, before you jump in, do a Google search on 'realtor best practices for FSBO" or whatever the niche. Watch some YouTube videos on the topic. Take a class at your brokerage on the topic. See what other agents are doing, what they are saying, how to be most authentic and get the best results. Do a little homework, a little practice of what to say, then jump in. You will get better faster by doing than you will by studying and then studying some more.

FASTEST ROUTE ACTION ITEM 3
Open Houses Can Make a Million

We have top producers whose whole careers were built on nothing but open houses and stellar follow up. Now they work by referral. I love seeing all those stories where agents started their career simply all-in on open houses, and that is how they grew their business to where it is today to a referral-based business. Open houses get you in front of buyers and neighbors. It puts you in the role of qualified professional super fast, and no one who walks through the door knows that you're new.

The job with an open house is to first know about the house and neighborhood, make the listing agent look good to the seller, and for you to gain leads. I know many successful agents who got their start cranking it out with open houses. This is an especially solid option if you are new to town or do not have much of a local sphere. Talk with your broker about open-house opportunities in your office and how to line those up.

Here is some of the best advice I have heard over the years regarding open houses—your number one goal at an open house is to simply build rapport with the people who walk through the door. And how do you do that? It's simple. The fastest way to build rapport with anyone is by asking questions. You are not in telling mode where you are all talk, talk, talk, talk, talking about the house, the neighborhood, the stats, about you, your company, your awesome marketing. Telling mode tends to be ineffective.

Get into asking-questions mode. All you are doing is asking questions. What do you like about this neighborhood? What interests you about this house? What style do you like best? Where do you live now? Do you rent or own? It's all about rapport. I have a longer list for you on the next page.

Fastest Route

I list these three here because they are FAST opportunities, and that is good for your business. I could write an entire chapter on talking to your friends and sphere (your phone contact list), an entire chapter on FSBOs, an entire chapter on open houses. You could easily spend an hour online on each of these topics. Your broker most likely has a class on each topic. I will build on these topics throughout the book. The task at this point is simple... get started with action in each of these right away as they have a high likelihood of being your fastest route to your first ten clients.

Here is a recommended minimum schedule:

- Three open houses every month
- Ten conversations every day
- One FSBO outreach every day

Those are minimums. Specialist new agents' schedules may look like this:

- The open house specialist will do an open house every day, six days a week.
- The phone pro will have twenty real estate conversations every day.
- The FSBO specialist will have a goal to have an appointment with a FSBO every day.

Scripts for open houses? I'm so glad you asked. These are all open-ended and designed to get your visitors talking and to help you get into rapport. This is just a start. You can find so many more online, but here is a collection I like:

- "Hello. What brings you to the open house today?"
- "Have you seen any homes you really like yet?"
- "Who is your agent?"
- "What do you like best about the house?"
- "What neighborhoods are you considering?"
- "What is your timeline?"
- "What is most important to you?"
- "Have you been to other open houses? Any creepy or pushy agents?"

For neighbors:

- "How long have you lived in the neighborhood?"
- "What do you like best about the neighborhood?"
- "Are you looking to move or just curious?"

- "Who do you know who is considering moving to the neighborhood?"
- "When we list a house like this, we tend to get numerous buyers looking to move into the neighborhood. Do you know other neighbors that are considering selling?"

CHAPTER 11

Got Confidence?

Pretend you're good at it.

—*Furiously Happy*, Jenny Lawson

Confidence

One of my best friends said the most clever thing the other day. She said "I may not have been the smartest kid in the class, but I always made sure I sat next to them." I love this concept! The truth is she was probably the smartest kid in the class. She also said, "I may not have been the prettiest, but I was definitely top ten!" She was on a roll; there were, most likely, margaritas involved.

Confidence—it is one of my favorite topics for new agents and so critical with a new venture or a new audacious goal.

But new ventures and new careers and adventurous goals tend to come packaged with a decent learning curve, and confidence and steep learning curves are, well, not the best roommates. So how do you handle this confidence thing when you are first starting out or starting over or pushing through to a much bigger goal? We'll dig into that, but let's first take a quick inventory on how you're showing up in the world.

Let's take a simple quiz. Rate yourself on a scale from one to ten (one, low... ten, high) on the following:

- Overall on any given day, how is your energy level?
- Do you like talking to people?
- When your learning curve is steep, do you keep your energy up, do you lean in?
- Do you exude confidence, or do you just muster it up?
- Are you kind to yourself?

What about feeling stuck or in a rut or feeling a lack of meaningful progress or riding a plateau? We've all been there, and it impacts our confidence, our energy. Let's look at being stuck or plateaued from two angles. The first thing in the stuck category has to do with how we line up excuses. The bigger the rut, the bigger the excuse sandwich. I've been there, maybe you've been there. We loaded up the excuse sandwich, we stacked it high. We spent way too much time on that excuse sandwich. Consider dumping those excuses for the time being. This is really important because it helps you be kinder to yourself.

The second angle on stall or stuck is to encourage a perspective shift, from burden to opportunity. My friends, the stall is part of the business formula. Don't judge the stall. The stall gets us into a place where we recognize there is a missing piece, and then when the missing piece is identified, the path reveals itself again. So if it feels like a stall or a rut, shift your perspective. This is really important because it helps you be kinder to yourself.

This energy and confidence and personal kindness will play into your success and tends to walk into the room before you do; it always does, always will. We are going to call this your power score.

Power Score ... Success from the Inside Out

Why do some agents succeed, and other well-intentioned agents never really make it? In five intense and insanely rewarding years of training new agents, I realized there is this somewhat intangible yet moderately palpable thing that combines your energy, your confidence, your eye contact, your voice, your posture, your motivation, your nutrition, your internal dialogue, or, simply, how you're showing up in the world. A bit intensity score, a cousin to urgency score, say hello to your power score.

Most agents I talk with think they are confident and have a sense of urgency for the most important things. But in reality, many are afraid to jump in, pick up the phone, be direct in asking for business, or muster up the energy to go extrovert themselves all over town. They lack intensity and their sense of urgency is misplaced or misguided. I have this theory that some agents would benefit greatly from bumping their power score up a notch or two or five, summoning urgency for those two hours a day of driving the lead generation train. I think most agents apply urgency with client demands and situations, especially when the client is not happy, and then we have all sorts of on-point urgency, but I'm talking about urgency and intensity and strength with two hours of lead generation juju every day.

Let's not interpret power score as an introvert/extrovert thing. First, let's define introvert and extrovert in the simplest terms. An extrovert gains energy by being around people, an introvert is exhausted after a party or a big crowd. Introverts can be engaging and talkative in a crowd, they just need a nap the next day. Conversely, quiet time builds energy for the introvert while it unsettles the extrovert. The extrovert will gain energy with their lead generation conversations, the introvert will need a break after two hours.

Introvert/extrovert is not static; it moves around a bit, it's more of a spectrum or a continuum. You may move around the spectrum, somewhat, depending on the circumstance, your day, your mood, how hard you have been working, how you felt about the news that day. Perhaps you're in the middle somewhere. Perhaps you're adaptable. I know strong and confident introverts. I know extroverts who are negative or flirt with depression. I know extroverts with health issues so energy is a challenge. I know extroverts who have shifted toward more introvert over the years; I count myself in this last category, a waning extrovert or a waxing introvert, or at least a bit in the middle. Maybe I am an introverted extrovert. Or an extroverted introvert.

Because real estate is a people business dependent upon attracting opportunity and having effective conversations, how you're showing up in the world, your personal ecosystem, is a foundational piece of your success formula. You could go through every ACTION ITEM in the book, not skip a one, possibly complete everything faster than everyone else, but if your power score consistently dips into the low zone, you'll have trouble gaining clients and traction.

So here is a little task for you today: Rate yourself on your power score. How are you showing up? This really is an ongoing activity and is rarely a straight line; rather, it's more a process of ongoing course corrections. It's life, right? Tweaking what is working and what is not. Again, you are starting (or re-starting) a new chapter in your life, or you are pushing through to a new goal, and we are addressing your foundation. Remember my sabbatical? I was addressing my foundation; my sabbatical was a solid course correction and helped me stabilize my power score that was waning at the time.

Be true with this exercise, be true with yourself, as you may have blinders on in some aspects of your life. I certainly have had my phases of denying something or a delayed dealing with things, delayed course corrections. To remove the blinders, you may want to have this conversation with a trusted friend or two... how am I showing up? Narcissists typically do not know they are narcissistic (and will think this exercise is completely unnecessary), depressives may be in denial of how their energy is showing up in their lives, egotists are likely unaware of their self-absorption, the unhealthy may avoid the doctor. A good friend (or in some cases a skilled therapist) can help remove the blinders and get your energy moving in the right direction.

Putting our energy together, putting our lives together in order to move solidly toward a new goal—it makes so much sense. You don't put expensive hubcaps on a crappy car or build a victory garden without supplementing the soil. If your energy and attitude are not in the right place, you risk self-sabotaging your plans. I have heard the stories of many successful agents who first had to put their lives together in order for their businesses to materialize.

So how are you showing up? Let's go through an exercise here where you are assessing if your power score is low, medium, or high. It can be situational, we know that, but we are looking for your general state of being.

You could use the low, medium, high categories or a one through ten rating, if you prefer.

I find that this exercise is most useful for the medium zone people, and here's why. The high zone power score people pretty much know who they are. And then everyone else thinks they are middle. My case and observation is this: If you think you are middle, are you at risk of flirting with the low zone? The reason this is important is—and I'll be really straightforward here—low power score people tend to be ineffective in a sales environment where the job is to quickly develop rapport and confidently deliver expertise.

Let's take a closer look.

The Low Power Zone

In the low power zone, you're having a hard time showing up with confidence and energy. You are uncomfortable asking direct questions. When making business phone calls, you have a bit of a knot in your stomach. Perhaps you do not feel well. Your immediate circle leans negative and pessimistic and consistently attempts to sabotage your drive and optimism. Motivation is elusive, eye contact inconsistent, diet may have issues, optimism is a distant cousin. Obviously, this is not a good campsite.

If this is situational, then you may need to embrace the "fake it till you make it" mantra. (You can double-down on the fake-it mantra by replacing it with "fake it till you believe it!") You still need to believe. Believing leads to motivation. If you're in a funk (and we all know a funk now and then), find your funk reduction tools and push through it. If this is an ongoing pattern, talk with some valuable people in your life STAT and push this into the medium range ASAP.

Here's the deal: if you embody a low power score, you will have a hard time attracting clients or gaining rapport and trust. Address this ASAP.

The Medium Power Zone

Your status in the medium power zone can be situational. You may be naturally high power zone, but maybe there are challenges at home, and you have to muster up your energy and decide every day to bring your best self.

Medium can also be that nice and steady person of few words, the keen observer who is rarely the outspoken cheerleader but rather the reliable and consistent authority. Never the loudest voice in the room, medium can be the steady team player everyone relies on to get things done, often with little to no credit. Be careful about rating yourself medium when really you are a strong introvert. Remember, power score is not an introvert—extrovert thing. Rather, it is an indication of the extent to which you are attracting people.

Medium indicates that high is possible. If you are hanging out in the medium zone, pick one thing you can focus on this week that may bump your score up a point or two . . . we like incremental changes and tweaks. For example, this week I am going to call my two most positive friends because I always feel so much better after we talk. Or this week I am going to start each day off with a good breakfast and a walk. Or this week I am going to attend the neighborhood meeting like I said I would. Or Sunday I am going to clean my desk because the clutter is messing up my brain. Hey, you started a new really big chapter in your life . . . sometimes confidence is a bit elusive in times of something big and new, so figure out what you need to tweak and make it happen.

And, by the way, medium power zone can be quite successful in sales and real estate. It may just be how you are wired—you get things done.

The High Power Zone
You rock the room, you attract people, you raise your hand often, you are consistently engaging. Most days, your energy is solid. You are your own best advocate. If you are an introvert (yes, introverts can have a high power score), you are attentive and articulate, a leader. You move quickly. If you hit a bump, you keep moving forward. You are willing to try things, you are positive and optimistic. You are consistently giving yourself that internal nod of approval. Swagger comes easy. You most likely have decent sleep, eat, and exercise habits. Obviously, a high power score is good; it's where you want to hang out. Hanging out in the high power zone is super effective in attracting people and converting opportunity into actual clients.

Take a moment to identify two or three things that help you stay in this zone. This will be different for everyone. For me, my stay-in-high-power-zone formula is hugely dependent upon my sleep habits (I am a lifelong member of the eight-hour club): breakfast with protein (we have chickens), exercise (gardening, swimming, cycling), affirmations, loose-end management, and helping other agents. Like a compound pharmacy, it is my customized prescription. What is your prescription? It may involve coffee; no coffee, no talky-talky. What keeps you in the zone and, contrarily, what compromises your zone, your power score?

Power Score Agility

> If you're trying to be perfect, you're going to fail every time, but if you're lucky, you'll learn to be yourself. Feeling the need to be perfect doesn't make you perfect; it just makes you paralyzed. So the sooner you can let go of that, the better off you'll be. If you think I'll never be like that person, or I'll never be successful like that person, well you're actually probably right because you'll never be that person, but if you're lucky, you'll end up being the best version of yourself possible. Needing to be perfect is a real curse.
> —DAVID SEDARIS MASTER CLASS (PARAPHRASED A BIT)

We all have things that can throw us off our game. A big culprit for me is when there is too much on my plate. Then I get busy-head, my self-talk gets messy, and I misplace my A-plus confidence. I get frustrated, my compass goes sideways, my grounding loses ground. Having an awareness of those things doesn't necessarily mean we avoid them or order a second donut; it often means we can course-correct faster. I know this impacts business, but I swear that power score agility may be the secret of life... your ability to course-correct and adjust is key. Life, success, happiness—it's never a straight line; it's a bit of a moving target.

Drop your perfection, and embrace agility. What a relief when we can finally embrace this concept and give ourselves a break, relax a little, and simply course-correct. And then course-correct again, course-correct on the fly, course-correct your week, course-correct your month. This is what agility is. Your mindset, your energy, your production, your self-talk, your habits, your diet, your exercise program, it's never a straight line.

Your power score can change from day to day. This would be normal. What we are looking for is awareness and consistency and your ability to course-correct faster. Let's call this power score agility. To show up solid in your business (well, really, in your life), you need to consistently land in the medium-to-high range. Too much low and you'll be out of the business before you know it. Hang out in the high range, and you'll gain traction faster than everyone else.

Your power score is all about success from the inside out. Starting with you, your thoughts, your internal compass, your internal dialogue, how you're showing up. Your energy walks in the room before you do. Your swagger speaks louder than your words. How you think matters. What you think matters. Whatever you're thinking about is literally like planning a future event. When you're worrying, you are planning. When you're appreciating, you are planning. When you are dreaming, you are planning. What are you planning?

Success-from-the-inside-out is a foundational piece of your success formula and worthy of our time. The inside is how and what you think and feel, the outside is your behavior and your action. So let's tackle the next two ACTION ITEMS, your TOP 100 and what to say.

> ✔ **ACTION ITEM**
> **Identifying Your TOP 100**

Get out your phone. Get your neighborhood list. Your church directory. Your Christmas card list. Your kids' school directory. Your former colleagues. Your golf league. Don't forget your family. In town or out of town or out of state . . . all of them. Your college friends. I have brand-new agents who got their first or second client because they called their cousin or college friend halfway across the country. You know a LOT of people! Let's identify your TOP 100 because I promise you, there is business in there. Your immediate job is to cultivate and coax the leads out of that TOP 100 list.

You don't know 100 people? Call the ten you do know!

Who are your besties? If you had a party, they would be on the list. You follow these folks on Facebook. They know you. Get super clear on who your TOP 100 are, and get them on the phone. The faster you have a meaningful conversation with them about your new business, the faster you'll gain their trust and their referrals. And they want to help you. They love you and want you to succeed.

Ask for their support. Tell them you intend to earn their referrals. Ask if they anticipate any real estate needs this year. Who do they call when they have a real estate question?

When I started my real estate business in 1999, I threw a little party. When there is a new store or restaurant in town, they have a grand opening event, right? I figured I should do the same for my new business.

At the time, I rented this lovely little basement apartment in the woods on Shoal Creek in central Austin. I had just sold my house in north Austin, and this was my interim landing place. It was serene with an amazing patio in the woods. It was a nicely situated gathering place.

I knew I needed to engage my sphere to launch my real estate career. I invited my top 40 friends to my home for a happy hour (the landlord, owner, upstairs occupant was on the list). I stopped the party in the middle, announced my new business, told them why I was excited about real estate, asked them for their support, gave them all my new business card, threatened to not let anyone go home without a referral, told them I was going to send them all an email with my current contact information, told them I intended to earn their referrals, told them I loved them all, toasted to new beginnings, then got on with the party. The whole speech and toast took five minutes. That party and my post-party outreach (the email and a personal call thanking them for coming) jump started my career. Six of my first ten clients came directly or indirectly from that party outreach.

> ✓ ACTION ITEM
> TOP 100, What to Say When You Call

Remember that I told you in the introduction that this book was actionable? And that your results, your ability to gain traction will be directly related to your ability to tackle the action? Start paying very close attention to getting the ACTION ITEMS done in each chapter. Put your foot on the gas pedal, don't let up, and crank out these calls, these conversations. You want a raise in real estate? You give yourself a raise by having more conversations.

So today's ACTION ITEM is this: Call one to twenty of your TOP 100, and here's what to say:

"Hey, Robert, it's [me]. Do you have a minute? I know you're at work, so I'll be fast. I wanted to let you know what I'm doing. I've thought about this for years, finally pulled the trigger, and I am now an associate with XYZ Realty. Love it, wish I had done this sooner! So a couple of quick questions: 1. Do you have a go-to agent when you have a real estate question? [NO: Great, you do now! Or YES: Great, happy to be the second person on your list.] Second question: Are you anticipating any real estate needs this year or know anyone who may need my services? I appreciate you keeping me in mind. I'll send you an email right away so you have my contact info. Everything good with you? Would love to do lunch or happy hour sometime, catch up. What's your schedule like the next couple of weeks?"

CHAPTER 12

More Conversations = More Income

If you are not moving closer to what you want in sales (or in life), you probably aren't doing enough asking.

—Jack Canfield, *Chicken Soup for the Soul*

Conversations

Chit chat is ok. Socializing is ok. But to talk on purpose for business? THIS is how it works: You have to line up meaningful real estate conversations and you have to ask for business. Falling short on either of those will seriously impact your bank account.

You are in the business of talking to people about real estate. This is the most fundamental income producing activity (IPA) you will do. Some of you may think IPA is a beer, and you would be correct. In the context of business and business coaching, it's income producing activity. I like the idea of asking myself at the end of each day, how much IPA did I have today? Not beverages, but how many calls? How many conversations? How many appointments? How many follow-ups? I like starting out each day, spending the majority of my mornings, only with IPA. If it sounds like I am drinking beer regularly in the morning, I am pretty much a chai and water gal and would never mix those two IPA's into the same time block. Let income producing activities anchor your day. More conversations, more income; fewer conversations, less income. Whoever has the most conversations, banks the most money... and wins the game, when cash is the score.

In the last chapter, we addressed your power score and how you talk to yourself. In this chapter and the next and a couple more after that, we dig into the practicalities and specifics of talking to people about real estate. You can talk to yourself all day long, but the last I checked, unless you are personally buying twenty properties this year, your internal dialogue does not directly lead to new client opportunities.

You are in the business of talking to people about real estate.

You may be amazing online and capturing leads via various techy strategies, but you still need to talk to those people. The goal with any online lead, any lead, is to get them on the phone, to get into a conversation. Sometimes the script is simply, "What's your phone number?" Keep this principle in mind, take your online leads offline, and your offline leads online.

The fastest route to rapport and ideally an appointment is an actual conversation. If you have an online lead, and all of your communication is electronic, there will be a greater chance of that person disappearing, no-showing, or simply not responding. In sales and in real estate, keep this principle close at hand: The person who talks to the most people will have the most opportunities, will make the most money. And, all too often, the agent who talks to the person FIRST, wins the client... there is that fast concept again.

And, again, you do not have to be an extrovert to make it in this business. It helps, but it is not a rule. If you lean shy or lean introvert, this is a critical point. I know one of the top agents in the country (he now coaches top agents in the country), and have actually heard him say on stage something about not really being a people person. He prefers solitude over crowds. But what he realized very quickly when he first got started thirty-some years ago was that he liked going to the bank. And he made peace, quickly, with the concept that he was in the business of having conversations with people about real estate.

The consistent number and quality of your real estate conversations is everything; it is the cornerstone of your success. I believe this so strongly that when I talk about making a certain number of contacts per day, I do not get to count voicemail messages left, text messages, emails, or Facebook exchanges. While those touches add up and will be a solid piece of your overall strategy to connect, do not confuse online and text interactions with actual conversations. If you get hung up in text or online communication, you may miss out to the agent who gets them on the phone first.

Do not create the illusion of income producing activity when all you are really doing is building up to it, especially you perfectionists out there. I am particularly skilled at pointing that perfectionist finger because I am one. Sometimes this perfectionist thing serves me well, and sometimes it's a curse. Sometimes my mantra to myself is simply get busy with the right things, dammit!

What to Say . . . And How . . . And Why
Power Questions

By now you understand that you are in the business of talking to people about real estate. Yes, this is a repetitive message. But what do you say? Notice the subtitle does not say power conversations or power presentations. While those have their place, this is about POWER QUESTIONS. When you realize that the majority of effective communication in this business (and in life, marriage, parenting, leading, being a good friend) is simply asking good questions versus you doing all the talking and sounding amazing, brilliant, and experienced, your relationships improve, things start leaning seriously in your favor, and you'll be good at parties. This question approach takes a lot of the pressure off and begins to put you in control of the conversation. It also puts you on the rapport fast-track. Just ask questions, powerful questions. Some questions are more strategic, more effective than others. Let's scuba dive into this topic.

Being a question pro is a handy tool for so many situations, a handy tool for life, a particularly handy tool with children, teenagers, and spouses. Ask more questions. Are they teaching this in schools these days? They should. It's such a skill to everything working better. Asking good questions and having the patience to listen to the answers is the great ego-moderator skill.

Once you get the hang of this, not just professionally, but even more importantly personally, it becomes part of your natural style. Notice the people in your life that you love to be around, that make you feel good, that always seem to get you talking, talking about your day, your experience, your opinion, your story, your challenges. They get you, you feel heard. The people that are really good listeners, I bet those feel-good skilled-listener people in your world consistently ask a lot of questions; it's how they operate. Start observing this. Also, notice the style of people you know who are successful in some sort of sales or leadership. Notice their style of communication. I bet they are asking a lot of questions.

On the converse, the folks who annoy you, that you don't really care to be around or that wear on you or that you simply tune out, they're never asking questions. It's all about them; it's a lopsided conversation all the time. It's annoying and seriously limiting in sales and people businesses.

> **🗡 NINJA TRICK**
> **Get in the Three-Question Habit**

The Three-Question Rule
Experiment with this a bit. Without telling anyone what you are doing or allowing them to read this chapter, try it out on your kids, your spouse, the grocery store check-out clerk. Before you can say anything about yourself, your day, or your opinion, you have to ask three questions. You do not have a green light to talk (and in some cases talk, talk, talk, talk . . . we'll address that somewhat annoying behavior later), until you have asked three questions.

The grocery store clerk says, "How are you?" You say, "I'm good. How are you?" (question #1). Listen to the answer. "How long have you worked here?" (question #2). Listen to the answer. "You're always so pleasant, and I appreciate that. What do you like best about working here?" (question #3). Listen to the answer. They'll remember you. If I ran a retail store, I would totally train the three-question rule into my customer-facing team. I would make it a standard of how we operate.

The teenager. That's another book. I don't have kids, but I was one once. Try it on teenagers, the three-question technique. And then keep trying it. Do not tell them what you are doing. If the teen response is "I don't know," then with a smile try, "Well, if you did know, what would it be?" Keep it up. This may drive them crazy, but they'll eventually come along. Ultimately, they may start using it on you, or you'll observe them using it on their friends. It will be a great day when you overhear your teen actually say to a teen friend, "Well, if you did know, what would it be?"

The spouse. I have one of those. Start trying the three-question approach on your beloved. When your spouse or significant other says something along the lines of, "Whew, what a day!" And your typical response, "I know! I was up at 5:30. I felt rushed all day, traffic was rough, and you know that meeting I told you about? Well, let me tell you what happened." Uh, no! You do not get to talk about your day until you have asked Mr. or Mrs. or BFF three questions about "Whew, what a day!" Seriously, this three-question red light/green light can transform a stalled or stuck or flat relationship. Eventually, tell your spouse or significant other about your three-question experiment, and the two of you can start working on this approach together. We have done this in my household. It's not a perfect record, and sometimes we joke about it . . . "Hey, you only asked me one question. I need my three on this topic." It's a bit of a game-changer.

How does this apply in business? Earlier, we addressed your power score. Now, in this chapter, we are going to talk about the POWER QUESTIONS, what they are, and what they can do for your business success. The power questions are a supply of conversation-yielding go-to questions that will be the core of how you engage folks in effective real estate conversations. Tweak these to make them authentic to you and your style.

POWER QUESTIONS (we'll call these PQ's):
PQ #1: I WOULDN'T BE DOING MY JOB
"Hey, real quick . . . I wouldn't be doing my job if I didn't ask you this question. Who do you know who may need my services this year? I appreciate you keeping me in mind. I'll send you a quick email with my contact information. Are you anticipating any real estate needs this year?"

PQ #2: EARN YOUR REFERRALS

"I know you know a number of Realtors. I just want you to know that it is my goal to earn your referrals. Just planting the seed. So what's the most important thing that you value in an agent? While we're on the topic, are you guys anticipating any real estate needs this year?"

PQ #3: THE SECOND ON YOUR LIST

"I respect that you know another Realtor [or that your sister is licensed or that you like your old agent]. I'd love to be the second on your list. Not everyone is the right match, so keep me in mind. While we're on the topic, are you anticipating any real estate needs this year?"

PQ #4: THE ONLY PROPERTY?

> ⊗ **WARNING LABEL!**
> Frequent use of this PQ will make you a bunch of money:
> "Is this the only property you have to sell, or are there others?"

> 🥷 **NINJA TRICK**
> Always ask this is-this-the-only-property question with all sellers.

PQ #5: WHO DO YOU KNOW?

"We are already setting appointments for fall. Who do you know who may need my services this year?"

PQ #6: MENTIONED REAL ESTATE?

"Who do you know who has recently mentioned real estate?"

PQ #7: WHO DO YOU CALL?

"Who do you call when you have a real estate question?"

You need to find yourself asking the POWER QUESTIONS as often as possible. Get super comfortable with this. The more you ask these, the more comfortable, natural, and effective you will be. Start counting how many times you asked one of the POWER QUESTIONS every day. It's your job to ask these questions. The more you ask them, the more money you make. You could treat this like a game. The person asking these questions the most, without being annoying, wins.

I do want to touch base real quick on the naysayers. There will always be naysayers, people who say no, and your job is not to do the work for them. Your job is to do the work for everyone else. It is not about how to convert those who say no; it is the art of ignoring them, the art of moving on, the art of keeping going until you find the yeses that will drive your success. Don't let the naysayers tap into your lizard brain.

Seth Godin loves to talk about the lizard brain, the part of your brain that is trying to stay alive and doesn't think critically about anything. It's all breathe or not breathe, swim or be eaten. He says the lizard brain is capable of subverting your magic and sabotaging your progress. The lizard brain delivers a false agenda and talks you out of things that are imperfect because lizard brain is all about safety. Lizard brain shows up for all of us, especially the breathe or not breathe piece, but take inventory on how often that scaly skinned reptilian is in charge or not. Sometimes, especially with pushing through new things or maneuvering around naysayers, we need to tell the lizard brain to sit down and shut up.

Pretend that you are the national sales manager of your real estate business (because you are). What does a sales manager do? Sales managers set the sales targets for their team or division, establish a structure to support those goals, and then hold the team accountable for hitting those targets. Right? So what is your target? How many buyers and sellers do you need to help this year in order to hit your financial goals? Simple business plan, right? So as the national sales manager of your real estate business, shouldn't you know if your team is doing the work? You are the team. Keep a tally. Set a target.

Let's apply this concept to one of the top agents in the country . . . actually, let's clarify . . . one of the top under-30 agents in the country, Tim Heyl in Austin, TX. He made this very simple when he first started in real estate fresh out of college. He called his client leads "nurtures." Every day, five days a week, he started his day talking to people about real estate. He would not allow himself to consider it a day worked until he had identified five nurtures that day. That means he was adding twenty-five leads to his pipeline every week—not all of them quality leads, but he was feeding his pipeline. And then he knew his math... five nurtures usually equaled one appointment. He was being a very good national sales manager of his young real estate business.

Here's another example, the A–Z approach. I know agents who use this approach every day. They pick up their phone, open contacts and today is the letters A & B... they are calling everyone in their contacts with a first name that starts with A or B. Then tomorrow is C & D. And so on. What the heck do you say? Uh, POWER QUESTIONS? Text them, tell them you have a quick business question, ask them when do they have a couple minutes today, then call. "I'm reaching out to make sure we are driving our business this summer and fall and to check in with our A-plus friends. What real estate needs are you anticipating this year or next for you or your company (family, friends)?" That is just one example of what to say.

And one more example. Drive real estate conversations on Facebook by posting super open & engaging questions, something like this:

- "What home improvement is on your bucket list?"
- "How's this working from home thing working for you?"
- "Privacy fences, yes or no?"
- "What was your first car?"
- "Who is the best cook in the family?"
- "How old were you when you bought your first house?"
- "If you could do one upgrade to your kitchen, what would that be?"
- "Who are my green thumb friends? Post something we may all enjoy!"

And then you COMMENT on EVERY comment and the goal with ANY of these questions is to then ENGAGE with some of them in private message and then the goal is to take some of those PM's to a PHONE CALL. I know, it seems like I am YELLING in that last sentence.

All of this is designed to get you into CONVERSATIONS WITH PEOPLE (sorry, I'll stop yelling) and create opportunities to ask some version of a POWER QUESTION. You have to drive the conversation lead generation bus, rather than just being a passenger. And in those conversations, a bunch of folks will ask you this question...

How's the Market?

In this chapter of what to say, the how's-the-market question is foundational. Your mastery of this question is critical. Every day, you must have a solid answer to this question. And you should be getting this question every day. If you are not getting this question every day, then you are not having enough real estate conversations.

You should be getting this question every place you show up. You should be getting it at church, at the kids' soccer games, at the gas station, grocery store, neighborhood picnic, family dinners, open houses. Everywhere, every day. If you are not getting this question all the time, then no one knows you're in real estate. This is hands-down the most common and popular question and conversation-starter. So how is your market?

As quickly as possible, you need to be a subject matter expert on this topic. It's your job to get on top of this and stay on top of this. Pay attention, study, read, talk to other agents, talk to lenders, engage your friends on the topic, watch stats daily or weekly in your MLS. For example, I know that in the Austin MLS there were 1,337 properties that went pending in the past seven days. (Well, at least when I wrote this; you get the point.) What about your market? You could get in the habit of posting something to social media every single Monday with a how's-the-market commentary (TIP: post it early morning, noon, or early evening when everyone is paying attention, not in the middle of the day when they're working).

So what do you say? There are two categories of approaching this topic. One is the subject matter expert where, for example, you may write a blog article or do a quick video online talking about the market and some of the statistical dynamics. Have pertinent facts ready to go. The more facts, the better you sound. The other approach is the engage-the-consumer approach, where the emphasis is less on stats, and more on why they are asking you the question.

And there's a little NINJA trick I want you to take in. It is NINJA for being an awesome human and effective in sales...

> **NINJA TRICK**
> Always End With a Question

When you end with a question, you take control of the conversation, you get to drive the conversation. This ask-questions approach takes the pressure off of you being an expert, the pressure of needing to relay facts and stats and advice and observations, and simply puts you in a position of gaining information and insight and clarification. It's less of speaking to an audience that you may lose the attention of, and more of being a skilled interviewer who comes across as caring. It's a huge difference. Always end with a question. Make sense?

See what I did there?

Let's take a closer look at what you can say and how to lead with questions.

Stats and Market Dynamics

Here are some common stats to monitor and work into your conversations:

Inventory: "Wow, there are fifty-six homes on the market in Shady Grove, and about twenty are selling per month. That means on average it will take two-to-three months to sell. Are you considering selling?"

Inventory: "Last month there were eighty homes for sale in the area, today there are ninety-three. Don't miss the market. Who do you know who is thinking of selling?"

Price Trends: "The average home price in Bay City went up 7 percent over this same time last year. This is influenced both by our strong economy, low inventory, and all the new construction in the area. It may be a good time to sell... let's chat. What's your schedule the next couple days?"

Interest Rates: "Interest rates bumped a tad recently, and the Fed is indicating another bump early next year (Hint: Lean on your lender for this.). Even a quarter or half point bump can significantly impact your monthly payment. Don't miss the market. Who do you know who is thinking of buying and would benefit from a decent strategy conversation?"

Engage the Consumer

Here are some handy engage-the-consumer responses to the popular how's-the-market question. Again, notice the question on the end of each response; get into this NINJA habit as it is crazy effective in gaining control of the conversation.

"The market? It's crazy awesome... why do you ask?"

"The market? It's great. Have you thought of selling?"

"Is it a good time to sell? It is for a lot of people, not so much for others . . . depends. What's up? What is your situation?"

"How's real estate? It's amazing! Wish I had done this years ago! You guys still live downtown?"

"Home sales are up x percent from this same time last year, and prices are up x percent in our neighborhood. That's solid. How long have you guys been in your home? Who do you know who is wanting to move into this area?"

"The market? It amazes me. You know, with interest rates as low as they are, a mortgage payment on a $220k home today is about the same as a mortgage payment on a $120k home in 1995. It's called the affordability factor. The folks out there that are still renting need to take a serious look at that. What's your email? I have a blog article on the topic I want you to see. When are you going to buy?"

> ✔ **ACTION ITEM**
> Practice! The **POWER QUESTIONS (PQ'S)**

Curse me now or love me later, but the repetition and action throughout the book is by design. Trust me on this . . . practice the questions, the scripts, the conversations, practice again and again and again. Why is this important? Once again and, this time, with just a little more flavor, I will be in-your-face enough to say that the people who practice more, who do the exercises more . . .

- make more money,
- go on more vacations,
- change more lives,
- win more games.

That can be you, but it does not magically happen. That can be you, but opportunity does not just materialize out of thin air. With the right action and putting in the time, and then more action and more time, that can be you and your bank account.

What will your life look like when you win your business game? What will your life look like when you pay down your debt? What will your life look like when you create a financial foundation for your kids? A foundation that you never knew growing up? How will your success change things? How will your success impact the messages your children learn and take with them into adulthood? What vacations will you go on? How will you feel when you are helping more and more families change their lives?

> "Practice is just as valuable as making a sale. The sale will make you a living, the skill and practice will make you a fortune." —MIKE FERRY

ACTION ITEMS, POWER QUESTIONS, time on task, practice, and more time on task, and then more time on task, honestly...

Repetition is where you make your money.

Repetition is where you change your life.

Repetition is where you move toward On Fire Hot!

Repetition actually works best when it is spaced out over time, frequency and effort spaced out over time. So this practice-the-power-questions-exercise is not a one-time thing or something you worked on a bit in the first few months of your career. Stephen Curry still practices free throws. Tiger Woods spends hours on the putting green. Ed Sheeran spends hours and hours on one transition, years after a song has been released.

Let's have a little science moment around why repetition works. The topic is neural pathways. We need to build these up and keep building. The goal with practice, with repetition, is to stimulate the neurons that create the pathways, neural pathways. Your brain will believe and build muscle around anything you repetitively feed it. So feed it good things and true things and useful things. In this case, the muscle is actually myelin which is the insulation around the axon which improves how well signals travel from one neuron to the next. The stronger this connection, this myelin, this neural pathway, then the greater the likelihood that you'll actually be able to say the right thing at the right time and be more and more effective and confident as a salesperson because your ability to ask the right questions, really effective questions at the right time, your skill is well-developed. You own it. You own it because you put in the time to build the muscle.

THE EXERCISE

Read the PQ's again and the how's-the-market responses above out loud ten times fast. And then read them faster. You probably want to be by yourself when you do this. Another option is to pair up with another agent and plow through this exercise together. There are quite a few ways to do this repetitive exercise. You can say it out loud, say it with an accent, say it in front of a mirror. Pace while you're doing this, record yourself and listen on replay a hundred times, write it out on a sticky note and put it on the bathroom mirror or your computer monitor, handwrite it twenty times, type it fifty times. Are you more visual, more auditory, more kinesthetic? Pick one but make sure that some of the time is auditory because that's the physical part.

The goal of this quick exercise is simply speed and repetition. In fact, you may want to do this simple exercise every day this week and next week and the week after. Go over and over and over and over these questions. Speak them out loud, write them out on a notepad, type them out, record yourself on your phone and listen to them in your car (hands-free, of course). Speed and repetition.

THE CALL

Pick one of the PQ's in this chapter and call someone, call five, call twenty ... heck, walk your block and ask your neighbors. This is not an email; it is not a post on Facebook. You must have conversations with people. Do not move on to the next chapter without this ACTION ITEM checked off.

So, for example, you would call ten friends and ask them real quick:

"Hey there, I have a quick business question for you. Who do you know who may need my services this year? We are already setting appointments for Fall."

Or you would call all of your family members and ask them this:

"Hey, I am really hustling to build my business this week. I need your help. Who do you know who has mentioned real estate lately?"

CHECK-IN: How Are You Doing?

How are you showing up on the ACTION ITEMS? We are well into *Success Faster On Fire Hot!* and your success will be directly related to your ACTION versus time spent reading. Your reading or listening time will build knowledge, clarity, and motivation, but it is the ACTION, the doing, that is the income-producing activity. Reading equals knowledge. Action equals make more money. Think of this paragraph as the teacher checking on your homework progress. It's the teacher that you love checking on your progress. Remember your most favorite, kind teacher or professor you ever had? When Mrs. Favorite or Professor Kind genuinely checked in on your progress, that was a good thing. Right? They cared. I care. Consider this a nudge.

We are all busy; I'm busy, you're busy, but is it the right busy? What if most of your activity is social media, yet there are very few actual conversations? Have I mentioned lately that you are in the business of having meaningful conversations about real estate?

I know, you may be working your tail off. You may be cranking out open houses, taking as many broker classes as you can fit in, preparing awesome newsletters to send to your friends and neighbors, working on your buyer packets, spending hours on your social media profiles and campaigns. All of that matters. And none of that matters without conversations.

I see this all the time. And every broker and trainer in the country would say the same thing . . . busy with the wrong things.

I am not immune to this busy-with-the-wrong-things thing. In fact, I am sufficiently experienced. I can be completely together one minute and an hour later all over the place with distractions and wondering how I traveled that distance in such a short amount of time to only repeat the pattern multiple times throughout the day. This creates a bit of chaos. I pride myself in being somewhat measured and rational, but there are days that steadfast Julie is completely thrown out the window. I need a deeper understanding of the disruptions and the noise and the patterns. Or do I? Perhaps I just need two squirrel-free hours every day to crush my A-plus tasks, then I can immerse myself in whatever squirrel farm presents itself that day.

To navigate around my tendency to run a frickin' squirrel farm, a rodeo without rules, my coach introduced me to this simple concept of having a daily three-item checklist. The three items are the non-negotiable business items that I must complete that day, the A-plus tasks. The A-plus tasks earn me money or represent solid progress toward my goals, and I get these things done first. Or, I can review the three-item list toward the end of the day, and if they are not all complete, then I realize the squirrel farm was alive and well that day, and I turn on the hustle and get it done in the last hour of the day. Either way, the three items are done. And if I can be more and more and more consistent with this over time, even with squirrel sightings everywhere, it doesn't matter because I keep getting my three things done. I have good days with this and not so good days with this. Just line up the good days. Two in a row, three in a row, four out of five. Build some consistency. Line up the good days.

You can succeed by doing the right things with consistency. Every day, you have an opportunity to start or restart this pattern. Simply start building consistency with the things that matter the most. Do the things that matter most first. Every day. You can do this.

Again, *Success Faster* works best if you're doing the action. Maybe you're reading the book through quickly first, then you're going to circle around and read it again doing the actual work. I get it. I scan material all the time. My point is this . . . if you're not doing the work of consistently having real estate conversations, you'll be at risk. If you delay, you may be at risk. If you are two weeks in or two months in and are still getting ready to get ready, you'll be at risk. I coached a Rookie of the Year where she had six clients lined up the day she got her license. She had been talking to everyone she knew for months, doing a countdown to license day.

Here's the deal. On any given day, your actions could be high action or they could be low action. We all experience this. I experience this. On any given day, I may be totally in the game, and on another day not even close, or, worse yet, in denial that I was in the game when I was actually on the sidelines feeling busy. No one has efficiency immunity; it comes and goes. It is an ongoing process of being more and more accountable, more and more in the game. So don't beat yourself up on this stuff, just line up the good days.

Simply take inventory every day. How did I do today? How was my IPA (income producing activity)? Did I complete my three items? Was I on the sidelines, or was I on the field? Was I a good boss today? Based on today, would I hire me? How many conversations did I have today? Did I add anyone to my pipeline today? If you track your number of conversations, track the health of your pipeline, or somehow rate yourself each day, your patterns will show up, and this awareness is so incredibly valuable. Pay attention. Keep improving week after week. Were you off track on Monday? Fix it on Tuesday. Did you have an off week? It happens. Let go of perfection and embrace improvement. What course correction do you need to make next week?

CHAPTER 13

More on Practice

I felt a cleaving in my mind
As if my brain had split;
I tried to match it, seam by seam,
But could not make them fit.
The thought behind I strove to join
Unto the thought before,
But sequence raveled out of reach
Like balls upon a floor.

—Emly Dickinson, "I felt a cleaving in my mind"

I think I'll make my life experience rearview mirror smaller (like tiny, as in those little round handheld dental mirrors) versus the full-size dressing room three-sided version that provides so little value and does little to no favors for my confidence or my ability to brilliantly move forward. How often do you find yourself assessing what you said, or did not say, in the rearview mirror? The committee in your head chiming in with *if only I had said this or that*. How often was there a missed opportunity for brilliance or gentleness or connectivity or a perfectly timed power punch or the perfect close? Or the times you simply forgot to ask the right, if any, POWER QUESTION, or stumbled over an objection? We have all obsessed over what we could have said. Let's take a closer look at building muscle memory on what to say.

Time on Task Over Time

You really do get smarter and better looking as you go; I believe this, and so it is true. In your new or renewed gig, you need to move toward expertise status swiftly and systematically. For those of you relaunching, you may need to brush up on your knowledge base and skills. I am twenty plus years in the business, and I still brush up on some of the basics.

What does time on task over time really mean? And how much time are we talking about here? Hermann Ebbinghaus in 1885 studied what would become known as the learning curve. We all understand a steep learning curve, the quick accumulation of knowledge, or a way to say "there is so much I need to learn!" and we know that a somewhat leveled learning curve is more of a gradual accumulation of knowing your stuff. What I find most interesting about the Ebbinghaus study of memory and recall is what he coined as the "forgetting curve." The forget-it curve notes that our retention fades over time, but when it is rehearsed and repeated at regular intervals, we forget less. So how quickly can you become an expert?

In Malcolm Gladwell's *Outliers: The Story of Success*, he presents the now popular 10,000-hour-rule of achieving expert status in anything. *Huffington Post* says it is a myth, that the 10,000-hour thing is only half-true. *Huff Post* says it's the 50-hour, good-enough level, "where amateurs and experts part ways." *Inman News* (add that to your must-read professional subscriptions) does the 10,000-hour math for us in "12 Tips for New Real Estate Agents": three hours a day, five days a week, that will roughly take you a decade to log 10,000 hours. That's a bit tiring.

My advice today is this . . . start building up your knowledge base, start moving toward expertise status as quickly as possible, speed up your business metabolism, speed up your learning curve, and reduce your forgetting curve. For those of you who are not yet licensed, start building now, start learning the language now, get ahead of the learning curve, start watching *YouTube* videos on agent best practices and what to say, block out the time and start building your muscle memory now so you will have a much easier time getting started and, frankly, will shorten the time it takes to get your first commission check.

We are not talking about perfection here. We are talking about getting better faster. Better is good. Perfection? She's annoying, fire her. (Unless she's a pharmacist or builds airplanes or is your bookkeeper, then definitely keep her on the team.) Commit to this, get started. Let's take a closer look.

Speed vs. Perfection

In your first year, you should be dedicating a minimum of five hours per week to practice. Practicing scripts, dialogues, what to say, your buyer presentation, your seller presentation . . . practicing until you sound confident. And then practice more. Want to get there faster? Double your hours of practice. In medical school, it's "see one, do one, teach one." Simply reading it once in this book or some other script source doesn't quite cut it. Watching one YouTube video, while hitting another area of your brain (the auditory cortex near your ears and the visual cortex in the occipital lobe in the back of the head), is just a start. Read it, say it, write it, practice it, use it. And then do it again.

Your brain needs all of these angles to move the material from input to processing the input to storing it in a meaningful and accessible file folder in your memory, so you easily know what to say when you need it. Remember the anatomy lesson earlier in the book? The myelin, which is the insulation around the axon, which improves how well signals travel from one neuron to the next? I knew you remembered exactly that, the myelin part. It is the muscle memory around what to say. Yes, we keep covering this off and on throughout the book. It is definitely one of the repetitive messages we are going to hammer home.

Put in the time.

Here's an example of what the increased hours can do for you. I met a San Antonio agent at a workshop a few years back. He was really good. Genuine, confident, solid. The guy was so smooth with what to say and how to say it, his confidence filled the room. He appeared to be one of the more experienced agents in the room. We were doing an exercise where we practiced scripts in a rapid-fire manner. Our conversation went something like this:

Me: "Andrew, wow . . . you're really good. How long have you been in the business?"

Andrew: "Two months."

Me: "No, how long have you been a licensed Realtor?"

Andrew: "Two months."

Me: [somewhat blank stare] "Seriously? Two months? Were you an assistant or something before? I mean, you're really good. How did you do it?"

Andrew: "They told me to do five hours a week of practice and role play. I'm really competitive, and I needed a paycheck faster than everyone else, so I've been doing fifteen."

He was two months in, sounded like a pro, already had five or six clients lined up, and five or six additional leads in the pipeline. He was practicing what to say fifteen hours every week. He got better faster than everyone else. Bye-bye learning curve.

NOTE: The top agents in the country still practice years into the business. Put it in your calendar and stick to it. Do the Andrew thing and get better faster. Get better, stronger, more confident, more competent faster.

I want to throw in a little tip here. It is a powerful question I learned to ask all sellers. I learned to do this with any of my seller consultations when I knew or suspected that they were interviewing more than one agent. Of course, in those appointments, I always wanted to make sure I asked all the right questions, wanted to make sure I did not forget to cover any pertinent detail. The scenario here is a seller consult, where you know the seller is interviewing more than one agent and, in the end, they choose the other agent. It happens.

Sometimes they want aggressive, and you may not come across as aggressive. Sometimes you are aggressive and that does not resonate with that seller. Sometimes they only want the lowest commission. Sometimes they choose the agent who suggests the highest list price (even if it is totally wrong and a horrible strategy). But what about the seller who did not choose you, and you thought the appointment had gone well? I remember years back, asking a seller if they could tell me what it was that differentiated me with the other agent they hired. I am forgetting all of the actual details here but am going to convey an important point. The seller said that the other agent said he would do [fill in the blank], and that [fill in the blank] thing is something you do with all of your listings, such as a geo-targeted Facebook ad or personally calling agents who have closed recently in the neighborhood! I seemingly lost the listing based on something I always do and yet failed to cover.

So the lesson was twofold. First, I made sure my listing presentation had every bullet item in our marketing plan clearly spelled out. Your listing material gets better and better over the years, and it always gets better when you make a mistake because you'll tweak it to make sure that you never forget to cover that detail again. Second, and this is the main tip I want to put out there, I learned to ask one simple question toward the end of a listing consult when I knew or suspected that they were talking with more than one agent. And that question is this . . .

"Is there anything the other agent said they would do that for some reason we have not covered?"

Nail that question in your learning curve, and it will save an opportunity or two every year.

✔ **ACTION ITEM**
Your Calendar Is Money

Plug the following non-negotiable recurring weekly appointments into your schedule:

- Ten hours per week of lead generation
- Five hours per week of practice; maybe one hour per week for experienced agents

The lead generation hours in your schedule, yours may be more, especially in your first two years, this is THE foundational piece to your successful real estate business.

The practice piece, five hours per week for launching agents, less for experienced agents. Let's keep this really simple. If you want the Andrew approach (remember his success story just a few months into the business?), pencil in fifteen hours per week.

Let's talk about your practice and what may work best. What is your best learning style? Are you visual, auditory, or tactile? Each of us learns best in different ways to tap into what works best for us—reading, speaking, or writing. Which one works best for you? Even if you are a visual learner or a tactile learner, make sure you spend time on the auditory, time actually saying the words out loud because that is what you will be doing in real life with clients. Tiger Woods can watch videos of himself putting or chipping, and that has value, but he needs to actually spend time on the putting green or in the sand trap to truly improve.

For most people, honoring this schedule takes discipline and accountability. It's not like you have a boss who is checking in on your progress every day or every week. These appointments, solidified and respected as a serious non-negotiable appointment in your calendar, will play a direct role in how quickly you start lining up your next client opportunity and your next paycheck.

> ✔ ACTION ITEM
> Call Your Biggest Advocate, Again

Yes, we already did this. And we're doing it again. That same person you called in the call-your-mother (or BFF) section, we're calling them again, and here's why. You need the close people in your life in your court. Some of them will forget that you are in real estate. Some of them are holding back, waiting to see if you are really moving forward with this real estate thing.

Sometimes your closest people can be your biggest advocates and your biggest critics. So the conversation may be as simple as giving that important person an update on how you're doing. It may look something like this:

"Hi. It's me. I wanted to give you a little report of how things are going at work. I want you to see how serious I am and tell you a couple things I have going on. [Or share a recent win.] Got a minute?

"First, I really appreciate your support. So I . . . " [then go on to tell them about your open houses, the buyer you're working with, that as the national sales manager of your real estate business you basically go to the office in the morning and do not leave until you have talked with x number of people about real estate . . . or some pertinent fact about what you're doing].

Then ask if you can practice a script or two with them over the phone.

"So I spend about an hour a day just practicing what to say, my presentations, and studying the market. I realized I would like a little real feedback, trying to get this to sound natural. I want to run this by you, get your feedback."

Then practice with them. They may laugh a little as it can be slightly awkward at first, but just roll with it. They usually offer a little advice like "be yourself," then half the time they'll mention someone who may have a real estate need.

You always want to end with a question something like this:

"Who have you come across recently who mentioned real estate?"

And then you need to train them HOW to help you:

"When you do hear of someone, don't just give them my card. Instead, say this: "You know what? I really want to introduce you to/have you talk to my friend [your name]. She's the friend I mentioned who is a Realtor. What's your email? I'm just going to send an email that introduces the two of you. No pressure; she'll treat you like family and may be able to help you. At the very least, she'll be a good resource."

CHAPTER 14

Bird Dogs and Your Next Few Clients

Call it a clan. Call it a network. Call it a tribe. Call it a family. Whatever you call it, whoever you are, you need one.

—Jane Howard, journalist

Five People

Over the years, I have observed a pattern in real estate where the majority of your leads and traction actually originate with a few key people. These are your people who always seem to be digging up new potential clients for you and sending them your way or drawing your attention to the opportunity. We'll call these your bird dogs.

So what is a bird dog? It is a hunting dog analogy for the people in your life who always seem to be spotting new client opportunities for you and your business. Bird dogs innately sniff out opportunities and point at them. Whether you hunt or not (I do not) or whether you own a Springer Spaniel, a German Shorthaired Pointer, or a Chesapeake Bay Retriever, even the couch-sitting kind, you need your bird dogs, your five opportunity-finding people.

I have helped many entrepreneurs over the years evaluate their businesses. I still do today. Specifically, I help them evaluate the source of their business. This is easy. Where are the leads coming from, and how can we make that work at a higher level? Time and time again, a pattern surfaces, a pattern of five people—five key people, and their introductions, their referrals, their referrals' referrals, their networks, and their support—resulted in a significant chunk of the agent's clients.

I'll give you a personal example. Early on in my business I kept an insanely detailed spreadsheet of all my closed clients. (I have a sample of this in my 456 Coaching Club on Facebook.) This was both a break-down-the-money ledger and a demographic log. Columns included the basics of name, address, zip, list and sales price, commission, broker split, fees, referrals, who the other agent was, the lender, where we closed it, and most importantly, how that client found me. It's the DNA of a transaction. Annually and early on, I tracked and analyzed that data and realized that there were key people who were sending me a lot of business. I recognized early on that I had a few bird dogs. I shifted my perspective as far as taking care of these key people, feeding the relationships, and cultivating a few others that had the potential of joining the VIP club. What if I poured more love and attention and lunch and happy hour and birthday flowers into these valuable assets? I have regular and purposeful business meetings with these people, including asking how can I help them. And SPOILER ALERT! It's not always about me! Some are friends, some are family, some are industry partners where business flows both ways, such as my mortgage partner. I pour all sorts of appreciation on them and shamelessly ask them how they think we could do even more business together next year.

Find Your Five People

Your five people, and your next client opportunity or the opportunity to increase your price point, may be closer than you think. Your key people could be your mother, your spouse, and his or her work network. Or your five may be in unsuspecting places—the guy you met at the coffee shop, the speech therapist at your kid's school, the quiet neighbor, your former boss.

My five people look like this:

My spouse. Knows everyone, retired teacher, has an antique business, super engaging on Facebook and Instagram, always meeting and attracting people.

My financial advisor and her spouse. These two know a lot of people and are both in the business of helping people make sound financial decisions. They understand referral business at a core level. I support them, they support me.

My lender. My top lender has been a dear friend for my entire career. Big community leader who knows everyone. She always seems to be looking out for people I should know.

The Susan Arbuckle Band. Yes, these are friends with a popular local band that draw nice complimentary crowds of more friends. They played at my business relaunch party, and together we sponsor a big annual community event. They always seem to be introducing me to the right people.

My agent network. This is a broad category on my list, but nearly 20 percent of my business comes from agent referrals around the country. My ability to love on these folks and stay top of mind is key to the sustainability of my pipeline.

I am always looking for the right opportunity to add to this list of five. But more importantly, I am always looking for the right opportunity to love on and double-down on these important people in my world. I would rather have my list of five and have that solid as a rock, than a list of twenty, and no one feels special.

Let's take a closer look at your five people (and yes, there is an exercise for this in the *Success Faster Workbook*):

Who are five people you know who know everyone? (Write it down.)

Who are five people who would give you the shirt off their back, who believe in you, who would not hesitate to help you if you asked? (Write it down.)

Who are five people you know who started their own business or have done something professionally impressive? (Write it down.)

What is your top community involvement or local network, and who are your favorite five people in that network? (Write it down.)

Train Your People

We have been talking about how the close people in your life can and will, in most cases, help you build your business. The majority of agents eventually end up with a referral-based business, meaning that the majority of their business comes from friends, family, and past clients simply spreading the word that you are the guy or gal they need to talk to. However, the majority of friends, family, and past clients are not particularly skilled or effective with how to really make the connection or the introduction. The majority of your people think that handing out your business card helps you build your business. It helps a little but is actually not all that effective. I know agents who actually believe they do not need business cards. And they're kind of right.

Your mother may be all excited that she gave your card to someone at the church social two weeks ago. But have you heard from that someone? Mom forgot to tell you.

Your spouse may have a few of your business cards in his or her desk drawer, but have you worked with any of his or her coworkers to help them buy or sell?

What if your significant other is a techy introvert? Is she telling other people about your business?

You need to train your closest people, and there are three important steps in that process. Each step sets the stage for the next.

> **🔥 NINJA TRICK**
> Train Your Best People

ONE

Share Your Goals, Vision and Dreams

With your close people, your family, your significant other, your BFF, your best close clients, these people deserve to know and see your vision and your dreams. And the more detailed, the better. Not just "It is my goal to help twenty-four families this year." Go deeper with something like "It is my goal to help twenty-four families this year so I can (fill in the blank) . . . help other people build their financial future, fund the kids' college education, take a meaningful step toward adopting a child next year, help my grandmother with her medical bills, make a difference at the local food shelf." Get personal with this.

TWO
Ask For Their Help and Support
Brene Brown does not like the term self-help; she doesn't think help is something we do on our own. Your people want to help you succeed. In sales we say you have to ask for the business. And with our close people we want to specifically ask for their help and support versus just assuming that that will materialize. Work hard, drive your business, ask for help.

What does that look like? Start simple: "I need your help." Explain how real estate sales is all about word of mouth and referrals, that the majority of experienced agents receive the majority of their client opportunities via personal referral and that you intend to build that type of business as quickly as possible. I often use the script that says something like, "I wouldn't be doing my job if I did not ask you about real estate every now and then. Who have you been around lately that mentioned real estate?"

THREE
Train Them What to Say When Someone Mentions Real Estate
You know your mother is going to say, "Of course I will help you, sweetie." But you need to train her. Tell her (ok, ask her) next time she hears someone talking real estate, do not give them your card. Let her know that cards are just not really effective, and it is totally passive. Instead, ask her, next time she hears someone talking real estate to say "Oh my gosh, I want to introduce you to my daughter, she's a Realtor. She is as straightforward and trustworthy as they come. She is not salesy or pushy and, at the very least, would be able to answer a few questions. What is your email? I'll send a quick email introducing the two of you." Or she can send a group text, same effect. The effect is that it puts you in the driver's seat of talking with and connecting with the other person. The business card exchange puts that other person in the driver's seat, and business cards get lost in the shuffle all the time.

> ✓ **ACTION ITEM**
> Find Your Five People

You guessed it. The quick lists you wrote down in this chapter? Call them. Do yourself and your bank account a favor, and do not move on to the next chapter until you have talked to these people, every single one of them. Call these people now. You can text them first to set up the call.

Here's what to say:

"I promised myself I would call you today. Do you have a second?"

OPTION 1
You Know Everyone

"You probably know more people than anyone I know. That's why I'm calling. I have big goals for my business this year. Here's my quick and easy question: Who do you know that I should know?"

OPTION 2
You Love Me, Right?

"I need your help. I have big goals for my business this year. Here's my quick and easy question: Who do you know that I should know?"

OPTION 3
Your Own Business

"You've started your own business/you've accomplished some impressive things. That's why I'm calling. I have big goals for my business this year. Come have coffee with me. I want to ask you about your success, advice for starting something new. I figure I should listen to successful people, and you're on my short list. What is your availability this week or next?"

OPTION 4
How Can I Help You?

"You have always been very supportive of me and my business. How can I help you? How is your business? What are you working on? Is there anyone I know that you would like to meet? Let's have coffee and catch up."

Mentors

Remember, we're looking for and cultivating bird dogs, raving fans, champions, your five people, folks who simply have their radar up all the time looking for opportunities for you.

You've just started this new amazing chapter in your life. Congratulations. Seriously, this is a big deal that you started this. So here's a little tip: Find a few mentors. Find someone outside of real estate, someone who has accomplished some sort of business success that you admire. They could be retired or full-on with some big expansion. Ask them out for coffee, or bring lunch to them at their place of work.

Think of it this way... you are always building relationships and on the lookout for key relationships. Having some focus and intention around this is key versus thinking it will just naturally happen. So identify some people in your world that you admire, and here's what to say:

"Alice, thank you so much for taking my call. I assume you're busy, so I'll be brief. I just recently started my new business (or I am relaunching my business), and I promised myself that I would meet with one successful business pro or entrepreneur or interesting person every week for the next two months. So that is eight amazing people, and you're on my short list. I intend to do this right. I just want to ask you how you got started, what advice you may have for someone just getting started, and if you were to do it all over again what you might do differently. I figure in the process I'll end up with a couple of mentors (no pressure). I simply really value your opinion and experience and would be honored if you would meet me for a cup of coffee, or better yet, I could bring sandwiches by your office sometime this week."

Friends, Easy Outreach

Friends who bought a home last year . . . I love this category for newer agents. It is a super low-pressure way to have a quality real estate conversation with a friend who already used another agent. Remember, you're looking for bird dogs, advocates, champions!

Call three (or one, or five, or ten) friends who bought or sold a home last year and ask them a few questions about their experience. The call might go something like this:

"Hey, it's [me]. Got a minute? You guys have been in your new home... what, six months now? Awesome! How is it? You love it? What's your favorite thing about the house? Any projects you're working on? Hey, the reason for my call... you know I just started in real estate, right? (I love it... wish I had done this sooner.) My question for you has to do with your experience buying your house. Can I ask you a couple of questions? What did your Realtor do really well? What could he or she have done better? Is she still in touch with you? What was most important to you in the process?

Do you have any questions on anything... home warranty, property taxes, filing for your homestead exemption? I can probably help, and if I do not know the answer, I'll go get it for you. No problem... call me anytime you have any question on your home... need a handyman, painter, plumber etc. I can help you. Hey, real quick before I get off the phone, is there anyone you know who may need my services this year? I appreciate you keeping me in mind. Hope to see you guys soon. Would love to see the house."

Why Should I Work with You?

Remember, this is a bonus section, and at this point, we are going to cover a critical question... Why should I work with you? Why should I hire you? You better know the answer. This is a good opportunity to stop for a hot minute or ten and write out some of your thoughts on your response, your elevator speech for why should I hire you? Get clear on what you bring to the table, knowing your value. More importantly, get clear on how to confidently take control of this conversation.

This business is very much a skill-based business, and your ability to handle the most common objections will not only be a big confidence booster, but it will also will help you convert your leads into actual clients.

Here is a starter list of some of the most common objections:

- Why should I hire you?
- I think we'll wait.
- Will you lower your commission?
- We're talking to two other agents.
- I have a friend who is an agent.
- Oh, that carpet is awful!

- We want to price it at $325k (when it's worth $290k).
- We want to offer $30k below the list price (when it's the coolest home and the market and homes are selling for full price in three days).
- We're just looking.
- We're going to try to sell it by ourselves first.
- We're not ready to talk to a lender.

We address these objections at length in the *Success Faster Workbook*. For now, here is my favorite response to the why-should-I-hire-you question:

"Why should you hire me? Maybe you should, maybe you shouldn't. I need to know more specifically what your needs are to make sure I am the right person and can deliver. You're interviewing me and I'm interviewing you; it needs to be the right match. What is your situation?"

Remember this key tip, end most everything you say with a question. Again, notice the pattern of this being an awesome human skill. Ending most everything in a question puts you in charge of the conversation, you in the driver's seat of the conversation.

Let's break down this response a bit:

- It's super honest.
- It is not salesy.
- It does not involve a monologue of my resume and skills.
- It's about them.
- It ends in a question that shifts the attention from me to them.
- It is offensive, not defensive ... I took control of the conversation with the strategically placed what-is-your-situation question.
- You can address your skill set later in your buyer consultation when you address some of the things you bring to the table to get the job done right.

CHAPTER 15

The Google
My dear friend, I tried to find you.

There is something very freeing about being anonymous because nothing is expected of you; nothing is getting back to anyone, and no one cares.

—Dolly Wells, British actress

> ⊗ **WARNING LABEL!**
> This is one of those "work" chapters I mentioned early on. It means we are going to dive into the work! Remember, and fair warning, this chapter is designed to hurt your brain a bit. So you may want to get a glass of water or turn on your best work music, quiet the kids . . . do whatever it is that helps you focus. This is IMPORTANT work that is designed to move you forward with your on fire hotness! Do I have your permission to help you actually move forward toward something better? I thought so.

f I searched for you online right now, how easy would it be to find you? Would I find you loud and proud online or more of the secret agent type? When your friends think of real estate, how easy is it to jump on your website or find your email or cell phone? We need to make sure you are easy to find and that it is easy to grab your email or cell phone. I figure agents miss opportunities all the time because a friend of a friend could not easily find your digits or connect with you online.

How you show up online falls into four main categories. Ease, accuracy, quality, and tools. Let's take a closer look.

The ease is how quickly can someone find you and your email and your cell and your website online? Can someone find that information with two clicks?

The accuracy is simple: Is it current, and does it show clearly that you are in real estate?

The quality is what information or content or flavor are people seeing when they do find you online?

The tools part has to do with your website—getting people using it to look at properties, and understanding where the information goes when they register on your website (if they register). Hint, you want people to register on your website.

So how well are you showing up online?

Whether you are a social media hound who could qualify for the Snapchat Olympics, a hold-out who only recently upgraded to a smartphone, or you fall into the social media love-hate club, your customers and potential customers are online, and they will check you out online before they pick up the phone and call you. Your friends will even do this to you. I cannot teach any class without spending a little time on this topic, and I certainly cannot complete *Success Faster* without a review of how you need to be showing up online. This is a somewhat brief yet very important chapter.

Think of this as building your reputation online. You're building it, you get to drive that bus.

Here's the deal, the first thing or the last thing prospective clients may do before they call you is check you out online. What if you don't look like a solid serious real estate professional on a simple Google search? What if they cannot find your phone or email with a simple Google search or a click on your Facebook About Me link? I would hate to see you do all the pipeline-development work outlined in the previous chapters, then the client doesn't hire you or call you because your LinkedIn profile still says you are an account supervisor at ABC Company, or a teacher at Garcia Middle School, or a barista at Starbucks, or your Facebook page has zero real estate related content. You must look good and legit online.

Find Yourself

While this could be a self-help mantra or an invitation to a spiritual retreat, in the context of *Success Faster*, it is an invitation to find yourself online. Let's do a simple Google search. Try this exercise... pretend you are someone, even a friend, who needs to quickly find your personal phone number and your email address online. Or pretend that you are, very quickly, trying to find another agent's contact information so you can connect with them regarding a potential client referral. Try a simple Google search and try Facebook ABOUT ME to get the contact information. How many clicks does it take you to get that information? Was it easier to find the broker information and a bit elusive to find the agent email and cell phone? This last broker info versus agent info is an important and potentially costly difference. Are your friends or friends of friends landing in the broker's inbox or yours? Is it the broker's lead or yours?

Let's see how easy it is to find you online, how easy it is to find your basic contact information; let's see if you actually look like a full-time real estate professional online. Regardless of your love or hate for social media, your disdain for mixing business and personal, your tight grasp on your other career or gig, or your need or desire for privacy, these are common highly used business tools, and you need to be aware of how you are showing up. If you choose to clamp down on your privacy online, just know that being a secret agent will cost you some business, and you'll need to make up for it in some other arena.

Stop and actually do this simple online audit exercise. TIP: You may want to try this with your browser in incognito mode because your laptop and its cache and browsing history know who you are and where you've been.

Google Search

- Type in First Last Realtor (meaning your first name, your last name, and the word Realtor; hopefully I did not need to point that out).
- How easily do you pop up on the top of the search results?
- What websites are you on?
- What does it say about you?
- Is it you or is it your broker?
- What websites are you on?
- Is it accurate? Is it current?
- Type in First Last City, hit enter.
- Type in First Last Brokerage, hit enter.
- Type in your email address; how many websites are you on?
- Type in your cell phone, any results?
- Type in your old phone number or old email address; any results that need updating?
- Your Facebook About Me page—You need an email, a phone number, and a website listed, and you most likely are required by your state to show your broker affiliation upfront.
- LinkedIn—In today's online driven world, you are expected to have a current LinkedIn profile. Do not fail this LinkedIn test.

Your Business Website

Is your information easily located? Is it only your broker's number and contact information, or are you easily found? I say this in particular because what if a friend of a friend is trying to find you online and, instead, lands on your broker's page and simply clicks the button to talk to an agent? Any agent. Or they click the form for more information, and that form either lands in the broker's inbox or goes to the agent on duty at the time? You may have just lost a lead and did not even know it. Many brokerages are designed to funnel as many leads as possible through the brokerage, especially those leads that the broker is spending money to generate. I want as many leads as possible coming directly to me versus funneling through my broker's system or both. How is the broker's technology set up? Do you have your own website within their website? Or is it just their website, and people find you on the meet-the-team page? Again, the question is how easy is it for someone to find me and connect directly to my home search tool?

Politics, Religion, and What You Ate for Dinner

While we're on the subject, let's talk about a little social media protocol. Politics, religion, opinions, hobbies, your culinary skills, your community involvement, your kids, your family, your insightful friends, your crazy cousin (who is one taco short of a combo plate) who posts stupid shit, and then tags you—your content matters. People will make decisions on hiring you or not based on your social media content. So who are you online, and does it matter?

Some people go completely neutral with their social media content, blending into everything, not standing out on anything, and this is by design.

Some people go all-in with their politics or religion or knitting hobby or soccer league, totally standing out, and this is, sometimes, by design.

Some people are business only with their social media, and this is by design. Not the best design, in my opinion.

Most people find a balance, and this is by design.

I know agents who have strong political views and are constantly posting content related to their political views. And they are fine with that because it is their intention to attract and work with people with similar beliefs and they do not worry about losing an opportunity or two with someone with opposing views.

I know gay agents who have no issue posting LGBT-related issues and content and photos of their gay lives, as the majority of their clients are LGBT, and they know that someone who is homophobic is not the right client for them. I also know gay agents who live in more rural areas, and they come across totally neutral on social media.

One of the first things I do with any new client lead is to look them up on Facebook. Same with the other agent, I check them out on social media. I want some insight on who I am about to talk to. And for the seller (or buyer) on the other side, the more insight the better. It's a tool. I think we all do this, brief stalking before picking up the phone. The point here is there is value in you taking inventory of and some responsibility for your social media content as it relates to business.

Make sure you are aware of the rules and regulations in your area, state, and brokerage for how you identify yourself online. Compliance is a big deal. Your broker holds your license (and takes on liability on your behalf), and some state board issued that license (and their purpose is to regulate the industry and protect the public). So these important people and entities have a say, an important legal say, in what you do and how you present yourself both in print and online.

Working through this exercise can help you find old information online. Clean it up, make sure you look good online, make sure you are compliant with your broker and state. One thing I did earlier in my career and do occasionally now and then is search online for a top agent, or an agent I admire, or an agent that I know is pretty techy to see how they are showing up. It's a little online research but borders on stalking. What websites are they on, how do they describe themselves in their bios? I do this to get new ideas for how to present myself, to find new websites that I should consider, and to simply study the top or cool agents so I can have some awareness of how things are evolving online.

I am always sharpening and tweaking my presence online. It is never perfect, and I have little to no control over Google analytics or algorithms. But I do have control over my content. Oh, and you need a professional or professional-looking photo.

And don't fall for those solicitation emails or phone calls from some company that promises, for a bunch of money, to help you improve your ranking on Google. I swear I get five of those calls or emails per week. Don't fall for that stuff.

As you go through an online review and updating your profiles, you will thank me for this next section.

> ✔ **ACTION ITEM**
> **Start Your Bio Document**

This to-do will save you a lot of time and frustration down the road. You are going to create a document that has two or three versions of your bio paragraph, as well as all of your critical URL links. The beauty of having this document at your fingertips is that you never again have to go on a hunting mission to find your LinkedIn profile URL, your Facebook business page URL, or your NRDS ID number. And you maybe did not even know that you had an NRDS number, but some critical member profile page is asking you for it. (Hint: it's on your NAR member card and somewhere in your NAR profile. You will want it in your bio document so you never have to go hunt for it again.)

My bio file is a Word file, conveniently called "BIO.doc," and I have it pinned in my favorites list (and backed up) so it is super accessible. I access this document all the time. It has three primary sections. First, ID numbers. Second, critical links. And third, every bio paragraph I have ever written. Here is a run-down of mine (yours will vary):

ID Numbers

- my license number
- my NRDS number
- my CRS member number

Links

- my main website link
- my blog link
- my personal Facebook link
- my business Facebook page link
- my LinkedIn public profile link
- my Twitter profile link
- my YouTube channel link
- my YouTube promotional video
- my Google+ link
- my Pinterest link
- my Zillow profile link
- my Yelp business profile link
- my Inman News author page link
- my Instagram link

- my Skype handle
- my 456 Coaching Club link
- my coaching intake form link
- my online audit intake form link
- my client intake form link
- my business consult intake form
- and https://linktr.ee/julienelson, which is a super-easy way to get contact info & multiple links into your Instagram profile.

NOTE: tools like this can easily change over the years, so if you are reading this three, four, or five years after *Success Faster On Fire Hot!* was published, we'll see if that link still works . . . but I think you get the point. It's hard to put tech advice in print, as the tech changes often. My blog at thenelsonproject.org is really the best place for current techy tips.

Bio

This section of your document will build and grow. I use this document any time I am filling out a bio on a new website or refreshing an existing online professional bio paragraph. This is so I am not having to re-write it every single time and hope that it is complete and as brilliant as the last time I wrote one. Here is where you can start:

- **Short**—Write a three-to-four sentence version of who you are professionally.
- **Medium**—Write a two-to-three paragraph version of who you are professionally.
- **Long**—Write a longer version of who you are, including background, skills, areas of expertise, what you bring to the table, why you are in real estate, what's in it for the client, and wrap it up with some personal interests.

One tip is that you can go online, maybe in Zillow or your brokerage agent directory or LinkedIn, and look up other agents to find examples of well-written and interesting bios. Go ahead, look up mine. No, you cannot copy and paste someone else's brilliant bio. You can, however, find inspiration, keywords, and examples of above-average well-written bio's.

What you will also find in this online treasure hunt is plenty of examples of poorly written or non-existent bio's. You need to look good online.

Photos

You definitely need a good photo online. For entertainment purposes, you will find plenty of really bad agent profile photos. Go to Google images and type in "bad Realtor profile photos." Seriously, that fluffy boa feather thing went out in like 1985. And if your profile photo is sixty pounds lighter, 15 years younger, and three hairstyles ago, you may want to upgrade. It's called truth in advertising.

Conversely, type in "best Realtor profile photos," and you will see a dramatic difference. Your photo matters. I would be curious if there is an income-to-photo-quality correlation. I suspect there may be. This may seem like a stretch, but if you look up some of the best agents in your area, your state, your brokerage, I bet they have a fabulous professional photo. As much as we may not want to admit it, first impressions matter.

This does not mean wear a suit and tie when you are not that guy and your sphere is not that guy and your clients expect you to show up authentically. I know entire brokerages, successful brokerages, that brand themselves on being super authentic. And I know entire brokerages that brand themselves on expensive black suits, ties, high heels. This will vary from area to area. Austin, Texas is a somewhat casual business environment, and millionaires wear torn jeans and flip flops. Downtown Chicago may be a suit and tie environment. If your target audience is millennial, it may be a different scene than if you are rural farm and ranch. So whoever you are, whatever your target audience, whatever the professional standards in your area or brokerage, match those up as best you can.

Yes, I recommend a professional photo. But a cool, happy, high resolution, personal photo will do on day one; you can upgrade later. And, by the way, most smartphones will allow you to change the resolution on your camera, and you can pull off a high res photo on your phone. And then change the resolution back to a moderate setting so you do not use up all the space on your phone with super high-resolution photos of everything. I used an informal photo for years. The kiss of death online is no photo at all.

CHAPTER 16

Rinse and Repeat
The Not-so-sexy Yet Incredibly Simple Ingredient to On Fire Hot!

Opportunity is missed because it is dressed in overalls and looks like work.

—Thomas Edison

Sexy

Let's talk about all the cool reasons you got into real estate in the first place.

You get to help people, keep a flexible schedule, and be your own boss. You have no financial ceiling, you like negotiating, you love design and architecture, you get to look at cool houses, you have no rush hour. While your friends are in a cubicle, you're driving around town with the top down. You get to meet people in the middle of the day for coffee, you're looking at cool properties, studying design and architecture. You get to work from home, no commute, no traffic jams. You get to help people change their lives.

You may start the day off working in your pajamas. You may take every Thursday off. You get to meet the kids at school lunch every Friday and sponsor the monthly school field trip. Yesterday you took the kayak out at 3:00 P.M. because you felt like it. Your car is your office, and you have this general sense of freedom on any given day. This is part of what is most attractive about real estate. Life is good.

Let's call this sexy real estate. It's most likely what attracted you to real estate and is what the public thinks you do. It's what your friends think you do.

Not So Sexy

And then there is the not-so-sexy part of real estate. Anyone who has spent any sort of time with me in a classroom setting has heard me give this speech, the sexy versus the not-so-sexy part of real estate.

The not-so-sexy part of real estate is the part we will refer to as a job. The job is the two to three hours per day, five days a week of lead generation and lead follow-up. It is lead pipeline building and lead pipeline nurturing. This is the job.

This is the foundation of your business, the frontal cortex of real estate, the DNA of sales. It is the day in and day out of always finding, generating, nurturing, and converting leads and potential clients. It is being busy with the right things.

Make peace with this.

Make peace with two to three hours first every day of doing the most important thing in your business. You must lead with this. Is this the most exciting part of your real estate business? No, not at all. But it is the work that creates the opportunity for awesome. Some of the most boring people in real estate are the most successful.

One of the biggest mistakes agents make is leading with sexy. You must lead with the job, lead with getting the most important things done first every day versus running your squirrel farm.

This foundational component of the success formula is especially pertinent for the highly distracted, the perfectionists, and the do-gooders. You may relate to one of all of these categories, and if you have equity or strong tendencies in all three—distraction, perfection, and people-pleasing—then you may want to read this chapter twice.

The Highly Distracted

The highly distracted bounce from one shiny object to the next all day long. You can get to the end of the working day and realize you got all sorts of things done. You may feel accomplished that day. Yet you accomplished little to nothing with your client pipeline. This sense of accomplishment is misdirected because you celebrate the wrong activity. Progress on shiny objects may look and feel good, and you get to cross things off a list. Oh, we love to cross things off lists, don't we? Done, done, and done. But what about progress with the thing that creates the most stability, predictability, and cash flow in your business? What would it look and feel like to cross that off your list on most days before noon?

The Perfectionists

The perfectionists have a tendency to spend countless hours on a spreadsheet or a new system or revisiting their LinkedIn strategy. If you are a perfectionist, you can be at risk of your perfection getting in the way of your progress. Progress on the right things. You have a tendency to think that all progress is good progress because you think all the details are important, and you will work hard to convince yourself of that. At the end of the day, the progress that matters most is your client pipeline. Not progress with your system or tools or software that supports your client pipeline. You see, perfectionists will argue that the system and software are just as, if not more important. And while you are arguing this point, some messy agent with a lousy system and loose notes all over their desk is closing more deals, building a stronger business, and building bank faster than you are. Yes, the messy agent needs a system, and their lack of organization may bite back, but the premise and title of this book is success faster. Faster. Perfectionists can be slow.

The People-Pleasers

The do-gooder-people-pleasers (I have this gene) are always saying yes to anything that comes their way. We fill up our plate with hundreds of smalls, all the while postponing the big. Yes to the committee, yes to the extra project, read all the e-newsletter subscriptions (fear of missing some important content), last-minute yeses, lots of "Sure I'll do that." Yes to nearly every request that comes along, yet we delay the dream.

When this pattern gets in the way of consistently hitting two to three hours per day of tending to your client pipeline, then it can be a problem. If this is you, you are always saying yes to something other than real estate sales. Saying yes to most everything that comes along, yet you delay the dream; *yes* is keeping you from *wow*. It's a formula for mediocrity, exhaustion, and disappointing yourself.

I personally relate to all of these profiles and have fallen victim to their traps throughout my career. I am not doomed, yet it is an ongoing challenge. There are a few tools I use, and you can too, that help me avoid shiny, perfection, and my saying yes tendencies.

One, I have a sticky note on my monitor that simply says, "Julie, what is your fastest route today to a lead, client, contract, or paycheck? Do that thing first." This works for me.

Two, I keep a three-item list almost every day. What are the three items I must get done today that are non-negotiable, and at least one of them has to have something to do with my client pipeline? This works for me.

Three, I have a coach who helps hold me accountable. I have worked with her for years, and I attribute much of my progress to her ability to help me stay on track, help me do what I say I am going to do. Accountability works for me.

What works for you?

Renew Your Joy

> He discovered his reset button early on, & there were not many things that bothered him all the rest of his days just because of that.
> —STORYPEOPLE

I think of joy as a business topic that does not get anywhere near the amount of airtime it deserves. This is a particularly poignant topic for agents feeling a little stuck, pushing through a rough patch, questioning their career path, at a mid-year check-up, assessing a lackluster bank account, or simply hitting the reset button on their business.

When I relaunched my business in 2017, this was where I started. I started with joy. I anchored my restart by asking myself a few questions. I anchored by going introspective first. I asked myself these questions:

- Why did I get into real estate in the first place?
- What do I like best about real estate?
- What am I good at?
- Who is my favorite client ever?

My answers looked something like this:

Why

Why did I get into real estate? I know this is a hugely broad statement, but I was looking for my life mission. I was looking for a career that spoke to me like no other had in my life up to that point. I wanted to have fun with my work, I wanted a thing, a product (like homes and people's lives) that mattered. I wanted to be jazzed every morning. I wanted something that pleased both sides of my brain. And I wanted to make more money than I had before without any sort of perceived ceiling, and I wanted to make a difference in people's lives.

What

So what do I like best about real estate? That's easy. I like . . . no, I love making a difference in people's lives, and I really like making great money. And I love design and architecture and outdoor living and finding and winning the best properties.

What am I good at? Finding and winning the best properties. And I am increasingly good at making great money. And I am a skilled negotiator, and I am really good at helping people navigate complex situations and make really good decisions.

Who

I asked this question because it is at the heart of what we do as real estate professionals. We are agents of change for the individuals and families that we serve. We get to help them change their lives by helping them change their address, helping them add space, helping them downsize, helping them sell mom & dad's house, helping them invest, helping them move to another city for a new opportunity, helping them move across town for a new school for their kids.

Who is my favorite client ever? It may be who has been the most meaningful or the most memorable. Meaningful is the new parents where we signed the offer in the maternity ward. Meaningful is the Army retiree starting his next chapter. Meaningful is the recently widowed moving to town to be near the kids. Meaningful is the first-time homeowner. Memorable is the BFF having a blast exploring property. Memorable is the grotto discovered viewing a rural acreage outside of Austin. Memorable is the wasp down the shirt showing property with my clients-turned-friends.

This who-is exercise is a gateway to the joy we feel when we know we have made a difference.

Recommit to the joy.

Business, and life, works best when the joy factor is solidly in place. Life and relationships and business and clients, they have their ups and downs. If you have misplaced your joy, your next potential client can read that energy a mile away. And the opposite is true. When your joy factor is solidly in place, your next potential client can read that magic a mile away. If you ever find yourself out of sorts, off your path, misplaced juju, questioning what you are doing, searching or re-searching for the meaning and the fun, take a deep breath and reconnect with why you started this in the first place.

Your joy, your energy, your eye contact, it all matters. It's your mindset, your personality capital, and will have a tremendous impact on your traction and success. The right mindset will gain you clients, the wrong mindset will cost you clients... this is sales 101. Find your joy.

Rinse and Repeat

Rinse and repeat. Rinse and repeat. Go back to the beginning of the book or simply camp yourself in the ACTION section at the back of the book, and just keep doing it and doing it and doing it. This is the not-so-sexy part of real estate. It's work. It's repetitive work. The sexy part starts when you have built a beautiful, healthy, and sustainable pipeline, and the referrals are consistently rolling in. More job, less sexy. Nail this foundational principle now, the principle that you are in a lead generation business first and a real estate business second.

Your success in this business will have a heck of a lot to do with building your stamina around this simple principle, this core repetitive activity. Stop overcomplicating this business. Get on the offense with this. You are always building your pipeline; you are always looking for and nurturing your next five to ten leads.

Rinse and repeat because there is so much material in this book that you could simply recycle all the ACTION ITEMS and do it over and over and over again ten to fifteen hours per week, and that alone can build a successful real estate pipeline.

> *We are what we repeatedly do.*
> *Excellence then, is not an act,*
> *but a habit.*
> —COMMONLY CREDITED TO ARISTOTLE, BUT REALLY THE WORDS OF WILL DURANT, *THE STORY OF PHILOSOPHY*, PUBLISHED 1926

✔ **ACTION ITEM**
Your Calendar and My True Story

Time-Block for Practice

Let's revisit your calendar and putting time in on building your what-to-say skill. For new agents, it's those five hours of practice every week; for experienced agents, just a few minutes per day. Did you already put it on your calendar, or did you blow through that chapter? One appointment with yourself per day. Your confidence and your results will have a direct correlation to the amount of time you put into practicing what to say.

Let's unpack this topic a bit. But first, let's take care of this simple action list immediately:

Block your time every day Monday through Friday and call it "practice." Put it in your calendar right now. An hour a day or a few minutes first thing in the morning is best. Treat this appointment as if it is one of the most important appointments on your calendar. It is an appointment with you. Tell yourself that you have to hit four of them; five is the goal for a perfect week, four is acceptable. Do this for a minimum of two months. More is better. Remember the San Antonio rookie story earlier in the book? Do more hours for a couple of months if you're newish and you intend to accomplish skill and confidence faster than the rest of the pack.

Set a recurring appointment with at least two of these daily practice appointments where you are practicing with another agent. This will be the most time effective if you do it over the phone. Try Skype or Facetime or Google Hangout or Zoom. This agent becomes one of your accountability partners. If this practice partner starts becoming unreliable, missing more and more appointments, or gets off topic all the time, then fire them as your practice partner and find another with a commitment that matches yours. Don't worry about firing a practice partner; you can still keep them as your friend. Just make this clear in the beginning. You may have to go through multiple practice partners until you find one as committed to mastery as you are. Your practice partner could be in another city or state. These practice appointments need to be on-task and can be as little as fifteen to twenty minutes, if you are on-task. Limit the real estate chit chat (Why say blah blah blah blah blah, when blah will do?), and simply practice what to say; role play with the other agent.

Tell someone about this plan, this task, this goal. Someone in your household works nicely, or a good friend or family member, or your broker. Tell them that you are telling them so that they'll help you stay accountable. When you tell someone else, you raise the bar on your seriousness, and you increase the likelihood of hitting the goal. When you tell no one, then you are your only accountability partner... and how is that working for you so far?

Print out a two-month calendar, and post it on the wall somewhere. For every day that you hit your appointment, highlight the day, or get little star stickers like the kids do at school. This way you have a visual of your progress, you become your own accountability partner, and anyone else living in your home or coming by your office will ask you about it.

Time-Block for Progress

True story, I did this to write the original book. 6:00–8:00 A.M., four to five days a week for four months. I had gotten off track with my writing, immersed in my business, and had put the book aside for a while. If you are a writer or have a book in you, putting it aside for a while to simmer is actually a valuable tool, but at some point you have to have keyboard time. So I started with a July plan, my focus for the month, a theme for July. For the entire month of July 2017, I had this plan: alarm 5:50 A.M.; at my desk with coffee by 6:00 A.M.; perfect week five days, ten hours, minimum four days, posted on the wall; posted a video on Facebook talking about it; kept at it until it was complete.

I did the calendar-on-the-wall exercise. I liked the task of highlighting each day I hit the 6:00 A.M. two-hour writing target. At one point, I shifted to 5:30 A.M., and occasionally 5:00 A.M., as I needed to log more keyboard time. Five o'clock is not my natural thing. I am an eight-hour sleeper, so this pushed me.

Occasionally, I got off track, but I had three accountability partners who would ask me how I was doing with my writing program. And, get this . . . because of the Facebook video I posted? I really had about 400 accountability partners. I posted that video on Facebook for a couple of reasons . . . one, I knew it would help motivate a few people to tackle a project; and two, it would raise the bar on my own accountability. It accomplished both.

I am not super hard-wired for this sort of push. I had to be very intentional about it. Sure, I have a history of getting things done, and I have all sorts of athletic training in my past. So it may look, on the surface, like this comes naturally. That would be an illusion. I am not the most disciplined person on the planet. I love a shiny object or twelve. I need some structure. In team sports, the team is the structure. But in solo situations, like the solo athlete long-distance runner, or the writer, or the person learning to play the guitar, most of us need a tool or two in place to help us put in the hours, to help us produce and accomplish. I needed to build in a tool to help me produce. So what do you need?

Some of you reading this book are crazy hard-wired for discipline and structure; you have savant-level get-things-done built into your DNA. This will be an easy section for you. And, frankly, you may have clients faster than everyone else because of your discipline and your record of getting the most important things done first every day. You're built for sales.

Most of you reading this book are a bit like me. You're capable of discipline, but given a choice, you're off doing all sorts of other things. You are shiny-object oriented, so some structure is supercritical. If you are like me, a little structure and accountability can go a long way.

Some of my friends commented on my Facebook video, the video about this 6:00 A.M. writing project, with things like "your discipline is inspiring!" The reality is, my discipline is a challenge.

Until it becomes a habit.

CHAPTER 17

Where Are They Now?

If you just start dancing, I can assure you, by the powers vested in me (more than you could ever imagine), the music will be added. As will the partners, the giant disco ball, and whatever else you like.

But I must warn you, "start" is not to be confused with "start and then stop to see if anything happens." Nope, that's "I'm scared, tired, and not sure what I really want."

I mean "start" as in "never stop, never look back, because even if I make a 'mistake,' at least I still get to dance."

Do your thing and I'll do mine.

—The Universe (tut.com)

Fast-forward Five Years

Remember the stories at the beginning of the book? The vignettes of agents just getting a start? Let's fast-forward and see where they are today.

STEPHANIE
Newly Divorced Mama Bear

Stephanie is in her eighth year, has two designations under her belt as well as some investment properties, and I think her daughters are, by now, college-educated. She hired some administrative help (contract-to-close, marketing) and is now focused mostly on investment properties and short-term rentals. Oh, and I think she's in love. The majority of her business comes from her inner circle, a tight network of lifelong friends.

WILLIAM
A Vision for His Life

William is looking for land north of town to build a home and get his boys into a top-rated school district (and baseball program). His real estate success is creating that financial opportunity. For William, everything is about doing the right thing, keeping his mama happy, and providing a solid foundation and future for his boys.

William continues to network with the old men, the founders, in east Austin. He recently spoke at the Elks Club regarding east Austin real estate trends. One of the east Austin founders, one of the old men, believes so much in what William is doing that he wants to set up a college fund for William's boys. As I re-read this, it sounds a bit fairy tale, but it's true. William is an inspiration. As I write this, William is now in his fifth year in real estate and has become a proficient flipper.

MELANIE
VP Level Marketing Pro

Melanie is in her ninth year in the business and has steadily increased her sales and her price point, year after year. Slowly and steadily. A brainiac and analyst, Melanie runs circles around market statistics and can recite current economic trends with ease. She is definitely a market expert. She built her business on very high levels of service that generate consistent referrals. In fact, her business is now almost exclusively from referrals and she is selling more real estate than ever. Melanie has developed several niches, including working with a growing international company to help its incoming hires with real estate purchases, and becoming the go-to agent for a busy investor. She has developed savant-level systems to ensure the same high level of service that got her to the high volume her business enjoys today. Melanie is also spending more time helping the agents on her team become more successful with coaching and referrals.

SAM
Sixty-Something Non-Profit Executive

I wanted to make sure I included at least one story of a new agent who, after a few years in the business, chose not to renew his license. This is not uncommon, even for a successful newer agent. Choosing not to renew, to leave the business, is not a failure. Sam was succeeding in real estate; he was building a decent pipeline. He had skills, was a good advocate, a solid negotiator, and was plugged in. Problem was, he wasn't loving the business. He didn't like it as much as he thought he would. I had coffee with Sam recently to better understand his story.

I asked him what happened, why the shift back into the job market. He immediately told me about a couple of buyer clients who ran him ragged, were tough as nails, sucked the oxygen out of rooms. The buyers were frustrated, and joy was seriously elusive, with the process of finding the right home, negotiating, and navigating the process. Every agent knows this scenario. Sam quickly said that it wasn't that he couldn't handle a tough client He understood that was part of the package. Rather, the joy-deprived experience with these particular back-to-back buyers helped Sam realize that his motivation for succeeding in real estate was not big enough to push through some of the more challenging aspects of the business. He truly wanted to make a difference in people's lives, and while real estate provided the opportunity to do so, it did not match Sam's version of it.

A few other things Sam said are worthy of note. He said he should have done more due diligence before he started in real estate: "I didn't know teams existed. If I had known teams existed, I would have seriously considered that path. I do not lean entrepreneurial; I work better in a team environment."

Another thing he noted was that his three years in real estate had too much emphasis on cold calling. "It wasn't the right model for me," he said. The ironic thing here is that teams tend to follow the high-volume phone model. Sam felt a more relational model would have been a better fit for him—higher quality conversations, more personal connections. While Sam was succeeding in having a high volume of conversations every day, he said he failed with follow-up. He said he was good at initiating the conversation, and pretty much sucked with follow-up (his words). My immediate thought on this dynamic was that if the conversations had been with people he actually knew, had some relationship with, some rapport, a referral from a friend, or someone he had clicked with at an open house, Sam's follow-up would have come easily and naturally. Follow-up with cold calls—it's a numbers game. Follow-up with referrals, friends of friends, former colleagues, is common courtesy. In the midst of his third year, the numbers game was wearing thin for Sam.

Sam is sincerely grateful for his three years in real estate—the training, the opportunity, and how he developed as a professional. And he is happily back in the nonprofit world.

The Roadmap

Throughout the book, I have attempted to share a variety of new and launching and relaunching agent stories so you can find the one or two that resonate with you, your experience, your personality, your goals, your place in the world. In my two decades in this business, I have found that the larger body of real estate training material and advice and speakers and podcasts was so heavily laden with top 1 percent stories, with savant-level success stories, with mega this, and the super successful that, that agents who struggled their first year or two (which is almost everyone) or agents who had moderate financial goals were often questioning if they were good enough or thinking that they had to become someone or something they were not to be successful in this business. It's like looking at a fashion magazine and only seeing supermodels. Where are the models with grey hair or the models who fit into a size twelve? Can you at least show us photos of the supermodels when they were in high school before they were super?

Don't get me wrong. Those top 1 percent superstar stories represent some of the best practices in this business. They provide an inspiring vision of what is possible and are worthy of your time. When studying an industry, look at the best practices, not the average practices. The thing is that the best practices apply to everyone, whether you sell six or thirty-six homes. But where are you right now in your business, and what advice, motivation, tools, action do you need to move forward?

> Acting like something you're not is not only emotionally, spiritually, and frequently financially exhausting, it's unsustainable.
> —DANIELLE LAPORTE, *THE FIRE STARTER SESSIONS*

I believe you have to see yourself in the mix, in the shoes, in the story. While the top 1% may motivate and inspire you, where is the roadmap for years one, two, and three, the roadmap to starting over? There are times when you have to stretch yourself beyond your current framework. Is there a mismatch between your current state of being and your goals? There are more times when you have to get in touch with your authentic self, capitalizing on what you do best, what you like, what you're good at, your style, your DNA. Be you. The old adage of "be true to yourself" applies here. Merge that mantra with "What best version of myself do I need to manifest to meet my goals?" and you create a pretty powerful balancing act and success formula.

Let's sum this up. Here are some of the key points, the roadmap, for starting or restarting (pretty sure these will all land as memes on Instagram):

- Find clients fast.
- Take action that matters.
- What you did sixty to ninety days back matters most; what you do today matters next.
- Start your momentum now.
- Practice doing vs. studying.
- Have conversations every day.
- Track it.
- Call your mother.
- Follow your joy . . . do more of what you like to do, do more of what comes naturally, double down on what is already working.
- Check your power score . . . how are you showing up?
- Don't be a lousy boss.
- Attend to the job first.

- Review your TOP 100, your most likely source of clients and referrals.
- Get busy with the right things.
- Know what to say... practice.
- Stay in touch with your birddogs.
- Remove shiny objects.
- Drop your perfection, and embrace improvement.
- Build in accountability.
- Your greatest sales tool has always been simply showing up as an authentic, decent human.
- Be you.

If you stick to these basics with a sense of urgency, I would place a bet on your success. Let's reflect back on this foundational premise... that you are in the process of creating something amazing in your life, that your success will change the world. My sacred mission is to help you do that.

> ✔ ACTION ITEM
> Write It Down

This ACTION ITEM is introspective and practical. Research shows that writing down your goals, as opposed to just in your head, significantly increases the likelihood of you actually hitting that goal. Empirical evidence and all, Dr. Gail Matthews, a psychology professor at the Dominican University, found that the likelihood of hitting your goals increases a whopping 42 percent if you write them down. So let's do that.

If you have not yet done so, put some words down in your journal or in your workbook addressing the following:

- What success looks like to me:
- What success will do for me and my family:
- My financial goals are:
- My personal goals are:
- My five-year vacation plan is:
- Here's how I will change the world:
- My sacred mission is:

CHAPTER 18

The $100,000 Recipe

I was 32 when I started cooking; up until then, I just ate.

—Julia Child

There is this hip coffee shop in central Austin that has killer cookies. Similar in size to your outstretched hand (unless you're LeBron James, then that would be a cookie pie), fingers wide, these oversized calorie mongers are slightly crisp on the outside, soft on the inside. You know the ones. We eye them every time, hard to miss their alluring massive presence in the glass display just below your credit card. I bet I could find that recipe online.

Speaking of recipes, I have one for you. Whether you have foodie skills or not, everyone can follow a recipe because you can read. Much like a monster cookie recipe, you can double or triple this formula to match your appetite. You can throw in walnuts or chocolate chips to match your style. I prefer peanut butter. Let's look at the formula for making $100,000 this year in your real estate business.

I do want to mention that there is more than one $100,000 recipe out there. There is the one where you are flipping houses, and, if done right, you can get to $100k much faster, but you can also lose $100k in no time if not done well. The risks can be high with flipping, until you have a formula. And a stable market. The most experienced flipper rehabbers have a formula and an awesome spreadsheet. Yet many of them started out with a wing and a prayer, quite often, by stumbling upon a crazy deal because the old family friend siblings reached out to sell mom's old house quickly. Foundational tip numero uno with flipping profitability: You make your money by what you pay for the house. But someone else wrote that flipper book. That's another meeting.

There is another $100,000 recipe that involves massive online leads, the funds to generate them, and the systems to go after these low conversion, low loyalty leads with three to four hours on the phone every day. That's another meeting.

There is the $100,000 recipe that involves luxury real estate, fewer transactions, and expensive shoes. That's another meeting.

In this chapter, we are going to cover the $100,000 recipe with traditional real estate serving buyers and sellers. So channel your inner Julia Child, and let's review the recipe. We'll cover the ingredients first and then the directions. We also dig into this in the *Success Faster Workbook* with hands-on exercises for breaking down your numbers.

Ingredients

1 C. vision	1 C. drive
1 C. grit	1 C. butter
1 C. talk	1 C. sugar

INGREDIENT 1

Vision

Always start your recipes, your goal, your plan, your year, your month, your diet, your meal, with a vision. I am an aspiring foodie. I like to cook. While I am nowhere near Top Chef or Junior Chef or The Great American

Baking Show material, I love those shows. I learn by watching and quickly recognize how much I do not know. I have a killer (and simple) artisan bread recipe, I grow a lot of vegetables, and I am perfecting the reverse sear ribeye on the smoker. And I almost always start with Pinterest.

Pinterest, the image-sharing app. I guess Pinterest falls into the social media category, but I am not especially social with it, except for following my niece who is an exceptional cook, and following barbeque boss, Hey, Grill Hey.

Here's why Pinterest works for me with recipes. Besides staying organized, I have different categories like foodie, Big Green Egg, garden reference, real estate basics, Austin architects. It's the photos, it's the vision that does the heavy lifting on Pinterest.

So what is your vision? Your vision for that $100,000? How do you see it materializing and evolving; but even more so, what does it look like when you get there?

Vision 101 can be as simple as a sticky note on the bathroom mirror or on the edge of your computer monitor that says $100,000. Or simply writing it down.

Vision 201 takes it a step further by telling someone else your goal; this adds accountability. Or doing a vision board. Your subconscious, and the universe, will respond to what you feed it, whether it is something you're observing; or something you're remembering, or imagining, or doing; or something someone else is telling you; or simply some images you are feeding it every day. All of it. Your brain believes what you feed it (talk to yourself more, listen to yourself less), so feed it the vision of what it is going to look like when you are on pace for $100k and when you hit it. What car will you drive? What vacation will you create? What debt will you pay? What backsplash will you choose? What suit will you wear? What clients will benefit from your success?

So write it down. Write down the vision. Write it down as if you mean it. Even if you don't fully believe it, yet, write it down. Write down the goal, the prize, the results, the clients. Your brain believes what you feed it. Feed it the vision.

INGREDIENT 2

Grit

Vision 301 takes it one critical step further. Consider grit as part of advanced vision manifestation, wrapping the vision with some grit and the wherewithal to persist.

I have mentioned Angela Duckworth a couple of times. Duckworth delivered one of the best Ted Talks ever, "Grit: the power of passion and perseverance," in 2013. With her grit talk, she revealed one of the basic findings of her research, the finding that grit beats talent. And that talent does not make you gritty. It is why sometimes it is the scrappiest agent, who has had all sorts of hardship or uphill battles or personal challenges to overcome in life, who wins the race. Grit matters. "Our data show very clearly that there are many talented individuals who simply do not follow through on their commitments. In fact, in our data, grit is usually unrelated or even inversely related to measures of talent."

Duckworth researched it, but Calvin Coolidge observed the grit factor over one hundred years ago:

> "Nothing in this world can take the place of persistence. Talent will not; nothing is more common than unsuccessful men with talent. Genius will not; unrewarded genius is almost a proverb. Education will not; the world is full of educated derelicts. Persistence and determination alone are omnipotent."

Expertise and IQ and care and hard work and perhaps your competitive nature may get you there; but grit will push you through, grit will knock down barriers, grit is a difference-maker.

I know a very successful broker who was homeless as a kid. I know a millionaire broker-owner executive who grew up dirt poor. I know a top producer who was on food stamps as a kid and had her electricity shut off in her early twenties. I know an industry leader who failed out of college, twice.

But it doesn't take hardship to generate grit. Grit can be nature or nurture. I think my grit is more of either my competitive nature, or a prove-myself to anyone who may have underestimated me, or a desire to make my parents proud. Michael Jordan was cut from his high school basketball team; I think his grit was all sorts of competition wrapped into his incredibly skilled physical being.

What is the source of your grit, persistence, and determination? A critical part of the recipe is, one way or another, tapping into and owning your grit.

When you hit the goal, what will it feel like? What energy will you possess? Who will you impress? Who will you become? What unapologetic and non-negotiable and infectious space will you own? What mountain will bow down?

So ingredient two is grit. Vision first and then grit.

INGREDIENT 3
Talk

Now that you have your visual check and your gut check, let's map out the specifics.

Math, my friends. It's all math for the $100,000 recipe. And we'll keep this as simple as possible by focusing on the lowest common denominator in your real estate success equation, conversations. Let's break it down.

We will run through a detailed example of this here in a bit, but here are the basics.

If you want to make $100,000, and you know that you need a certain number of closings to accomplish that and a certain number of appointments to get to those closings, and then a certain even higher number of leads to get to those appointments, and then a certain number of conversations in order to get to those leads, then we can do this math progression, starting with conversations:

→ that drive leads
→ that drive appointments
→ that drive clients
→ that drive contracts
→ that drive closings
→ that drive commission checks
→ that drive $100,000

You could arguably add one more initial layer of people; people drive conversations. But we are going to stick with conversations as the foundation, as that is basically the goal—meaning, I would rather you add more conversations than add more people. Just because you have more people in your database or your neighborhood or your mailing list or your volunteer organizations or you're attending more community events doesn't mean you're having more conversations. So for the $100,000 recipe, we are going to focus on simply driving conversations and, in most cases, having more and better and more purposeful conversations.

Put that sticky note on your monitor: conversations!

INGREDIENT 4
Drive

Drive belongs right here after Ingredient 3: Talk, as we need to tap into your drive to drive more conversations. If I told you on your first day on the job as an agent on my team that in order to stay on the team or earn your spot on the team, you had to talk to enough people every day to create three solid leads, and that is what successful agents do. Would you do it? Sometimes all it takes is someone giving a directive. If a directive is what you need to get into the conversation habit and flow, consider this paragraph the directive.

Maybe your drive is related to grit and having something to prove.

Maybe your drive is financial freedom and escaping the stress of just scraping by, or the pit of too much credit card debt. Maybe your drive is wondering how you are going to pay your rent in three or four months.

Maybe your drive is your family, maybe your new family, and creating an amazing life.

Identify and stay tuned in to your drive.

INGREDIENT 5
Butter

Butter, in a recipe, is that most excellent flavor factor and what tends to hold all the other ingredients together. If the other ingredients are your vision, your grit, your conversations, and your drive, what is holding those together? Or maybe that is the problem; you have these ingredients and have not been able to get them working together in one cohesive effort.

What is stopping you? What holds you back? What is the story you have been telling yourself? Mindset, life events, dual career, your story is real... it's just super important for us to acknowledge what is going on right now so we can move into what is next. When you can identify and own where you are right now with your mindset and the stories you tell yourself and have possibly been telling yourself for years, then you can accept where you are so we can invite you to where you go next. It's like forgiving your ex so you can be fully present with the one you're with (thank you, Lisa Nichols).

So the butter represents the story you tell yourself. And if the $100,000 income (or maybe yours is the 3x or 5x version of that goal) is that thing that has been elusive and unattainable, then you may need a new story. Your story may be holding you back. Same stories, same lessons, same resentment, same results. The old adage, "If you keep doing what you've always done, then you'll always get what you've always got" (Henry Ford, Albert Einstein, my high school track coach), applies to how you think. It's a new goal, so it may need a new story.

And it's not that you have to get rid of your old story (well, maybe the one that suggests you're not worthy; I would dump that one). Your old story may simply be the story of your life; or it could be the learned stories you tell yourself, something that happened to you, versus the meaning you assign it and have packed all nicely into that thing we so lovingly, ahem, call baggage.

What do you tell yourself when your confidence is down? What is the committee in your head telling you? That voice that is uncertain, that annoying voice that questions your qualifications and goals, the voice that holds you back, the voice that is the little kid in you showing up at the wrong party; this is human nature. And who is in charge of that voice, that committee? Not the little kid. Tell that negative committee that meets inside your head, that lizard brain, that little kid, to sit down and shut up. You can thank them for showing up, as they may have served you well in the past, but now your stronger voice is in charge, so be in charge. This may be old AA stuff that can be really useful for everyday life and driving your business.

So what is your story, and is it serving you and your goal? If yes, then wrap your arms around it and keep going. If not, then time for a new story.

INGREDIENT 6

Sugar

Have fun! It's the sugar, baby! Remember the "renew your joy" concept earlier in the book? Let's tap into that.

Having a goal and making progress on it every day and every week is fun! What if you started each day with the question, "What is one thing I can do first thing this morning that will move me closer to my $100,000 goal? What is one thing I can do this morning that will move me closer to that dream vacation?"

Helping buyers find the right house is fun! What if you reminded yourself every day that you get to help someone change their life today?

Making loads of money is awesome because it builds your life and creates amazing options and experiences! What if you look at your vision board every day?

Don't forget the sugar!

Directions

A recipe always starts with ingredients and then the directions. So here are the directions, and, remember, it's really about the math. And how you apply yourself.

First, recognize that with the recipe there is one key ingredient right in the middle. That ingredient is talk or conversations. It's the meat in the recipe. Could you skip all the other ingredients and simply jump to talk and conversations? Yes, for some, and no for most of us. For each of us, there will be one or two "support" ingredients that really do some heavy lifting, so it is important to identify yours. My personal do-not-skip ingredients are the vision and the drive; those two ingredients do a lot of heavy lifting for me. Yours may be different. But to nail the $100,000 recipe, the one thing we all have in common is talk, talk and conversations.

Let's break it down.

The Goal: $100,000 Gross Commission Income

First, what is your average price point? What is your current average price point, or your market average price point, or your market niche average price point? You can use one of those. If you want to be conservative, and conservative is helpful with this exercise, just take the number down a notch. Let's say my average sold price point is $465,000, but I had two million-plus clients this past six months, so I am going to use $420k or $400k for this exercise, just to be conservative. We are going to use $300,000 as an average price point in this example. (The online book resources at thenelsonproject.org have this formula in a downloadable worksheet.)

Average Price: $300,000

Average Commission: $7,500
(Using 2.5% to allow for some referral fees, broker splits, or for markets that draw a less than 3% commission; adjust yours up or down as needed.)

The Closings: $100,000/$7,500 = 13.33
... round up to 14 because you cannot sell a third of a house. So just barely over one closing per month and you hit that goal. That seems doable, right?

And if your goal is $200,000, with the above parameters, then it's just slightly over two closings per month and you hit the goal.

The Clients

Let's just agree that not everyone who starts out with you as a client ends up closing on a property. People change their minds; run into financing issues; maybe they are unrealistic; maybe they give up in a competitive market; maybe you took them on as a client, and it wasn't the right match in the first place; maybe they did not sign a buyer agreement with you, and you showed them 20 homes, then they disappeared on you. Just for some easy math, we are going to use an 80% ratio, that 80% of your clients end up with you getting paid. (Now hopefully your ratio will be higher than that, but I said I was going to go conservative on these numbers). So if we rounded up to 14 closings, using the 80% factor, you would need to have signed 17 or 18 clients; so we'll use 18.

The Appointments

How many appointments do you need to generate 18 clients? Let's keep it real simple and use 80% again (yours may be higher, we're going conservative). So you would need 22.5 appointments; so we'll use 23. Oh heck, any time you can round up to something that fits easily into a twelve-month calendar, please do. So we are going to use 24. Always round up, never round down on your goals, or your life.

The Leads

How many leads do you need to generate 24 appointments, to generate two appointments per month? Now this is where it gets a little tricky, and you will learn your ratio as you go, or perhaps you already know it, then amazing! I am going to suggest, for this recipe, that we use a 50% ratio of leads to appointments, partly because lots of folks are in no hurry at all. So 24 appointments will take 48 leads; two appointments per month will take four solid leads per month. A solid lead per week! OMG, is that all I have to do?! One solid lead per week?!

> **NINJA TRICK**
> Caveat here... don't confuse a solid lead with a not-so-solid lead. So the NINJA angle on this is to find a lead per day. If you have five leads per week, you'll be in good shape to move forward with the most solid lead, and then nurture the others.

The Conversations

How many conversations do you need to generate one solid lead per week? What if you knew that every working day it was your goal to have one solid bona fide serious lead generation conversation? I am suggesting to you, and this recipe supports it, that all it takes is one solid bona fide and serious lead generation conversation per day to make $100,000 in the next twelve months. If everyone knew this formula, there would be more agents out there. And knowing this formula may change the way you approach each workday. Tell your spouse, your BFF, your mother, your sister, your lender, friends who are in sales, tell them your business involves you having one decent real estate conversation per day, and ask them to help make that happen. Tell your spouse that one serious lead generation conversation per day equals $100,000 and more vacations, which tends to be effective with a significant other.

Remember the hip coffee shop with the killer cookies? Set an appointment to meet a friend there every day this week to support a local business and generate some quality conversations. Oh, and when you're there with your friend and an amazing cookie, share your goal with them and ask for their help. But only after you have tapped into one of their goals and how you can help them. And don't forget to make friends with the owner and manager of the shop; they may need a good agent who appreciates an amazing cookie and regularly brings people into their store.

Here is one of the WORK pieces I warned you about. I did not label this entire chapter a "work" chapter because I really do not think the $100,000 recipe hurts your brain at all. In fact, I think the recipe lights up your brain to the possibilities, the simplicity, and the overall appeal and doability of six figures. This ACTION ITEM only hurts it a little, because it's work, and I want you to dive in.

> ✓ **ACTION ITEM**
> **Do Your Math**

Besides meeting a friend every day this week at the coffee shop with a giant cookie and then going for a walk to burn off the monster calories (which I still recommend doing, all of that), do your math. Fill in the blanks:

- The goal:
- Average price:
- Average commission:
- The closings:
- The clients:
- The appointments:
- The leads:
- The conversations:

CHAPTER 19

Getting Your License

Nothing is more expensive than a missed opportunity.

—H. Jackson Brown, Jr.

If you are in years zero through two, this chapter is for you and is super practical.

First, a little English lesson.

Real-tor

There are two syllables in the word REALTOR®, not three. Whether you are in Michigan, NYC, or the deep south, drawing it out to three syllables, ree-luh-tor, is inaccurate. Perhaps I covered this earlier in the book, but always worth a second mention.

Speaking of vocabulary, let's cover some industry lingo. REALTOR®, salesperson, agent, broker, broker associate, associate broker, managing broker, manager, team leader, professional titles vary from state to state and some of the lingo can vary from firm to franchise. Remember that the term REALTOR® is trademarked and reserved only for those persons who are members of the National Association of REALTORS® (NAR). You can get your real estate license and not join NAR, but then, in most cases, you would not be eligible to join your local board and participate in the multiple listing service (MLS). If you are looking at traditional residential real estate, NAR membership is part of the package.

It Takes HOW Much Time?

The fastest I have seen someone get their real estate license is about two months. In this fast scenario, it is pretty much forty hours a week of classes and studying and hustle to move through the process. Most folks take longer, and this will vary considerably from state to state. Recently, I ran into an agent friend who moved from Texas back to California. She said she filed her CA license application six weeks ago and is still waiting. In some states, it is way too easy to get a real estate license (many industry pros think we should raise the bar of entry). Other states can involve a lot of time, steps, classes, background checks, fingerprints, forms, fees, bureaucratic runaround . . . all in the name of protecting the public from bad or unprepared or unethical real estate people, which is always a good idea.

The overall licensure timeline, which can vary from state to state, will typically include:

License Classes

This may take a month, or it could take a year, depending on your focus. If you are still assessing whether you want to move forward with licensure and real estate in general (you have read this far in the book, which is an indication that you are moving forward), consider taking one or two of the required classes, dipping your toe in the pool, to see if you like it. Most agents take the majority of their classes online and then, often, an in-person exam preparation class right before they are ready to take the state and national exam. Depending on whether they accept any of your college credits, you may have anywhere from four or five to maybe eight to ten classes to take. These classes will include topics such as principles 101, contracts, legal, finance, ethics, and the national exam prep. Keep in mind that most real estate license classes only help you pass a test (that is what they are supposed to do), and most of them do not teach you how to survive and thrive in the business. Pass a test prep, yes. Understand nuance, market analysis, and business 201 of how to be a real estate rock star, no.

License Test

Any real estate school where you are taking your license classes (whether online or in-person), will help you understand your state license procedures and how to move through that as expeditiously as possible.

License Application

In most states, you can begin this process before you have taken all of your classes. This is typically a good idea, as most state licensing boards will need time to do both a background check, maybe fingerprints, and, in most cases, assess college transcripts to see if your college credits can take the place of any of the licensure credit requirements. This will vary considerably from state to state.

License Acceptance

I have no idea how efficient your state is, but until they push the button that says you are now licensed, you cannot function as a real estate pro. This may or may not happen somewhat simultaneously with this next item.

Broker Choice

You may have known from day one what broker was going to hold your license. You may still be assessing your options. But, typically, the state will hold your license in some sort of inactive status until you tell them what broker to send your license to. This involves two pieces: 1.) the broker/brokerage, and 2.) the state licensing entity. Your broker will guide you in this process, they may have a specific form or required signature to make things happen at the state level.

Local Board Application

This is the typical flow of things, that once you are properly set up with both the state and your broker, then you are joining the local board, including your multiple listing service (MLS) subscription. In most cases, this happens somewhat simultaneously (and hopefully online).

Talk with your local resources, the local board, your real estate school, brokers, and the state to get clear on the smoothest process in your area. And, of course, most of these steps involve money.

It Costs HOW Much?

Every agent has experienced the fee-at-every-step experience of getting licensed. In most cases, you will pay for all of these, not your broker. In this section, I am going to outline some generalized costs so you can be realistic and prepared before you spend a dime. I have seen a handful of agents over the years have an actual "investor" help them get started in the business. In most of these cases, the "investor" was grandma or mom and dad helping a young professional get started. New businesses get started with seed money all the time, so why would your new career be any different? If someone is going to help you financially, be prepared to present them with a bit of a business plan of how much you need, what it goes toward, your plan to gain your first twenty clients, and your plan to pay the investor back. Most folks will fund this effort on their own.

First, a little perspective on the cost of getting started in real estate. There is pre-license, license, memberships and dues, and then the ongoing expense of actually running and marketing your business. Compared to almost any other business out there on the planet, it is relatively inexpensive to get started in real estate. Besides your car, your smartphone, your laptop, your license, your time, and an appropriate wardrobe (except in maybe Key West), there are pretty much no asset requirements to getting started in this business. If you were to start even a taco stand, a lawn service, or a children's clothing line, you would invest some serious funds into equipment, inventory, and space. So if you have any sort of gag response to the expenses outlined below, you may need to reassess or save up.

Let's take a closer look at fees, and then we'll add it up at the end. These are generalizations designed to give you a budget framework. I would always pad it a little to leave room for unsuspecting or supplemental fees that either no one told you about or you missed on the website or in the fine print.

Licensure Classes $400-$1,500

Again, things vary greatly from state to state. You may be required to take three classes, or ten, or somewhere in-between. With a simple perusing of online real estate schools and clicking on various states, I can see 180 classroom hours required in Texas, 135 in California, 90 in Minnesota and Oklahoma, 75 in Illinois, 60 in Iowa and Virginia. Some of those hours may include some of your college credits. Each of those states then have varying numbers for continuing education hours required in your first and second years, required for your first license renewal. Those numbers can change at any time, so do your homework and do not rely on this paragraph as the license hour bible.

In most locations, you will have options of in-person classes and online classes. You get to choose the option that works best for you. Online classes tend to be cheaper. Ask other agents in your area what they recommend for taking the license classes. Some of these real estate schools will offer some sort of discount if you also sign up (and pay for) the package deal that includes your first-year continuing education classes.

License Application $200-$400

Let's use Texas as an example. In July 2020, I found these fees on the Texas Real Estate Commission license fee page:

Sales Agent Application	$205
Fingerprint Fee	$38
Real Estate Recovery Fee	$10
Paper Processing Fee	$20

This is just one example. Your state may be cheaper, could be more. I do find, true to form with most government websites, that it can be easier to understand all the fees by referencing either the real estate school material or the brokers' informational recruiting packet versus the state agency website. The schools simply tend to spell it out in an easily understood format versus putting together a Rubix cube flowchart of if/then fee structures that take a half dozen clicks to find.

Board and MLS $1,000–$1,600

Austin Board of REALTORS®, Metropolitan Indianapolis Board of REALTORS®, Des Moines Area Association of REALTORS®, Marathon and Lower Keys Association Of REALTORS®, these are all examples of the local board you will join in order to practice in your area and join the multiple listing service (MLS). Some agents will join more than one board, especially if you live on a state border. Most of my New York City colleagues also have some sort of membership in New Jersey.

Again, do not rely on these numbers as the fee bible. I am providing these after considerable clicking around and as examples of what to expect. Fees are subject to change, and I may have missed a fee or two. Some Board web sites are certainly much easier to navigate and more informative than others.

Here is an example from the Austin Board of REALTORS®:

Primary Membership Application Fee	$200	(one-time fee)
Orientation Fee	$50	(one-time fee)
Access Fee	$175	
ABoR Dues	$125	(annual)
NAR Dues	$150	(annual)
Image Campaign	$35	
TAR Dues	$117	(annual)
TAR Legal	$5	
TAR Mobilization Fund	$30	
Total	$857	
MLS	$309	(semi-annual)
eKey	$142	(semi-annual)

And, after much clicking, an example from the Omaha Area Board of REALTORS®:

Application Fee	$150	
Local	$165	
State	$230	
National	$150	
PR Assessment	$35	
Total	$730	
MLS Initial Fee	$300	
MLS	$30	(per month)
eKey	$15	(per month)

Broker $0-$500

Does the broker have any one-time new agent set-up fees? Any new agent training fees? Or a fee for the training manual? Are the brokerage classes free? What are their monthly expenses? Do you pay for a desk? Is there a technology fee? Is there a per-transaction fee? Do you pay an E&O (errors and omissions) fee with every closing (most do)? And, of course, what is the commission split? Or is it a fixed amount per month? Or a per-transaction fee? Or some combination thereof. And is there an annual cap on the commission you pay your broker, a maximum you would pay in a year? For as many brokerages as there are out there, there are varying commission and fee structures.

And what do you get for your money? I believe you should get what you pay for. Keep in mind that your broker has to run a profitable business and that the broker takes on liability on your behalf. Any time someone takes on liability on your behalf, it's expensive.

Some concrete things that have been important to me over the years in terms of what I was paying for with my broker are that I wanted good people, quality education, an open environment with freely shared information, an effective and trendy website, current technology, and a financial model that provided opportunity. Your needs may be different. Your needs may change over time. Some agents simply want the absolute barebones, lowest cost option. No judgment here; figure out what you need, assess your options, and then be open to the possibility that your needs may change tomorrow or over time.

Totals $1,500-$4,000

Is it more than you thought or about right? You are starting a new business, so plan ahead. What exactly are the costs in your area? Then pad it some; heck, double it because I promise you there will be costs that you did not anticipate.

Commission Structure, Do the Math

As for how we get paid, there are different models and variations out there. There are fixed fee, per transaction, split, split on a scale, capping, salary (as in you are actually an employee versus an independent contractor), teams, and whatever you can negotiate with your broker options. There are brokerages with heavy expenses, staff, services, brick and mortar, brokerages that are low cost/low service, some in between, and there are lower expense cloud-based firms.

Whatever commission structure options you are staring down, do the math. Do YOUR math. On the surface, the commission structure being offered may seem attractive when comparing brokers around town, but how does it play out with different sales scenarios? You will benefit from running sample projections of split, cap, and fixed costs on a spreadsheet of how the different options play out. What is your take if you sold $1 million in sales, $3 million, $5 million, $8, $10, $12, $20 million? For example, a 90/10 split in perpetuity may be attractive for the $1–$3 million sales volume range, but a 70/30 split that "caps" at $2 million (you get 100% after $2 million for the rest of that year) will pay out way more to the agent at a higher sales volume. Or if the broker commission split never caps, that can be very expensive to the higher producing agents.

Let's look at "cap" a little closer. The cap means that once you sell a certain amount of real estate in one year, then you get to keep 100% of the commission the rest of the year usually with some per-transaction fees. Cap can be expressed in either sales volume such as a "two million cap"; you cap after you close $2 million in sales (four $500,000 homes). Or can be expressed in what you pay to the broker such as a "$16,000 cap"; meaning, as soon as you pay the broker $16,000 that year, then you're done paying the broker for the remainder of that year. In one brokerage the cap will vary from city to city, depending on how expensive it is to run an office in that city (for example, it is more expensive for a national franchise to run an office in San Francisco than it is for the same franchise to run an office in Des Moines). I have seen caps as high as $40–$60k. Some brokerages, such as mine, have the same cap, no matter where you live. And if you hold a license in two areas—for example, one in DC and another in Alexandria, Virginia, or you do business in both Chicago in the summer and Orlando in the winter, do you have one cap or two?

Remember, you get what you pay for (or at least you should). Your low-cost options may not have the tools and training and technology that you need to look good and gain momentum. If commission structure is your main brokerage choice determinant, then you may be starting your career with financial blinders. Personally, I would assess every other broker attribute first, and commission last.

Remember this basic financial premise . . . a brokerage is running a business, takes on liability on your behalf, and has to be profitable. The lowest split cheapest brokerage option out there in your town may not offer anything in return and may not have a sustainable business model. You get what you pay for.

60-90 Day Pay Cycle

The best-case scenario in traditional real estate sales is that you may have a paycheck sixty days after starting. That would happen if you wrote and executed a contract within two to three weeks of starting with your brokerage and if that contract saw its way all the way to the closing table and key exchange. Just because that client is under contract to purchase or sell doesn't mean the buyer's financing approval holds, or that the home meets the lender's appraisal requirements, or that the buyers' other home in Ft. Lauderdale closes on time. What if the Ft. Lauderdale buyer loses his job or buys a new car at the last minute?

Every seasoned agent on the planet has learned that you cannot bank on any single closing. You have to line them up for financial stability. If you are financing your life moving from commission check to commission check, let's just agree that it's stressful. If one deal falls through, and you were relying on that to pay your rent or mortgage or credit card or to take the family on vacation, if this becomes any sort of pattern, it can chase you right out of the business or back to grandma for an extension on her investment in your future.

Six-Month Reserve

I have seen brand new agents start with very little and have seen brand new agents start with a $10,000 first-year marketing budget. I have seen brand new agents have to scratch and claw and continue working night shifts at the bar downtown to get their bills paid (some make it, some don't; truth: some of the top agents in the country started this way) and other brand new agents with little to no financial concerns.

You can easily find variations on the right number for your reserve or cushion in getting started. Four to six months will be the most common advice.

Here are the basics... add up your monthly basic living expenses, and make sure you have a solid cushion that could cover your expenses for four to six months. And then work your tail off to not touch that reserve.

Vital Resources

A quick online search for the licensure process in your state will be the best place to start. I would look for both the state licensing entity (Texas Real Estate Commission, California Bureau of Real Estate, Iowa Professional Licensing Bureau) and well-known real estate schools. The school websites tend to be a little easier to navigate and understand versus the official state websites, but you should definitely set your eyes on both.

A quick note on schools and going with a private real estate school vs. actually getting college credit in the real estate program at the local community college. The private school will usually be cheaper and a great deal faster. These private schools can typically get you through all of the required classes for your state in under six months. Community college programs, while perhaps more in-depth and possibly a greater learning environment, can easily take a year or two depending on how often they offer each class and if they have sequential requirements.

Here are some simple resources that can help you get started:

realtor.com is the website for the National Association of REALTORS® (NAR). Someone who has a real estate license without joining NAR is an agent, while someone who does join is a licensed (and trademarked) REALTOR®. This site has a blog loaded with articles to guide you.

Google "How to get a real estate license in my state." I know, this is so basic I almost did not type it out. Fill in the blanks for the following:

- My state licensing entity:
- My local board and MLS source:
- My local real estate schools (brick and mortar):
- My top online real estate schools:

The next chapter will cover broker choice. Unless you have your broker license, a broker will hold your license or sponsor you. This is done through your state licensing board. That broker typically serves as your foundation for training, mentoring, compliance, technology, and building your business. Broker choice is a big decision, especially for new agents.

CHAPTER 20

Broker Choice

Just really, really believe in what you're trying to do. Don't let people alter that. Let people advise you and lead you down paths to make smart business decisions. But trust your instinct and trust that overwhelming drive that made you put all your dreams and everything on the line.

—Luke Bryan

This is a huge topic, and you will benefit from some introspection, needs analysis, and homework. My coach calls it finding your belonging place. Your professional belonging place can change from time to time, as your vision for what you need and want can shift over time. It can be seriously affirming to go through a period of reassessing your needs and your brokerage choice, and realizing you're in a good place that supports you, your financial goals, your business principles, and your vision of what you are building and where you are going.

I have changed brokerages two times in my twenty-plus year career. So three brokerages total in over twenty years. I spent my first two years with a small independent local brokerage, then sixteen years with a large national franchise, then I shifted to an emerging national brokerage in 2017. I'll cover all of those moves in more detail here in a bit.

I swear I reevaluated my broker choice every year or two in the business, sometimes just out of curiosity. Perhaps a bit like renewing your vows, sometimes a light exercise, sometimes it was more in-depth, but it was always reaffirming to come out of that inner-dialogue with a recommitment to my professional place in the world.

The National Association of REALTORS® 2019 Member Profile provides some valuable insight into broker affiliation. That NAR profile shows us that 54 percent of Realtors were affiliated with an independent company (so 46 percent were with a national brokerage); nearly nine in ten members were independent contractors at their firms (so approximately 10 percent were employees); and the median tenure for Realtors with their current firm was four years. In this 2019 profile, the typical Realtor had eight years of experience, so if the median tenure was four years, then we could interpret this as approximately half the agents had changed brokerages at least once. The profile also stated that nine percent of Realtors worked for a firm that was bought or merged in the past two years. This last finding, the bought or merged factor, is a reflection of how things shift in the industry, so your broker choice today could change because your broker made a move versus you initiating the move.

On this broker choice thing, I have a little disclosure... I have my biases (most agents do). I have purposefully laid out the majority of *Success Faster* with little mention of specific brokerages (a little here and there for clarification). This section is different, and I will tap into some specifics on a couple of brokerages I know well. The bottom line is I want you to do YOUR research and find YOUR place.

Keep this business fundamental in mind: Brokers are running businesses, and besides profit and investors and owners and stock valuation and quality customer service and reputation, there are two main factors that are foundational to real estate brokerage success (not including the mom and pop shop, which is a different model). One success factor is listing market share (homes for sale by that brokerage); the other is agent count. Besides serving and attracting the consumer (buyers and sellers), listings and agent count drive the broker side of the business. And agent count drives listings count. So agent count is the biggie. And then per agent production. Because of this, there is a lot of "recruiting" in the industry.

I have a little issue with recruiting. When recruiting is a big numbers game (think of a corporation that has to meet its sales quota), agents and brokerages do not always make the right decision. Whether new in the business or considering moving brokerages, remember you need to find your belonging place. Are you being recruited, or is the brokerage conversation consultative in nature? It should be consultative and information-based. You need to find the right place for you to build your business and lay the financial foundation for you and your family.

Here is part of my bias disclosure... I ran the largest single office new agent training program for the largest brokerage in the country for five years at Keller Williams Realty in Austin, Texas. At any given time, there were 100+ first-year agents in my program. I have lived the majority of my professional life in a large franchise environment that is all about training and coaching. So it is ingrained in me that training is important. And it is very important in this enormous and ever-changing business.

A lot of the big firms do training well—eXp Realty, Coldwell Banker, Keller Williams Realty, to name a few. There is a three-generation California firm, Tarbell Realtors, that has had a big reputation for training in southern California. Many firms have excellent training and mentoring programs; some have very little. Some folks will argue that the best training opportunity in the area is the local board; sometimes this is true, sometimes not even close. Do your research and identify the opportunities in your area.

And here is the second part of my bias disclosure: In 2017 I moved my license to eXp Realty, founded in 2008, and I had been watching this innovative brokerage. The eXp model shifts away from the traditional real estate model. eXp is agent-owned, cloud-based, publicly-traded (I like stock ownership), and has made training and coaching extremely accessible in their online campus. Part of the draw for me was the culture and the people; that was first. Then the next big draw was the technology. Because their expenses are so much lower than brick-and-mortar brokerages, they are able to sock some serious resources into their technology and delivering on that model. This also allows them to provide stock (publicly traded, agents are owners) and a revenue share program (passive income). So I was seriously drawn to three sources of income, versus one of just selling homes. I did a crazy amount of research when I was considering the move. I look forward to a sustainable future in my new belonging place. I am always looking for the right people to join my national team, so if you're curious, reach out online.

Literally, you could talk with every broker in your area. And maybe you should. Who are the players in your area? Who is up and coming? Who do you know? Who is hiring? Are there stock options or opportunities for passive income? What is important to you? I personally would talk to numerous brokers of all sizes and shapes and the agents who work with them.

In talking with other agents, be selective, and be prepared to screen their feedback. I have found that if the dominant tone in the thread is negative and complaint-filled, then I am talking to the wrong person, and I want out of that conversation. Right topic, wrong person. Seek out objective professionals who will help you see the values, versus the disgruntled who thrive on throwing the competition under the bus, or the super salesy who are just throwing up information about their brokerage instead of having a decent consultative conversation with you.

Talk with agents and brokers, gather your information, then decide for yourself. You are looking for YOUR belonging place and the right place with the right tools to build YOUR business and YOUR life.

From Denver to Destin, Toronto to Topeka, from Albany to Anaheim, and everywhere in between, you have options and opportunity. Analyze your needs, do your research, find your place.

Choosing a Broker, Newbies

Of course, you want to make a sound decision with your brokerage affiliation as you are establishing the foundation for your business, your branding, your marketing, your initial training and mentoring, and even your reputation. For brand new agents, let's cover a couple of important brokerage differences.

First, for a number of reasons, not all brokerages accept brand new agents. So the coolest, sexiest, high-end brokerage in town may not be hiring. Some firms may or may not take new agents because they do not have the appropriate first-year high-touch program in place. Or you may be required to be in the mentor program for a year or six transactions at a higher split. The small local broker may not be hiring unless you are a relative or your sister is the mayor. They may not be set up to train and mentor new agents, or the broker may not want to take on the liability and time commitment of the newly licensed.

I personally think your first brokerage should have training, education, mentoring, and/or a coaching program solidly in place. I have seen many new agents get started with little support (they chose the wrong broker or did not plug in), and they were still searching for a foundation one and two years in. I have also seen brokers, often the smaller brokers, take on a new or newish agent saying they will mentor, and then they are not available or too busy—they over-promised and under-delivered. Your license classes simply helped you pass a test; now you need to learn the business, and it takes a village and experience to do that.

Remember this important concept: It would be rare for your real estate license classes to have effectively covered local real estate, lead generation, database, marketing, market analysis, market and economic dynamics, new construction ins and outs, contract nuance, commercial versus ranch versus condo versus land, estates, divorce, joint tenancy, the title process, property taxes, and leasing background checks. Your license classes did not cover what to say, how to handle the most common objections, repair negotiations, wood rot, flashing, plumbing static tests, pet odors, broken window seals, old roofs, how to be an open house pro, how to talk to a FSBO, how to market luxury properties, or how to handle distressed properties and distressed owners. What do you do if there is an unresolved insurance claim on the property? What if the buyer's funds are in a foreign country? What if the real estate agent misses one critical deadline in the contract? Your license classes did not cover the bigger stuff of how to be an entrepreneur, how to set up your finances and taxes, technology musts, how to manage the challenging work/life balance in real estate, and on and on and on. Really, I could go on and on.

As a new agent, you need help; you need a village and resources. Do a little research and find out who in your area has a solid training, mentoring, coaching program. Ask questions about exactly what is involved and how much it costs. Are you assigned a mentor who doesn't really have time? Are you attached to a senior agent for a 50/50 commission split for your first five transactions? Are you more or less on your own? How often do they run their classes? Who teaches the classes? Are the classes and resources in-person or on-line, and how often are they available? Who do you turn to for all of your questions? How available is that person? Will your broker be there to help you, or are they super busy and occupied with buyers and sellers? There are managing brokers who work directly with buyers and sellers (or often just sellers), and there are managing brokers who only manage the office.

Changing Brokers, Maybe

> There does not have to be anything wrong with where you are to move toward something else.

If you are in the considering-changing-brokers or I-am-curious category, be careful with "the grass looks pretty green over there" concept and do your homework. I have seen agents shift to another brokerage, only to return two or six or twelve months later with some form of "it wasn't what I thought." It is certainly possible that the best brokerage for you is your current broker. Or is it? Take some time with this.

Understand what you love, understand what you need, understand your business pain points. Is your current brokerage the right brokerage for your five-year plan? Your ten-year plan? Your retirement plan? Are you making enough money? Is your business improving? Is your brokerage staying current with the market and the industry?

It can be costly to hop from broker to broker. The cost for broker-hopping is not so much the hard costs you may encounter, such as a fee your state or board may charge to file with a new broker, or possibly a new agent admin fee the brokerage may charge. Rather, changing brokers may have higher costs, as in the cost of your time and changes to your marketing. The biggie could be whether you get to take your listings with you or not. In most states, it is the broker who "owns" the listings. Those listings you worked so hard to obtain. Technically, the seller signed an agreement with the broker. If you change brokers, what is the broker's policy on releasing listings? If you have multiple listings, you need to somewhat discretely understand how this could impact you financially and plan accordingly.

Changing brokers can work in your favor with your friends, sphere, and database. When I made a move in 2017, it was a good excuse to reach out to my people with a powerful "I have a big announcement" marketing push. Facebook and LinkedIn played nicely in getting the word out with my announcement. They energized my business and stirred up curiosity, interest, phone calls, and leads. And honestly, none of my current clients were concerned with the brand on my sign; they just wanted to make sure they got to continue working with me. I had a new flag, new tools, and opportunity for me, and business as usual for my clients.

Bottom line, find your belonging place and own it.

Brokers and Client Leads

It is pretty rare that your broker will simply hand you client leads. Most agents with most firms will be in a position of building their own pipeline. This is the first reality of starting in the business. Take some time to understand what opportunities and tools exist within the brokerage for lead generation, and for leads to be distributed to agents, and if the commission split varies depending on the source of the lead or price point. A broker may have a split arrangement of 70/30 (you 70 percent of the commission, broker 30 percent) or 80/20 when it is your lead, or maybe higher once you are a superstar, but it's 50/50 if it is their lead. This has a big impact on your income projection and how many transactions you need to close in order to hit your target income for the year. Understanding how the brokerage handles these things makes sense at this stage of the game.

If there is a surplus of broker leads, new agents may get the bottom of the barrel . . . old leads, lease leads, lowest dollar leads, leads in a town an hour away. Brokers may spend a lot of money or have earned their reputation over many hard worked years so a lead that comes in will, in most cases, be assigned to an agent who has the highest likelihood of turning it into an actual client and then converting that into an actual close and, thus, income for the brokerage. You may have to prove yourself first.

Broker leads can come from many sources. Yard sign call-ins, online clicks and registrations, walk-in traffic, phone duty, social media and email campaigns, events, and other various marketing campaigns. These sources can be very helpful for new agents getting started but keep this very important business principle in mind... the agents who consistently generate their own leads are almost always the highest earners versus those agents who rely on the broker. So do you want to be dependent on iffy leads from someone, or do you want to learn how to create your own leads so that you are in control of your business?

More Things to Consider

What is important to you with where you hang your license? It may be as simple as a holding place with low costs and no bells and whistles, or it's the Full Monty foundation for your empire building. Let's take a closer look.

Broker Support

I believe broker support is key, so if you are not getting broker support or training, it could certainly impact your results. Before pointing any fingers, let's see how you're showing up.

Of everything that your broker is offering (whether in person or online), how much of that have you attended or plugged into in the last thirty-to-sixty days? Get clear on what your broker offers and how he or she can best help. Success leaves clues, and the top agents train and train and train. Make sure you're plugging in.

Broker support takes many different forms. Primarily, there is training, there is coaching, and there is brokering. Training is content and knowledge; coaching is business development; brokering is compliance & legal guidance. Training is skill; coaching is mindset and accountability; brokering is someone else taking on liability on your behalf. Training is understanding the many nuances of the real estate contract, negotiation, market, and process; coaching is obstacle maneuvering and building a lead pipeline; brokering is understanding the contract and how to best protect your client.

TRAINING	COACHING	BROKERING
content, knowledge	business development	compliance, legal
skill	mindset, accountability	contract liability
contract nuance, negotiation, process	obstacle maneuvering, building lead pipeline	contract questions, protecting the client

Mentors, when available, tend to be transactional and limited in scope. Their job, for a fee, is to help you through your first handful of contracts because you will have a hundred questions. The mentor's job is, typically, not to teach you the entire business and to help you build yours; rather, it is to help you do a good job with your first few clients and contracts.

One of the biggest mistakes I see new agents make is not plugging in or taking big-league responsibility for their mentor or new agent training program. They know they have a list of classes to attend, a checklist of industry readiness, technology to learn, broker and mentor meetings to attend, blogs to read, resources to tap into, scripts to practice, but they treat it casually and then all of a sudden they have a client opportunity and are unprepared. This puts the mentor in a tough spot (do not put your mentor in a tough spot) and is a set-up for frustration and then the agent thinks their mentor isn't all that great because they are not available for four hours today and tomorrow. Don't be that agent.

If you're not getting support and training and coaching or mentoring, then you may want to either shop brokers or find a nationally known training program (these can be expensive) and find the one that will support you at the highest level. If you interview top tier agents on their advice for high achievement in real estate, a lot of them will say get a coach. But hiring a coach, in my opinion, can be expensive and comes later for the high achievers. In the beginning of your career, you especially need solid support and training with your first five to ten clients and the hundreds of questions that you will have (or should have).

In the support arena, there is more and more online support, especially post-COVID. Is there online support? Do you access your broker only by knocking on their office door or sending an email, or can you access them online? And your broker or your mentor are not your only support, not even close. The majority of agents get more support and input from their colleagues than anywhere else so what are your tools—a Facebook group, an online portal, a searchable Q&A online database—to tap into your agent tribe? And yes, you need to get to know that tribe, make sure people know who you are by participating, contributing, and showing up.

Teams

Did you know that the model these days for the top, top mega agents is a team format? The team format is a bit of a brokerage within a brokerage. The general structure is the lead rainmaker agent (usually the face of the team), an admin or two, and a buyer specialist or two. The biggest teams may have five-to-twenty agents on the team, sometimes more, and thousands of dollars pumped into online advertising and neighborhood marketing. The big teams crush it on the phones. The big teams are script masters. There may be some big teams in your market.

The reason I bring this up is that for some agents, starting on a team (versus starting as a solo agent) can make a lot of sense. Agents who desire more structure, agents who do not want to tackle every single aspect of the business, agents who want to ramp up their skills and experience faster, may want to consider joining a team.

But are they hiring? And if they are hiring, are you the right fit? With most teams, it may not be exactly what you expected with your shiny new real estate license. With teams, you will be on a very specific schedule, will be on the phones a lot, will be expected to learn and use specific scripts fast, and will be expected to produce, and convert leads into clients. A new agent on a team is almost always a buyer specialist with high commission splits (I have seen as low as 40 percent). It is possible that you may not have any seller opportunity on a team; the rainmaker is usually the listing specialist. Your broker may have team opportunities and may have limitations on who qualifies for a team. Talk with your broker or interview with teams before you get started.

It is not a bad way to get started in real estate, and for some agents, it is the perfect place. For other agents, it is not anywhere close to what they want. I have met many agents over the years who tried the team thing and hated it or underperformed and left. I have also met agents who thrive in that environment. If this interests you, do your research.

Reputation: It's Not What It Used to Be!

Broker reputation and training are no longer limited to a brick and mortar address. We live in a mobile world. A great many people conduct their digital lives on their phones now, not their computers, and certainly not by walking into an office on main street (except for maybe in a resort community, but those folks are online first). So find the company that will help YOU be the agent of choice. Ultimately, it's YOUR reputation, YOUR brand, YOUR following, YOUR ability to attract client opportunities!

In smaller towns or niche markets, the brokerage brand can be a big deal. But for the majority of agents, at the end of the day it is the individual's name, reputation, and following that drive the success.

Training: You Don't Know What You Don't Know

Your license classes helped you pass a test. But how will you learn the business? How will you become a contract expert? A market analysis pro? The ramp-up of your skills and knowledge base in your first few years is extensive. The truth is, you are always learning in this business. Is your brokerage set up to support that? Is your brokerage set up to train? Perhaps more importantly, is your broker set up to train and develop talent? To help the new agent become the middle agent? To help the middle agent become the mega agent?

Training matters, and the reality is that most of it is online these days. These days, most of us learn without the limits of location (think cloud-based). Take full advantage of classes offered, not only by your brokerage, but by your local Board of Realtors, your state organizations, other industry organizations, and the plethora of what NAR has to offer online.

Culture Matters

What are the core values of the brokerage? Is there a mission statement that resonates with you? Is it cut-throat, super competitive, expensive suits only, or is there an everyone-wins-when-each-of-us-succeeds environment? Is it low-pressure or high? Is it micromanage or how-can-we-support you? Publicly owned, privately held, stock, profit share, revenue share, open books? Some of the best corporations out there attract and retain talent by culture first, service second, product third. Zappos, Apple, Southwest Airlines, REI, Wholefoods... these places feel good, the employees appear happy, the environment is up. Culture matters.

Space, Cloud, Conducting Business

Some brokerages are shifting to more of a virtual model. Virtual as in cloud-based, no office, work from home, figure out where to meet with your clients model. I write in the midst of the COVID-19 pandemic that forced nearly every business and nearly every agent worldwide into a virtual model. I am thankful that my firm was already virtual, no adjustments necessary when the pandemic hit; our agents were way ahead of the curve.

Fully virtual keeps a brokerage's expenses low. The most expensive thing for a brokerage is, typically, the expensive commercial lease for their office space and the infrastructure to support that. Most agents work from home, so a cloud-based model can make a lot of sense. If this is your model, you may be meeting clients at Starbucks, or in their home, or maybe some shared workspace, or at your lender's office, or a title company conference room, or, increasingly, on Zoom. This works for an increasing number of agents in our cloud-based world, and it works well for me.

Or you may need a storefront. If you are in an area with a lot of walking traffic or where drop-in traffic makes sense, such as a beachside vacation destination, the visibility of a storefront on main street can be important.

Are there meeting rooms? Training rooms? Professional conference rooms? Copiers for agent use? Rentable office space for your team? In some cases, space matters. In many cases, it does not. I know agents who, when COVID hit and their office shut down, cancelled their office space, shifted to at-home only, and saved thousands of dollars and never looked back; they wondered really why they had been paying for office space for so long. For me, I work from home, I meet my sellers at their properties, and I meet buyers all over the place. I do most of my training and meetings online, but I do some in person, and I meet with colleagues in person once or twice a month to talk shop or meet with our broker and leaders. Cloud works for me and has saved me so much time, money, and gas.

Marketing and Branding

Some brokerages will be very, very specific about your branding (it's their branding, not yours), and other firms will give you all sorts of leeway with how you market yourself, your signs, your outreach, and how you can or how the brokerage will regularly communicate with your database. Your state will definitely have its requirements on branding, including what words you can use or not, and the size of the font on your signs; make sure you know the requirements for your area.

Let's talk about yard signs for a minute. You can gain more traction and opportunity from listings that you can from buyers. This is because listings usually include a yard sign and are the vehicle that puts your name all over the Internet when that for-sale is syndicated, via your MLS or your broker, to hundreds of websites. So on the yard sign or the online listing, is it the broker's phone number, or yours, or both? Is your name on the sign? Is it more likely for a drive-by neighbor to call the broker's main office number or your cell phone directly? It is your listing in the neighborhood you grew up in, that you worked your tail off for a year following up and following up and following up and coaching your cousin or best friend or neighbor to get their home ready to go on the market and list with you, their trusted advisor. It's your listing. But, in most states, it is technically the broker's listing. The broker owns the listing (and takes on liability for that contract).

The information on the sign and your ability to gain additional opportunity from that listing is huge for building your business and something to take into consideration when choosing a broker. There is an industry saying "list to last," meaning that the agents who have more sellers than they have buyers will have more pipeline-building opportunities, more staying power.

Let's talk about logos and branding for a minute. Can you have your own logo? Branding within the brand? I am The Circle Property Group at eXp Realty. I am a brand within my brand with a dba filed with the county and with the Texas Real Estate Commission. My sign and marketing include both my personal logo and my brokerage logo and have been approved by my broker. Not all brokers allow this—you use their sign and their logo, period. I figure I am building my business first and my broker's business second, so marketing flexibility is my preference.

Database is Gold

I put this in here specifically right after marketing so that you can focus in on an important business detail. In real estate, you have two primary assets: your time and your database. Who you know, that relationship, and all their contact information, is the biggest asset in your business. Your ability to add to and communicate with your database will play a huge role in building your business and creating more and more opportunity, stability, and financial predictability.

I consult with agents all the time, and it surprises me the times when an agent really does not have a database or a database tool in place. An excel spreadsheet is not much of a business-building tool. While it can track some pertinent detail, it is far from a customer relationship management (CRM) system. If your database is your biggest asset, are you treating it with that much value? Does your broker or local association provide these technology tools? Who pays for them? Is it a highly rated and easy to use system? Is it your database or the brokers? Or do you even have one? Database is different from I-have-a-list. The list starts the database.

So what is the broker's policy on your database? Do you own it, or do they? If you leave the company (a prenuptial sort of mature business question), do you get to take the database with you? Does the broker continue to market to those people if you leave? If you left the firm, are all your friends, family, and former clients going to continue to receive regular emails from ABC Realty (without your name on them) when you now work for Sunshine Realty?

Technology, Tools, and Resources

Speaking of database, does the broker have quality tools in place that allow either you or them to effectively email blast the database with quality information or new listings or market updates? And is the brokerage providing that to you for free, or for a basic technology fee, or high splits to pay for their tech? There is usually a non-negotiable fee. Are they running online ads or have technology in place to help you do that? Do they have a social media presence? What tools do they provide? Is that important to you? You will have a ton of options with tools and software, some free, some with price tags. While some of these tools originate with your local board, agents tend to rely on their brokerage to lead the way in the tech arena.

Is your broker current? Are they using the same technology tools they were using fifteen years ago with a "seems to work for us" mentality, or are they evolving with the all-things-mobile business and consumer environment? Are you the techiest person in the firm and somewhat on your own, or does the broker lead the way? Again, what is important to YOU?

So what tools do YOU really need? Your needed-tools list will evolve, and the reality is that most brokerages or boards will pretty much provide some or most of the following:

- Customer Relationship Management (CRM) software
- Contract-writing software with electronic signature tools
- Virtual storage of all transactions, online vault
- Some form of branded home-search website with your name on it
- A customizable listing presentation and other marketing material

Is it important to you that the broker provides these tools? As for me, I like a robust technology and marketing platform, and those tools can be expensive if I went out on my own to fill my basket. I like the power of leveraging the company to be successful. Make sure you can do that too. eXp Realty, ReMax, Compass, and other big companies offer all or most of these tools. But make no mistake. They are just tools. YOU have to use them, and YOU are the "product" that clients will be "buying."

How Are Brokerages Structured?

Brokerages come in all shapes and sizes. Let's take a brief look.

The Mom and Pop, the Independents

Mom and Pop real estate offices go way back in real estate history, and there may be hundreds of them in your area. Some of these brokerages may have been in the same family for multiple generations, some are very specialized. If it's your family, then it is most likely your landing place. Many of these are two to ten agent operations, some larger. Some of these have reputations for being way out of date, some are cutting edge.

The Boutique, the Specialized Independents

This is a generalized term for, typically, small to medium-sized local market-specific brokerages. Some may have originated as a mom and pop. Boutiques tend to be highly specialized. Many boutiques serve a specific neighborhood, sometimes a specific high price point, sometimes a niche market such as downtown condos. Maybe the boutique spreads its geographic wings to more than one office; often the boutique is one well-placed office.

The Local-Only Firm

Realty Austin, Port Aransas Realty—these are very geographic name specific. They may have more than one location, but the geographic name defines them. They can be big players, especially in smaller towns.

The Big Brokerages

These are the big players, many of them franchised. Some are publicly-owned and traded, some privately held. You will find them coast to coast and, in some cases, internationally. From eXp Realty to ReMax, to Coldwell Banker, to Berkshire Hathaway (Warren Buffett, purchased Prudential), to Keller Williams Realty, to Compass, one or more of these may dominate in your market. The massive Realogy Holdings Corporation owns Better Homes and Gardens Real Estate, CENTURY 21, Coldwell Banker, ERA, and Sotheby's International Realty.

Franchise Big Office

There are franchise real estate offices that have over 500 agents in them. I was a member of one with over 800 agents. This rarely means that all those agents actually have a desk in that office; it means they hang their license there with that specific broker and address. This type of office can completely dominate a market by dominating the listing inventory. But agent count does not equal agent productivity, which may be something for you to consider. These big shops tend to have big staffs and resources.

Franchise Not-So-Big Office

Some franchise offices may have twenty or thirty agents. The models are different. Some franchises strive for a fifty-agent office; some franchises consider their break-even profitability line to be a minimum of 150 agents. Each of these offices will have their own personalities.

Cloud-Based

This is a newer category and is a sign of the times. eXp Realty launched in 2008, and I think it deserves its own category. (Yes, I disclosed my bias earlier.) There may be other emerging players in this arena. I would expect that, as it is simply how we operate these days (hello Netflix, hello Uber). I will use eXp and me, personally, as an example. eXp has its headquarters in Washington state. My broker has a small office in Austin, mostly for mail because everything is online. I work online and from home and can meet my clients in their home (sellers), in Regus office space, at my favorite lender's office, at Starbucks, or pretty much anywhere—or virtually.

I have a network of fellow local eXp agents that I meet with, in person, once or twice a month to mastermind our businesses, and I meet with my national team every week online. I do all of my training and client processing online, and I access the headquarter services easily online (no commute) all the time. Cloud-based means that expenses are kept low (brick and mortar is very expensive for a brokerage office) so resources can be heavily loaded into services, technology, and revenue share.

Ownership

Who owns the brokerages? Well, that varies. Often, it is a broker-owner. Many are franchised, so there would be a franchise owner who paid a lot of money up-front to become the owner, and they pull in a large portion of the profits, with the majority going to the mothership. When it is a franchise, there is often a monthly or annual franchise fee that is passed on to the agents. Some brokerages are publicly held, with agents as owners, stock awards, and stock purchase programs. I have experienced each of these—the broker-owner, the franchise, and the publicly held; I prefer the latter, as the agent-owner concept makes sense to me, and I get to build equity versus just earning commission. I talk to a lot of agents who think they may want to start their own brokerage; let's look at that.

Starting Your Own Brokerage

I run into agents all the time who are considering starting their own brokerage or always thought it may be something they may want to do. I have mixed feelings on this.

If you would be a mom and pop shop working from home, just the two of you, then that is one thing. But if you are thinking of office space and working with a few or more agents, then when you go from individual to broker owner, you automatically take a pay cut, and you take on liability for your agents. You would have overhead like never before (and overhead is heavy when sales and agent production are down) and would likely be pulled away from your personal sales activity to build out, and pay for, systems, tools, software, training, and support for your agents. From my observation and quite a few conversations, many small brokerages are more broke than anything, but the brokers won't admit they're on the edge of broke because they have too much ego tied up in this brokerage that they built. The reality for many of them is that they are three-agents-leaving or one lawsuit away from shutting down.

Hybrids and Trends

Real estate is a big and evolving industry, and really big money (like really, really big money) is being pumped into development as I write. So if I were to outline today's hybrid brokerages, like a 100 percent brokerage, or the latest discount brokerage option, or what Zillow is up to today, or who merged with whom, that landscape would likely change by the time you are reading this a few years down the road. While hybrids have come and gone, especially over the last ten years, they can represent the cutting-edge, and occasionally one stays, hits it big, and changes the industry.

Same goes with industry trends. Some trends we have seen include rocket ship growth of new cutting-edge firms, smaller offices closing in the midst of economic uncertainty, independents merging with the big firms, a shift toward more cloud-based practices, and more options for consumers. We see new technology, iBuyer programs, and more institutional buyers. If you lean geeky or dream about giant what-if's for this industry, then, sure, go to town on studying the latest industry trends and hybrid development in our great big world. But for the purposes of *Success Faster* and your process of choosing a broker in a relatively timely manner, understand the options in your city and get busy assessing which one is the best fit for you and your vision.

> ✔ **ACTION ITEM**
> Assess Broker Choice

Pick which category you fit into, new agent or not new agent, and walk yourself through a review of your options and what works best for you.

CATEGORY 1
Broker Assessment for Not New Agents

NOTE FOR NEW AGENTS: Please read this section; it's packed with valuable information and perspective!

In my opinion, the broker assessment for a not-new agent is very different than it is for the brand-new agent. For the currently licensed agent reassessing brokerage affiliation or just reviewing their options, we'll split this assessment into two important sub-categories, introspective and business. The grass may be greener on the other side of the brokerage fence, or maybe not. You may simply be moving to another town and need to reassess, or you are just not happy and thriving where you are and need to fix that. Or maybe the market is shifting, and you need new solutions, or you need an exit or retirement strategy, or maybe you're just in a casual review. Take your time, and work yourself through this process.

INTROSPECTION
Always start within. Take inventory and ownership of who you are and how you behave in your business. This is sort of the pointing-a-finger exercise.

The finger you are pointing at your brokerage for something that is not a fit or not working... you know the exercise... there are four fingers, or at least three, pointing back at you, and that is where we want to start.

If you move to another brokerage, you will be taking yourself with you. So would you agree that it is possible, even highly likely, that your problems may follow you? Ask yourself these questions:

- Am I fully engaged in my business?
- How is my energy?
- Am I having fun?
- Have I fully engaged in what the brokerage has to offer?
- What do I like best about my brokerage, broker, office?
- Have my business needs changed?
- Has my brokerage or broker or office dynamic changed? And does it still fit?
- Did something specific happen or change, or has this been a gradual evolution of new or emerging needs and preferences?
- Am I serious about lead generation?
- If I take my existing business habits and practices with me, is that ok, or do I need to step up?
- What is missing?
- What am I seeking?

BUSINESS

Are you considering changing brokerages or offices because a new opportunity is presenting itself, a positive pull? Or are you considering a change because something is not quite working in your current campsite, a negative push? Or maybe a combination of the two. This is an important awareness. Rank your current needs regarding these business considerations:

Leads and Sales Opportunities—The top line on an income statement is gross sales, income. Are there new or greater client lead opportunities or tools at the other brokerage and, if so, what does that look like?

Training—Are you getting what you need?

Mentoring—Do you need more? or better? or more accessible?

Support—Are you getting the support that you need? And are you sure you will get it at the next brokerage? What exactly does the brokerage provide? Do they make your business easier and more enjoyable?

Tools—Are you missing some critical tools in your business that another brokerage can deliver?

Technology—What are you using? What is your brokerage using?

Environment and Culture—Ask most agents, and this is actually a biggie. In so many cases, your work environment and colleagues form a bit of a tribe, an extended family. Are you feeling the love? Is this your belonging place? Is there a values match? Is it positive and supportive? Or competitive and cut-throat? Are you included? Are you feeling aligned with the overall message from the brokerage, or is there a mismatch?

Diversity and Inclusion—Is this important to you, what does that look like at the brokerage? Are there networks of agents within the organization, such as a young professional group, a Latino group, an LGBTQ network, a veterans' network, or a seniors group? Is there a diverse and inclusive culture, do they walk the walk, do you feel included?

Broker Love—Supportive is one thing, but is your business growing? I have met many agents who have a great relationship with and are very loyal to their broker, yet they are barely selling any real estate, barely making it financially. Honoring the person who took a chance with you when you were brand new makes sense. But is your business growing? Are you making it financially? Are you loyal to a fault?

Physical Location—Sometimes big-time important, sometimes not at all. Most agents work from home. What do you need?

Virtual—Are you in need of more cloud-based solutions? Virtual business is a big deal in 2020. We'll see how that plays out over the next ten years.

Specialties—Are you needing a brokerage that supports a specific specialty—commercial, farm and ranch, leasing, new construction, investors, waterfront? Or do they have a system or networks in place to help you tap into agents with similar specialties or interests as yours? For example, how would I communicate with or ask questions with agents in my firm who specialize in short sales?

Health Insurance—Are there options?

National Network—Is there a national network of agents available to build referral opportunities? This can be done through various national industry organizations, if you get involved, or can be done through your brokerage, if it is available and you plug in. I live in Austin, Texas, with a hundred people a day moving here. Approximately half of my business comes from other agents referring people to me. So for my business, this is an important factor, and I build my network through my national brokerage, through a couple national organizations, and through my friends and clients.

Costs and Profit—Yes, purposefully near the bottom of the list. While not every business decision is bottom line, many are.

- If your sales increase significantly, do your cost concerns go away?
- What did you pay your brokerage last year and how was the return on investment?
- When your business doubles, what will you pay your brokerage?
- Would you make a brokerage move for a $10,000 pay increase? $20,000? $30,000? $100,000?
- Profit—Does the next broker have a more profitable model or additional financial opportunities?

OTHER

- Ownership, Stock, Career Advancement—Are these important to you?
- Ownership—Is this an option?
- Stock—Is this an option?
- Career Advancement—Is this important?

If you are an experienced agent considering changing brokers, we should probably connect, as I am always looking for the right people to join my national team. Check out my website thenelsonproject.org.

CATEGORY 2

Broker Choice Assessment for New Agents

Step 1: Write a list of what is most important to you in your first few years in the business. Assume massive success. Identify what is most important to you in your brokerage choice, and recognize that this can change considerably in your first couple years as you learn the business.

Step 2: Write a list of all the brokerages that interest you.

Step 3: While you can certainly analyze every single brokerage, most of us do not have that sort of time. (Remember the over-analysis, getting-ready-to-get-ready discussions earlier in the book and how that can seriously slow you down?) Circle your top two or three brokerages from your list.

Step 4: For your brokerage shortlist, gather information from numerous sources, including directly from that brokerage. Do they have a new agent page on their website?

Step 5: Grade them on what is most important to you. Keep it simple. It may be yes, no, maybe, I-don't-know. Or plus or minus. Or A, B, C. Here are some suggested categories:

TRAINING/MENTORING

- Technology tools provided
- Website—mine or theirs? Does it have lead capture?
- Lead opportunities—Careful with this. Brokers will tell agents they get leads but never reveal the terribly poor quality of those leads IF those leads ever happen.
- Open house opportunities
- Number of agents—do you like the idea of being with a small group, or does a large group excite you and provide more opportunity?
- Average production of the agents, how many are full-time? Research tells us that we become the average of the five people we are around the most—this applies personally and professionally. So if the office has eight agents and only two are full-time or only three have sold much if any real estate this past year, is that the right place for you and your aspirations?
- Cost

Step 6: Talk with agents. What do they love most about the firm? How much real estate are they selling and what is their goal?

Step 7: Set an appointment to visit with the brokerage manager or talk in-depth with the person you know at the brokerage. Ask questions, find the right fit, find your belonging place.

Step 8: File an application. I want to comment a bit on cost. I find that so many new agents simply make their first brokerage decision on cost, cost and training/mentoring. I purposefully put costs lower on the list above, as I want to encourage you to assess everything else first. The cheapest bare-bones model out there is not typically a good place for a new agent to start. You need tools and training, and these always have a price.

> **🥷 NINJA TRICK**
> **Bonus Step in Your Brokerage Choice Process**

Stir the pot with your family, friends, and sphere and get ten of them on the phone or face-to-face and engage them on the broker choice or broker switch topic. Your conversation may go something like this:

"I want to run something really important by you, get your opinion. Do you have a few minutes to chat? (You can message them to set up the call.) As you know (they should because you have been doing a good job of talking about what you are doing), I am very close to being fully licensed in real estate. I am beside myself excited about getting started! I have to decide on a broker, and, before I do that, I wanted to run a few things by some of my most valued advisors, and you're on the shortlist. So I have a few questions for you . . . ready?"

And then go through the conversational process of asking some or all of these questions:

- "When did you buy or sell your last property?
- What was most important to you in that process?
- Who did you work with at the time? What brokerage were they with?
- Would you work with them again? Are you still in contact with them?
- Have you worked with other Realtors?
- How did you choose them?
- Did you choose the agent or the brokerage or both?

- If you were about to build a real estate business, what brokerage would you consider? Do you have an opinion? Do you have any favorites around town?
- Is there a broker you know and trust that I should consider?
- Do you have any advice for someone starting a new business?"

And wrap it up with something like, "I have big goals for my business. When I get started, will you give me a shot? I appreciate your support."

If you are an experienced agent considering changing brokers, do a similar version of this exercise with a few trusted friends. Tell them you respect them as level-headed business professionals, and you would value their opinion on a business decision you are about to make.

Then send them a thank you note or a bouquet of flowers if they were amazing and generous and gracious in the conversation. You are pre-building your business. These conversations matter and can often be the differentiating factor between the superstars, the rapid starters, the first-year success stories, and everyone else. Start heating up that pot before you have your license. Always be looking for opportunities to have quality conversations with your favorite people.

CHAPTER 21

On Fire Hot!

Where does your money meet the meaningfulness of your life?

—Danielle LaPorte, *The Fire Starter Sessions*

On Fire Hot! is you with your strongest, most inspired, unapologetic voice calling the shots. On Fire Hot! is you when your life and business are clicking, all cylinders firing. On Fire Hot! is that internal fire that gets you out of bed. It's optimism without assistance, courage without chemicals. It's pushing through the bullshit story you've been telling yourself and truly owning the success you knew you could be all along. It's your bank account and profitability and net worth like never before. Can we agree that cash solves so many things? On Fire Hot! is that new car when that new car is not even a financial stretch. On Fire Hot! is joy solidly in place in your life and business, often in that order. *Success Faster On Fire Hot!* is you truly becoming the on fire hottest version of yourself.

Sacred Pact

I made a sacred pact with myself to make a difference.

The earliest version of this book was an ongoing newsletter, then a series of blog articles, and then a self-published e-book that was more or less a brain dump of everything I had pieced together on the topic. If you have a book in you, start there. Then I published *Success Faster* in 2018, then the workbook followed, then *Success Faster On Fire Hot!* in 2020.

I know from experience and from being a decent observer that success with a new endeavor, a new project, a new relationship, a new business, can simply change your life. And when you change your life, it inevitably changes someone else's life. It is a beautiful pattern of ascending meaning and value rewarded with additional trips to Adventureland.

I have seen new parents succeed in real estate because it supported their vision of how they saw themselves parenting, how they envisioned their new family, and their ability to be fully present and involved.

I have seen the newly divorced create financial independence and a new lease on life.

I have seen newish agents whose family history and personal experience was one of ongoing financial scarcity. Their upbringing, their family histories, their entire lives had an ongoing theme of financial instability. Their real estate success represented not only their personal financial freedom with savings, a decent credit score, and options, it represented a new vision for the siblings, the nieces and nephews, the next generation. Similar to the first child in the family with a college degree, this business success financial freedom thing would set a new standard, a new vision for the family of what is possible.

Whose life and vision will your success impact? What difference will you make?

Even moderate success can change your life and can change the world. Moderate success indicates that moderate plus is possible. And moderate plus indicates that massive success is possible. Just make sure you are using your definition of success and not a borrowed version of someone else's ... your success on your terms.

Success is incremental; it builds upon itself. Often it is one tweak that shifts us from ordinary and toward extraordinary. Rarely linear, often a curvy path, sometimes success goes in reverse before it moves forward... the back and forth with its beautiful imperfection, it's a bit of an awkward dance, yet the dance moves us forward.

You get to decide what On Fire Hot! looks like for you. You may define your success in financial terms, perhaps in more personal lifestyle terms. Maybe you have something to prove. It's your goal and your life. In this red-hot moment, I invite you to step into your success, step into the version of yourself that makes things happen.

My intention, my hope, my sacred mission, is that this book, this voice, and one small portion of the On Fire Hot! message is the catalyst, the nudge that will change your life. The world is ready for your On Fire Hot!.

The end.

Not really, you just started! Honestly, I don't think there is ever an end. And instead of perceiving that non-end concept as an exhaustion formula, I choose to think it just may be the secret of life, and the secret to always moving forward, and the secret to always creating something amazing in your life. There are cycles and rebirths and starts and restarts and launches and relaunches, and it all adds up to the beautiful and messy and imperfect and sometimes gradual and sometimes fast and sometimes small and sometimes massive but always an inevitable evolution of you and your mission and your place on this great planet. When I have influenced you with just one small nudge in your evolution, your dance, then we are both in the right place at the right time.

Who else do you know who could use a little encouragement and a real estate roadmap? Pass it on.

I wish you joy and success in your On Fire Hot! journey.

Oh, one more thing. Earlier in the book, I said I would mention the chicken farm thing. My professional journey, of course, involves my personal journey. As I look back over the years and the various homes I have owned and the gardens I have developed (and honed and nurtured and sculpted and weeded), each address tells a story. I adore this aspect of real estate, that every address has a story, many stories. Remember the dream home modern farmhouse we built on three acres on the edge of Austin? Well, the house has become so much of a home that, in addition to the customary dogs and cat, it is now home to about thirty gardens, a bunch of chickens, ducks, and two miniature donkeys. You may give wine and gift baskets to your clients; we give fresh eggs and vegetables.

What's Next?

In the next series of pages, you will find a powerful ACTION ITEM reference, a BONUS ACTION section, and an easy-to-access SCRIPT reference. The all-in with the action and knowing what to say is where you do the heavy lifting of gaining clients faster. I would like to encourage you to use the ACTION section as a tool to build your pipeline. You could simply open the book once a week, grab one ACTION ITEM, and all you do is focus that week on that one ACTION. THIS IS YOUR ROADMAP. The habitual weekly activity of ACTION ITEM action could single-handedly build your pipeline and build your business and your life.

Just know that this is where the serious get serious, this is where your on fire hotness begins. You have a decision to make, or perhaps you already made it, and that decision is this:

Today I am all-in with building my business and my life, and I am committed to the daily work and mindset it takes to get there.

Oh, and ps . . . please let me know how you're doing, please share your On Fire Hot! successes. One of the easiest ways to do that is through the 456 Coaching Club on Facebook or through my website. You'll find detail in the resources section at the back of the book.

And there's more.

Workbook

I mentioned in the first couple pages that the 2018 *Success Faster* had no mention of the workbook. That is because the workbook did not yet exist. So we now have a companion workbook available on Amazon called, of all things, *Success Faster Workbook*. Get yourself, your accountability partner, your mastermind group, your book club, your team, your brokerage a copy on Amazon today.

Also, there are a couple of free workbook downloads—Who's the boss? performance review and ACTION ITEMS—available in the book resources section of thenelsonproject.org.

Resources Page

If you flip to the back of the book, you will see an online resources page, with links where you can learn more and participate in conversations with other professionals who are on a similar journey. The main *Success Faster* landing page can be found at thenelsonproject.org, where you will find various resources, tools, and blog articles.

I am honored to deliver this to you . . . and then beyond blessed when something in these pages made a difference in your business and your life. Whether that difference-maker was totally On Fire Hot! and life-changing or simply a modest course-correction, either way, I have done my job. If you want more of what you found in these pages, check things out online.

Reference: Action Items

> ⊗ **WARNING LABEL!**
> This is DEFINITELY one of those "work" chapters I mentioned early on. It means we dramatically dive into the work! This is the MOST IMPORTANT work that will move you forward with your on fire hotness! I will ask this once again: Do I have your permission to hurt your brain a bit AND help you actually move forward toward something better? Do I have your permission to help you build your bank account? I thought so.

You are now in the most important section of *Success Faster On Fire Hot!* Your success in this business will have everything to do with building your stamina and consistency around the simple principle of pipeline building, this core repetitive activity of talking with people and cultivating opportunity. Stop overcomplicating this business. Get on the offense with this. You are always building your pipeline; you are always looking for and nurturing your next five to ten leads.

Park it right here in this section, and rinse and repeat. Rinse and repeat the ACTION ITEMS, and do it over and over and over again ten to fifteen hours per week, and that alone will build your successful real estate pipeline. And then when you get busy with clients, DO NOT STOP the ten to fifteen hours . . . never ever compromise those hours, as they are your ticket to success and freedom.

There is a free download of all the ACTION ITEMS plus BONUS ACTION ITEMS on the Book Resources page at thenelsonrproject.org.

✔ **Call Your Mother**　　　　　　　　　　　　　　　　　　　　　　**Chapter 9**

Call your mother. Seriously, call your mother (or your sister or BFF), and here's what you are going to say:

> "Mom (sister, BFF), I just started at [broker name] today! OMG, I am so excited! Wish I had done this earlier. I need your help. This is day one of the training program, and the very first assignment they gave me was to call you! This business is seriously referral-based, and I have big goals. Will you help me? It's now my job to know the real estate needs of my friends and family and their friends and families, so there is a basic question, actually two questions, that I need to ask you. 1.) Are you anticipating any real estate needs this year? 2.) Who do you know who may need my services this year? It's pretty much my job to ask this question, and who better to start with than you? I really super appreciate your support."

✔ **Identify Your TOP 100**　　　　　　　　　　　　　　　　　　　**Chapter 11**

Get out your phone. Get your neighborhood list. Your church directory. Your Christmas card list. Your kids' school directory. Your former colleagues. Your golf league. Don't forget your family. In town or out of town or out of state . . . all of them. Your college friends. I have brand-new agents who got their first or second client because they called their cousin or college friend halfway across the country. You know a LOT of people! Let's identify your TOP 100 because I promise you, there is business in there. Your immediate job is to cultivate and coax the leads out of that TOP 100 list.

✔ **Call Your TOP 100**　　　　　　　　　　　　　　　　　　　　　**Chapter 11**

Call one to twenty of your TOP 100, and here's what to say:

> "Hey, Sam, it's [me]. Do you have a minute? I know you're at work, so I'll be fast. I wanted to let you know what I'm doing. I've thought about this for years, finally pulled the trigger, and I am now an associate with XYZ Realty. Love it, wish I had done this sooner! So a couple of quick questions: 1. Do you have a go-to Realtor when you have a real estate question? [NO: Great, you do now! Or YES: Great, happy to be the second person on your list.] Second question: Are you anticipating any real estate needs this year? Who do you know who may need my services? I appreciate you keeping me in mind. I'll send you an email right away so you have my contact info. Everything good with you? Would love to do lunch or happy hour sometime, catch up. What's your schedule like the next couple of weeks?"

✓ **Practice! The POWER QUESTIONS (PQ's)**   Chapter 12

Read the PQ's again and the how's-the-market responses out loud ten times fast. Another option is to pair up with another agent and plow through this exercise together. The goal of this quick exercise is simply speed and repetition. Speed and repetition. In fact, you may want to do this simple exercise every day this week and next week and the week after. Go over and over and over and over these questions. Speak them out loud, write them out on a notepad, type them out, record yourself on your phone and listen to them in your car (hands-free, of course). Speed and repetition.

    THE CALL: Pick one of the POWER QUESTIONS and call someone, call five, call twenty . . . heck, walk your block and ask your neighbors. This is not an email; it is not a post on Facebook. You must have conversations with people. Do not move on to the next chapter without this ACTION ITEM checked off.

✓ **Your Calendar Is Money**   Chapter 13

Plug the following non-negotiable recurring weekly appointments into your schedule:

- Ten hours per week of lead generation
- Five hours per week of practice; maybe one hour per week for experienced agents

    The lead generation hours in your schedule, yours may be more, especially in your first two years. This is THE foundational piece to a successful real estate business.

    The practice piece—five hours per week for launching agents, less for experienced agents. Let's keep this really simple. If you want the Andrew approach (remember his success story just a few months into the business?), pencil in fifteen hours per week.

    Let's talk about your practice and what may work best. What is your best learning style? Are you visual, auditory, or tactile? Each of us learns best in different ways, so tap into what works best for you—reading, speaking, or writing—which one works best for you? Even if you are a visual learner or a tactile learner, make sure you spend time on the auditory, time actually saying the words out loud because that is what you will be doing in real life with clients. Tiger Woods can watch videos of himself putting or chipping, and that has value, but he needs to actually spend time on the putting green or in the sand trap to truly improve.

    For most people, honoring this schedule takes discipline and accountability. It's not like you have a boss who is checking in on your progress every day or every week. These appointments, solidified and respected as a serious non-negotiable appointment in your calendar, will play a direct role in how quickly you start lining up your next client opportunity and your next paycheck.

✔ Call Your Biggest Advocate, Again   Chapter 13

Sometimes your closest people can be your biggest advocates and your biggest critics. So the conversation may be as simple as giving that important person an update on how you're doing. It may look something like this:

> "Hi. It's me. I wanted to give you a little report on how things are going at work. I want you to see how serious I am and tell you a couple things I have going on. Got a minute?"

> "First, I really appreciate your support. So I [then go on to tell them about your open houses, the buyer you're working with, that as the national sales manager of your real estate business you basically go to the office in the morning and do not leave until you have talked with x number of people about real estate . . ."

Then ask if you can practice a script or two with them over the phone.

> "So I spend about an hour a day just practicing what to say, my presentations, and studying the market. I realized I would like a little real feedback, trying to get this to sound natural. I want to run this by you, get your feedback."

Then practice with them. They may laugh a little; they usually offer a little advice like "be yourself," then half the time they'll mention someone who may have a real estate need. You always want to end with a question something like this:

> "Who have you come across recently who mentioned real estate?"

And then you need to train them on HOW to help you:

> "When you do hear of someone, don't just give them my card. Instead, say this: "You know what? I really want to introduce you to/have you talk to my friend [your name]. She's the friend I mentioned who is a Realtor. What's your email? I'm just going to send an email that introduces the two of you. No pressure; she'll treat you like family and may be able to help you. At the very least, she'll be a good resource."

✔ Find Your Five People   Chapter 14

Your top five people, get them on the phone. Here's what to say:

> "I promised myself I would call you today. Do you have a second?"

OPTION 1: YOU KNOW EVERYONE

> "You probably know more people than anyone I know. That's why I'm calling. I have big goals for my business this year. Here's my quick and easy question: Who do you know that I should know?"

OPTION 2: YOU LOVE ME, RIGHT?

> "I need your help. I have big goals for my business this year. Here's my quick and easy question: Who do you know that I should know?"

OPTION 3: YOUR OWN BUSINESS
"You've started your own business/you've accomplished some impressive things. That's why I'm calling. I have big goals for my business this year. Come have coffee with me. I want to ask you about your success, advice for starting something new. I figure I should listen to successful people, and you're on my short list. What is your availability this week or next?"

OPTION 4: HOW CAN I HELP YOU?
"You have always been very supportive of me and my business. How can I help you? How is your business? What are you working on? Is there anyone I know that you would like to meet? Let's have coffee and catch up."

✔ Start Your Bio Document   Chapter 15

This to-do will save you a lot of time and frustration down the road. You are going to create a document that has two or three versions of your bio paragraph as well as all of your critical URL links. The beauty of having this document at your fingertips is that you never again have to go on a hunting mission to find your LinkedIn profile URL, your Facebook business page URL, or your NRDS ID number. And you maybe did not even know that you had an NRDS number, but some critical member profile page is asking you for it. (Hint, it's on your NAR member card and somewhere in your NAR profile. You will want it in your bio document so you never have to go hunt for it again.)

My bio file is a Word file, conveniently called "BIO.doc," and I have it pinned in my favorites list so it is super accessible. I access this document all the time. It has three primary sections. First, ID numbers. Second, critical links. And third, every bio paragraph I have ever written. Here is a run-down of mine (yours will vary):

ID NUMBERS

- my license number
- my NRDS number
- my CRS member number

LINKS

- my main website link
- my blog link
- my personal Facebook link
- my business Facebook page link
- my LinkedIn public profile link
- my Twitter profile link
- my YouTube channel link
- my YouTube promotional video
- my Google+ link
- my Pinterest link
- my Zillow profile link
- my Yelp business profile link
- my Inman News author page link
- my Instagram link
- my Skype handle
- my 456 Coaching Club link
- my coaching intake form link
- my online audit intake form link
- my client intake form link
- my business consult intake form and https://linktr.ee/julienelson, which is a super-easy way to get contact info & multiple links into your Instagram profile

BIO

This section of your document will build and grow. I use this document any time I am filling out a bio on a new website or refreshing an existing online professional bio paragraph. This is so I am not having to rewrite it every single time and hope that it is complete and as brilliant as the last time I wrote one. Here is where you can start:

- **SHORT**—Write a three-to four sentence version of who you are professionally.
- **MEDIUM**—Write a two-to-three paragraph version of who you are professionally.
- **LONG**—Write a longer version of who you are including background, skills, areas of expertise, what you bring to the table, why you are in real estate, what's in it for the client, and wrap it up with some personal interests.

One tip is that you can go online, maybe in Zillow or your brokerage agent directory or LinkedIn, and look up other agents to find examples of well-written and interesting bios. Go ahead, look up mine. No, you cannot copy and paste someone else's brilliant bio. You can, however, find inspiration, keywords, and examples of above-average well-written bio's. What you will also find in this online treasure hunt is plenty of examples of poorly written or non-existent bio's. You need to look good online.

✔ Write It Down   Chapter 17

If you have not yet done so, put some words down in your journal addressing the following:

- What success looks like to me:
- What success will do for me and my family:
- My financial goals are:

- My personal goals are:
- My five-year vacation plan is:
- Here's how I will change the world:
- My sacred mission is:

✔ Do Your Math   Chapter 18

Besides meeting a friend every day this week at the coffee shop with a giant cookie and then going for a walk to burn off the monster calories (which I still recommend doing, all of that), do your math. Fill in the blanks:

- The goal:
- Average price:
- Average commission:
- The closings:

- The clients:
- The appointments:
- The leads:
- The conversations:

Reference: Scripts

SCRIPT DISCLOSURE: The origin of most of these scripts is unknown. A few of them are my originals or modifications of scripts I have adopted and trained on over the years from many classes, many sources, many hours spent on YouTube and various online forums. I paid very close attention to NOT copy and paste from any copyrighted material. Ever. Understanding the origin of the majority of real estate scripts is like wondering about the origin of your favorite chocolate chip cookie recipe . . . they have been around for a very long time and have become our language. You should modify them to best fit your needs and authentic style.

Call Your Mother

Call your mother. Seriously, call your mother (or your sister or BFF), and here's what you are going to say:

"Mom (sister, BFF), I just started at [broker name] today! OMG, I am so excited! Wish I had done this earlier. I need your help. This is day one of the training program, and the very first assignment they gave me was to call you! This business is seriously referral-based, and I have big goals. Will you help me? It's now my job to know the real estate needs of my friends and family and their friends and families, so there is a basic question, actually, two questions, that I need to ask you. 1.) Are you anticipating any real estate needs this year? 2.) Who do you know who may need my services this year? It's pretty much my job to ask this question, and who better to start with than you? I really super appreciate your support."

Basic

The fastest route to gaining a client today is your phone, with your contact list already in your cell phone, the people you already know.

Keep this super simple; do not overthink. Here are some options of what to say:

"I have an announcement; do you have a minute?"

"I have a quick business question; do you have a minute?"

"I have two questions, one personal, one business; do you have a minute?"

"Did you see my Facebook post? Big announcement!"

"Are you anticipating any real estate needs this year or know of anyone who may be in need of my services?"

"I want to add my name to the list of people you call when you have a real estate question."

"I have big goals. I need your support."

To engage the people I know, I typically text first to set up the call. I shoot a text something along the lines of:

"Hey, it's Julie. Want to run something business by you real quick. Can you chat?"

For the best people in your phone—if they are on your speed dial, your favorites list, they deserve to hear your full story, your why; they deserve to hear your passion. What is your rocket fuel? What powers your determination? Tell your story. Engage them in your story and your motivation, and your goals, and your excitement.

FSBO

"I am Susan with ABC Realty (you always have to disclose your credentials). I live in the area and saw your sign. I wanted to ask you a couple of questions. Do you have a minute? Can you tell me a little about the house? What is the price? If I had a qualified buyer, are you prepared to pay a buyer agent commission? Are you considering hiring a Realtor? I'd like to come see the house real quick . . . can I swing by this afternoon?"

Open Houses

Scripts for open houses? I'm so glad you asked. These are all open-ended and designed to get them talking and to help you get into rapport. This is just a start; you can find so many more online, but here is a collection I like:

"Hello. What brings you to the open house today?"

"Have you seen any homes you really like yet?"

"Who is your agent?"

"What do you like best about the house?"

"What neighborhoods are you considering?"

"What is your timeline?"

"What is most important to you?"

"Have you been to other open houses? Any creepy or pushy agents?"

For neighbors:

"How long have you lived in the neighborhood?"

"What do you like best about the neighborhood?"

"Are you looking to move or just curious?"

"Who do you know who is considering moving to the neighborhood?"

"When we list a house like this, we tend to get numerous buyers looking to move into the neighborhood. Do you know other neighbors that are considering selling?"

TOP 100

Call one to twenty of your TOP 100, and here's what to say:

> "Hey, Robert, it's [me]. Do you have a minute? I know you're at work, so I'll be fast. I wanted to let you know what I'm doing. I've thought about this for years, finally pulled the trigger, and I am now an associate with XYZ Realty. Love it, wish I had done this sooner! So a couple of quick questions: 1. Do you have a go-to Realtor when you have a real estate question? [NO: Great, you do now! Or YES: Great, happy to be the second person on your list.] Second question: Are you anticipating any real estate needs this year or know anyone who may need my services? I appreciate you keeping me in mind. I'll send you an email right away so you have my contact info. Everything good with you? Would love to do lunch or happy hour sometime, catch up. What's your schedule like the next couple of weeks?"

Common Objections

What is your response to these basics?

- Why should I hire you?
- I think we'll wait.
- Will you lower your commission?
- We're talking to two other agents.
- I have a friend who is a Realtor.
- Oh, that carpet is awful!
- We want to price it at $325k (when it's worth $290k).
- We want to offer $30k below the list price (when it's the coolest home and the market and homes are selling for full price in three days).
- We're just looking.
- We're going to try to sell it by ourselves first.
- We're not ready to talk to a lender.
- Why-should-I-hire-you? My favorite response:

> "Maybe you should, maybe you shouldn't. I need to know more specifically what your needs are to make sure I am the right person and can deliver. You're interviewing me and I'm interviewing you; it needs to be the right match. What is your situation?"

Basics

The Basic Lead Gen Script

> **VERSION 1:** "Let me ask you a business question real quick . . . are you guys anticipating any real estate needs this coming year? We are already setting appointments for the first quarter and want to make sure we have you on our radar. Who do you know who mentioned real estate lately? I wouldn't be doing my job if I did not ask you this question every now and then."

> **VERSION 2:** "I know you know a number of Realtors. I just want you to know that it is my goal to earn your referrals. Just planting the seed. So what's the most important thing that you value in a Realtor? While we're on the topic, are you guys anticipating any real estate needs this year? Who do you know who mentioned real estate lately?"

Friends and Family

> "Hey there, I have a quick business question for you. Who do you know who may need my services this year? We are already setting appointments for Fall."

> "Hey, I am really hustling to build my business this week. I need your help. Who do you know who has mentioned real estate lately?"

Your Biggest Advocate

> "Hi. It's me. I wanted to give you a little report on how things are going at work. I want you to see how serious I am and tell you a couple things I have going on [or share a recent win]. Got a minute?

> "First, I really appreciate your support. So I [then go on to tell them about your open houses, the buyer you're working with, that as the national sales manager of your real estate business you basically go to the office in the morning and do not leave until you have talked with x number of people about real estate . . . or some pertinent fact about what you're doing].

Then ask if you can practice a script or two with them over the phone.

> "So I spend about an hour a day just practicing what to say, my presentations, and studying the market. I realized I would like a little real feedback, trying to get this to sound natural. I want to run this by you, get your feedback."

Then practice with them. They may laugh a little as it can be slightly awkward at first but just roll with it. They usually offer a little advice like "be yourself," then half the time they'll mention someone who may have a real estate need.

You always want to end with a question something like this:

"Who have you come across recently who mentioned real estate?"

And then you need to train them on HOW to help you:

"When you do hear of someone, don't just give them my card. Instead, say this: "You know what? I really want to introduce you to/have you talk to my friend [your name]. She's the friend I mentioned who is a Realtor. What's your email? I'm just going to send an email that introduces the two of you. No pressure; she'll treat you like family and may be able to help you. At the very least, she'll be a good resource."

Your Five People

"I promised myself I would call you today. Do you have a second?"

OPTION 1: YOU KNOW EVERYONE.

"You probably know more people than anyone I know. That's why I'm calling. I have big goals for my business this year. Here's my quick and easy question: Who do you know that I should know?"

OPTION 2: YOU LOVE ME, RIGHT?

"I need your help. I have big goals for my business this year. Here's my quick and easy question: Who do you know that I should know?"

OPTION 3: YOUR OWN BUSINESS

"You've started your own business/you've accomplished some impressive things. That's why I'm calling. I have big goals for my business this year. Come have coffee with me. I want to ask you about your success, advice for starting something new. I figure I should listen to successful people and you're on my shortlist. What is your availability this week or next?"

OPTION 4: HOW CAN I HELP YOU?

"You have always been very supportive of me and my business. How can I help you? How is your business? What are you working on? Is there anyone I know that you would like to meet? Let's have coffee and catch up."

OPTION 5: WRITE YOUR OWN.

How's the market?

Stats and Market Dynamics

Here are some common stats to monitor and work into your conversations:

> **INVENTORY:** "Wow, there are fifty-six homes on the market in Shady Grove, and about twenty are selling per month. That means on average it will take two-to-three months to sell. Are you considering selling?"
>
> **INVENTORY:** "Last month there were eighty homes for sale in the area; today there are ninety-three. Don't miss the market. Who do you know who is thinking of selling?"
>
> **PRICE TRENDS:** "The average home price in Bay City went up 7 percent over this same time last year. This is influenced both by our strong economy, low inventory, and all the new construction in the area. It may be a good time to sell . . . let's chat. What's your schedule the next couple days?"
>
> **INTEREST RATES:** "Interest rates bumped a tad recently and the Fed is indicating another bump early next year (Hint: you need to study this.). Even a quarter or half point bump can significantly impact your monthly payment. Don't miss the market. Who do you know who is thinking of buying and would benefit from a decent strategy conversation?"

Engage the Consumer

Here are some handy engage-the-consumer responses to the popular how's-the-market question. Again, notice the question at the end of each response; get into this NINJA habit as it is crazy effective in gaining control of the conversation.

> "The market? It's crazy awesome . . . why do you ask?"
>
> "The market? It's great. Have you thought of selling?"
>
> "Is it a good time to sell? It is for a lot of people, not so much for others . . . depends. What's up? What is your situation?"
>
> "How's real estate? It's amazing! Wish I had done this years ago! You guys still live downtown?"
>
> "Home sales are up x percent from this same time last year, and prices are up x percent in our neighborhood. That's solid. How long have you guys been in your home? Who do you know who is wanting to move into this area?"
>
> "The market? It amazes me. You know, with interest rates as low as they are, a mortgage payment on a $220k home today is about the same as a mortgage payment on a $120k home in 1995. It's called the affordability factor. The folks out there that are still renting need to take a serious look at that. What's your email? I have a blog article on the topic I want you to see. When are you going to buy?"

Mentors

"Alice, thank you so much for taking my call. I assume you're busy so I'll be brief. I just recently started my new business (or I am relaunching my business), and I promised myself that I would meet with one successful business pro or entrepreneur or interesting person every week for the next two months. So that is eight amazing people, and you're on my shortlist. I intend to do this right. I just want to ask you how you got started, what advice you may have for someone just getting started, and if you were to do it all over again what you might do differently. I figure in the process I'll end up with a couple of mentors (no pressure). I simply really value your opinion and experience and would be honored if you would meet me for a cup of coffee or better yet, I could bring sandwiches by your office sometime this week."

Friend Who Bought a Home Recently or Last Year

"Hey, it's [me]. Got a minute? You guys have been in your new home... what, six months now? Awesome! How is it? You love it? What's your favorite thing about the house? Any projects you're working on? Hey, the reason for my call... you know I just started in real estate, right? (I love it... wish I had done this sooner.) My question for you has to do with your experience buying your house. Can I ask you a couple of questions? What did your Realtor do really well? What could he or she have done better? Is she still in touch with you? What was most important to you in the process?

Do you have any questions on anything... home warranty, property taxes, filing for your homestead exemption? I can probably help, and if I do not know the answer, I'll go get it for you. No problem... call me anytime you have any question on your home... need a handyman, painter, plumber etc. I can help you. Hey, real quick before I get off the phone, is there anyone you know who may need my services this year? I appreciate you keeping me in mind. Hope to see you guys soon. Would love to see the house."

Listings

Listings, stick to your program:

> "Mr. and Mrs. Seller, the more we stick to our program, the more I can predict and control the outcome. Any deviation from this plan simply moves us from the A-plus plan toward the B plan; I can give you the best results with the A-plus plan."

Listing Questions to Ask

Having an online questionnaire you send to your sellers will save you a lot of time; then at the listing appointment, you are simply verifying the information. Here are some of your seller questions:

> "What is most important to you in this process?"
>
> "What is the best feature of your home?"
>
> "What is the best feature of the neighborhood/location?"
>
> "What upgrades or improvements have you made?"
>
> "Is there anything positive or negative about your house or neighborhood that could affect the price?"
>
> "Do you have any deferred maintenance?"
>
> "What is your budget to get the house market-ready?"
>
> "Is there anything the other agent said they would do that for some reason we have not covered?"

Pricing/Financial

> "What do you think the value of your house was at the peak of the market?"
>
> "What do you think the value is today?"
>
> "What is the price you will not go below?"
>
> "Do you have a mortgage balance on the home?"
>
> "Is there a second mortgage, or are there any liens on the property that will need to be paid upon sale of the property?"
>
> "Do you need the proceeds from this home for the purchase of your next home?"
>
> "Are you familiar with how buyers determine value in this area? Let's take a close look at that."

POWER QUESTIONS

PQ #1: I Wouldn't Be Doing My Job

"Hey, real quick . . . I wouldn't be doing my job if I didn't ask you this question. Who do you know who may need my services this year? I appreciate you keeping me in mind. I'll send you a quick email with my contact information. Are you anticipating any real estate needs this year?"

PQ #2: Earn Your Referrals

"I know you know a number of Realtors. I just want you to know that it is my goal to earn your referrals. Just planting the seed. So what's the most important thing that you value in a Realtor? While we're on the topic, are you guys anticipating any real estate needs this year?"

PQ #3: The Second on Your List

"I respect that you know another Realtor [or that your sister is a Realtor, or that you like your old Realtor]. I'd love to be the second on your list. Not everyone is the right match, so keep me in mind. While we're on the topic, are you anticipating any real estate needs this year?"

PQ #4: The only property?

"Is this the only home you have to sell, or are there others?"

PQ #5: Who do you know?

"We are already setting appointments for fall. Who do you know who may need my services this year?"

PQ #6: Mentioned real estate?

"Who do you know who has recently mentioned real estate?"

PQ #7: Who do you call?

"Who do you call when you have a real estate question?"

Online Resources

thenelsonproject.org

This is the best place to find all things Success Faster and all things Julie Nelson including all of the book resources and downloads mentioned throughout the book.

456 Coaching Club Facebook group

facebook.com/groups/456club ... come on in and engage with other real estate professionals from around the globe!

Julie's Austin, Texas Real Estate Business

thenelsonproject.com

Follow

Follow Julie Nelson and The Nelson Project and the 456 Coaching Club and thenelsonproject.org for future updates to this guide as well as best practices for new and emerging agents. If it is social and media, chances are you'll find me by searching The Nelson Project or thenelsonproject; in the case of Instagram, @thenelsonproject. And when I say follow, social is fine as in the Instagram or Facebook or LinkedIn thing, but what about really follow, as in go on a journey together, put our fires together to make one big fire, push through the noise and do something amazing? If the latter appeals, then dig into thenelsonproject.org, and let's figure out one way or another to connect.

Crazy Story

If you want to participate in the crazy story blog series that may, someday, be the next book, here's that link again: crazystory.info

Disclaimers and Disclosures

This book is not intended as financial, legal, or broker advice. Regulations, standards, license requirements, and license ethics may vary in your area, region, state, or brokerage. Licensed REALTORS® must consult their broker for legal, client, and contract advice. Unlicensed (pre-license) folks cannot give the impression that they may be licensed and, thus, cannot take the majority of actions outlined in this book. Acting like a licensed real estate agent when you are not licensed is illegal. Know the rules in your state, learn the nuances in your area. The author does not take any responsibility for the results of your actions as prescribed in this book.

Texas Compliance: Because Julie simply mentioned her Austin, Texas, real estate practice once or twice in *Success Faster On Fire Hot!* and because Julie is big on compliance, we are here to tell you that Texas law requires all licensees to provide the information in this link: http://tiny.cc/TRECcompliance470666

The author is legally and ethically bound by the standards and ethics of the National Association of REALTORS® and the Texas Real Estate Commission and personally bound by the golden rule. The author, Julie Nelson, is a licensed REALTOR® in the State of Texas.

Use of REALTOR®

A note on the National Association of REALTORS® (NAR) trademark, the ®: For readability purposes, I include the REALTOR® in the first reference in each chapter and omit it in the rest of the document. NAR says we can do this. REALTOR® is a federally registered collective membership mark that identifies a real estate professional who is a member of the National Association of REALTORS® and subscribes to its strict Code of Ethics. This book is intended for Realtors® and those considering real estate as a career.

REALTOR® Code of Ethics

The National Association of REALTORS® Code of Ethics has been in place since 1913. A lot has changed since then. The code changes with time and is updated annually. You can read the National Association of REALTORS® Code of Ethics in its entirety at nar.realtor/code-of-ethics.

The Author's Personal Code of Ethics

Be kind to yourself and others, take the high road, always return the grocery cart to the cart corral, open the door for others.

Acknowledgments

The *Success Faster On Fire Hot!* bus was packed with some amazing travelers. I must give a special shout-out to Portia—my coach, my mentor, my secret weapon, my chief encourager. Portia kept me on track when I most needed it and gave me space when my intuition said that was the right path. When my vision scattered or I lost my foothold, she was there to help assess the pieces and re-mold them into something even better and then gave me all the credit. And to Kay who has always believed in me and did some ongoing heavy lifting around the farm as I buckled up for marathon laptop sessions; I know I pushed the boundaries of "in manageable times and mania", and am forever grateful. And to Kate for leveling-up the look. And to the word fairies who placed words and phrases and inspiration in my path; to your credit I am now an obsessed collector. And to Fee, Sean, Michelle, Deanna, Di, and more . . . all the believers placed on my path to remind me of my mission and that my people are waiting.

About the Author

Julie Nelson and The Nelson Project Inc. created this guide to help real estate professionals and other entrepreneurs succeed. Julie Nelson is a twenty-plus year veteran of the real estate industry, including a five-year assignment running one of the largest new agent broker training programs in the country.

Julie is an active REALTOR® with eXp Realty in Austin, Texas. thenelsonproject.com is Julie's real estate business, thenelsonproject.org is everything else Julie Nelson including book resources, training, coaching, and blog. Julie lives on her somewhat urban farm in Austin, Texas with her spouse, Kay, two senior citizen dogs, one cat who likes to push mail off the table, two miniature donkeys, three ducks in a row, a collection of chickens, and thirty gardens. When not doing real estate stuff, you will find Julie in her gardens or on her bike.

Made in the USA
Middletown, DE
22 May 2022